Impossible Training

RELATIONAL PERSPECTIVES BOOK SERIES

LEWIS ARON AND ADRIENNE HARRIS
Series Editors

Impossible Training

A Relational View of Psychoanalytic Education

Emanuel Berman

THE ANALYTIC PRESS

2004   Hillsdale, NJ   London

Published by The Analytic Press, Inc.
101 West Street, Hillsdale, NJ 07642
www.analyticpress.com

Typeset in Book Antiqua 11/13 by
Christopher Jaworski, Qualitext, Bloomfield, NJ

Index by Mariana Gaitini
Supported by the Research Authority, University of Haifa

Library of Congress Cataloging-in-Publication Data

Berman, Emanuel, 1946–
    Impossible training : a relational view of psychoanalytic education /
Emanuel Berman
        p. cm.
    Includes bibliographical references and index.
    ISBN 0–88163–275–9
        1. Psychoanalysts—Training of. 2. Psychoanalysis—Study and teaching. 3.
Psychoanalysis—Study and teaching—Supervision. I. Title.

    RC502.B475 2004
    616.89'17'0711—dc22

                                                                    2004046259

Printed in the United States of America
10 9 8 7 6 5 4 3 2 1

Dedicated to Talia,

to the future

Contents

Thanks

When thinking of the many individuals who influenced my professional identity, I think first and foremost of my late parents. My father, Adolf Abraham Berman (1906–1978), received his Ph.D. in social psychology at the University of Warsaw. He worked as a school psychologist until World War II, when underground activities drew him into the political sphere, in which he remained active for the rest of his life, in Poland and in Israel (see Berman, 2002d). I never inherited his enthusiasm for the theories of Alfred Adler, but this book clearly expresses a search for my own way of integrating my interests in psychoanalysis and in sociopolitical processes.

My mother, Batia Berman (1907–1953), was a librarian. Her writings—through which I got to know her in my adulthood—conveyed a lively interest in people and in emotional nuance. Her wartime journal (Temkin-Bermanowa, 2000) counterbalances, in its subtle descriptions, my father's tendency to strive for an ideologic bottom line in his writing. I often contemplate the impact of these divergent styles on my own written work.

Many additional fertile influences accumulated during my studies, at Tel Aviv University (where I studied psychology, sociology, and social anthropology), at Michigan State University (where I specialized in clinical and social psychology) and at the Albert Einstein College of Medicine (where I interned, studied family and group therapy, and joined the staff as a clinical psychologist). Subsequently, I went twice through psychoanalytic training, a fascinating experience by itself. My first training was in the Postdoctoral Program in Psychotherapy and Psychoanalysis at New York University, where I enjoyed a broad range of theoretical approaches. I am grateful to my supervisors there, the late Emmanuel Ghent, as well as Ruth-Jean Eisenbud and Mark Grunes. My second training was at the Israel Psychoanalytic Institute; during this intense period, I deepened my analytic skills. My helpful supervisors were the late Shmuel Nagler, as well as Nomi Mibashan and Anne-Marie Sandler.

During each of these periods, I went through a valuable personal analysis, with Robert John Sayer in New York City, and with the late Vicky Bental in Haifa. Although both my analysts were predominantly classical, they were also flexible and caring individuals, and their dedication surely contributed to my image of what analysis should be like. I am grateful to them, as well as to the other analysts whom I consulted subsequently in professional and personal matters.

My years of analyzing, teaching, and supervising were most influential in helping me develop my thinking. I am indebted to all my patients, my students, and my supervisees. My central professional homes in Israel are the Department of Psychology at the University of Haifa, where I am involved in undergraduate teaching, in graduate studies of clinical psychology, and in postgraduate training of psychotherapists, and the Israel Psychoanalytic Institute, whose candidates helped me crystallize many of the ideas in this book. I also taught at the Tel Aviv University Program of Psychotherapy, at the Programs in Bibliotherapy and Counseling at the University of Haifa, and at the Tel Aviv Institute of Contemporary Psychoanalysis. In the United States, I taught and supervised during three sabbaticals at the New York University Postdoctoral Program in Psychotherapy and Psychoanalysis, and also taught at the graduate programs of Yeshiva University and Long Island University. I greatly benefited from discussing my work with colleagues at the Columbia Psychoanalytic Center, the Institute for Psychoanalytic Training and Research, the San Francisco Psychoanalytic Institute, the Psychoanalytic Center of California, the Institute for Contemporary Psychoanalysis (Los Angeles), the Los Angeles Institute and Society for Psychoanalytic Studies, Tufts University, the Polish Psychoanalytic Society, and in many clinical centers and professional conferences in Israel and in Europe, as well as at the congresses of the International Psychoanalytic Association and the International Association for Relational Psychoanalysis and Psychotherapy.

I am grateful to the editors, publishers, and reviewers of numerous psychoanalytic journals and edited books in which many of the ideas presented here were first developed in earlier versions.[1]

---

[1]Berman (1988b, 1994b, 1995a, 1997d, 1998, 2000c).

Many friends and colleagues read my work and responded with constructive criticism; I cannot list them all but must mention Ofra Eshel, Jay Frankel, Yoram Hazan, Rina Lazar, and Ruth Stein. The late Steve Mitchell encouraged me to write this book, and he and Paul Stepansky helped in planning it. Lewis Aron and Adrienne Harris, series editors, were most constructive in advising me how to improve the present manuscript, and Lenni Kobrin and all the staff at The Analytic Press were very helpful in following this project to its successful conclusion.

Thanks, too, to Israeli artist Michal Heiman for allowing me to use on the book cover her photograph *In Freud's Mirror* (taken at the Freud Museum in Vienna), which conveys so well my thinking about all the reflections and cross-identifications that characterize the training process.

Finally, I thank my readers for their interest.

Introduction:
On Training and History

There are two such histories. The official one, openly admitted and repeated . . . whenever anybody wanted to say anything about training . . . describes and explains the glorious successes of the system. The other history, mentioned only by Freud . . . explains the curse of strifes which seem to adhere inevitably to our training organizations.

—Michael Balint
"On the Psychoanalytic Training System"

"It almost looks," Freud (1937) commented, "as if analysis is the third of those 'impossible' professions in which one can be sure beforehand of achieving unsatisfying results. The other two, which have been known much longer, are education and government" (p. 248).

Psychoanalytically oriented clinical training, a form of education involving well-defined government (structure) and based on analytic thought, must therefore be impossible to the third degree. Or is it?

Having been deeply involved in conducting psychoanalytically oriented clinical training (of clinical psychologists, of trainees in postgraduate psychotherapy programs, of analytic candidates) for three decades, I admit that this book's title, declaring training to be impossible, must be taken with a grain of salt. Still, it reflects my experience that, though often exciting and gratifying, it is also a conflict-ridden, complex, difficult area characterized by many subtle emotional currents that are not always publicly acknowledged but that could be crucial in determining the fate of the endeavor. One of the major goals of this book is to shed light on these currents.

The subtitle of this book speaks of a relational psychoanalytic view. First, I simply mean a viewpoint that assigns great importance to the dynamics and the impact of relationships (in dyads,

1

triads, groups) while attempting to understand them with all the subtleties explored by psychoanalysis—unconscious and pre-conscious experiences, nuances of transferential–countertrans-ferential patterns, childhood issues that subtly mold adult life, inherent conflict, and so on. At the same time, though my work is surely influenced by my youthful interests in sociology, social anthropology, and social psychology, it is also an expression of a particular trend within the contemporary psychoanalytic scene—a trend variably represented by such labels as *relational psycho-analysis, intersubjective approach,* and *two-person psychology.* Here I outline my personal understanding of the historical roots of this trend and explore their implications and, in particular, their im-plications for clinical training and supervision.

Origins That Shape Our Present

One of the basic assumptions of psychoanalysis, across all theo-retical trends, is that one's infancy and childhood shape one's adult personality and life. A similar view may be relevant to so-cial phenomena, such as the psychoanalytic model of training and supervision. Its early origins still have a role in its present destiny, even if many trainees and even teachers are not aware of this influence.

Whereas Freud paid enormous attention to the technique of psychoanalytic treatment, he was not particularly invested in the topic of training. Many of the early analysts were never analyzed. Ferenczi was one of the first to undergo a brief analysis with Freud, but, as we shall discover, this happened several years after Ferenczi became an analyst. Freud himself was never analyzed; that he relied only on his self-analysis may have something to do with his pattern of creating close friendships—with Breuer, Fliess, Jung, Ferenczi, and Rank—and later finding them painfully dis-rupted. Jung, Abraham, and Rank were never in analysis. And, though Freud's soul-searching conversations with Breuer about Breuer's work with Bertha Pappenheim (Anna O) are often de-scribed as the first supervision, Freud never practiced supervision in a structured, continual way, so that most early analysts were never supervised either.

Moreover, though psychoanalysis originated in Vienna, no systematic psychoanalytic training was initiated there during the first decades of psychoanalytic practice. The first psychoanalytic institute was established by Ferenczi in Budapest in 1919. Unfortunately, it was short-lived owing to political upheavals — namely, the rise of the right-wing Horty regime, which put psychoanalysis into disfavor after it had been recognized and supported by the short-lived communist Kun regime, which had appointed Ferenczi a professor. As a result, the Berlin Institute, established in 1920 by Karl Abraham and Max Eitingon, became the worldwide model and influenced other institutes considerably. The impact of the "Eitingon model" may be felt most in countries in which immigrants from Berlin had a role in creating analytic training centers. These countries included the United States and Israel, where Eitingon immigrated in 1934. Prominent influences in the United States were Rado ("Eitingon's closest collaborator and shield-bearer"; Balint, 1948, p. 169) and Alexander — Berlin-trained Hungarians who were central in shaping analytic training in New York, Chicago, and Los Angeles (Kirsner, 2000).

Contemporary authors are sometimes oblivious to the major cultural and professional differences among Vienna, Budapest, and Berlin during the first decades of the 20th century. Ferenczi (often allied with Rank) and the Berlin group led by Abraham (often allied with Jones) were in constant conflict within Freud's "committee" in the early 1920s: Ferenczi and Rank strove for a freer, more experiential, and more experimental psychoanalysis, whereas Abraham presented more orthodox views, emphasized intellectual interpretation, and kept warning Freud against the dangerous "deviations" Ferenczi and Rank might introduce (just as he had striven to alienate Freud from Jung a decade earlier). Knowing Ferenczi's work, one can easily guess that the strict rules of the Berlin Institute were not to his liking either. And Freud, respecting Abraham, Jones, and Eitingon but emotionally much closer to Rank and Ferenczi, often aroused the envy of Abraham and Jones.

Frawley-O'Dea and Sarnat's (2001) slip, "Freud's Berlin Institute" (p. 21), is a good example of the confusion caused by paying insufficient attention to history. It seems to convey a misunderstanding of the gap between Viennese informality and Berlin-style formality at the time. Bernfeld (1962), a former Viennese who openly condemned "the Prussian spirit which rather flourished among the founders of the Berlin Institute" (p. 467), reported that, when he wanted to become an analyst and consulted Freud, Freud scornfully dismissed the Berlin structure (training analysis first, cases later): "Nonsense, go right ahead. You certainly will have difficulties. When you get into trouble, we will see what we can do about it" (p. 463). A week later, Freud referred Bernfeld's first analytic case to him.

With the rise of Hitler, most Central European analysts, many of them Jews, socialists, or liberals, sought to escape to safer places, notably the United States, Britain, and South America (though one group of analysts stayed in Berlin, tried to function within the structure of the Nazi regime, and turned a deaf ear to its atrocities, thereby giving the regime legitimacy; Berman, 2002d). This huge wave of immigration in the 1940s radically changed the cultural geography of psychoanalysis. Nevertheless, on closer scrutiny, we may find that some of the debates involving Vienna, Berlin, and Budapest were continued in subtle forms across the Channel and the Atlantic.

Another historical phase that still exerts influence is the near-split in the British Psychoanalytic Society in the early 1940s. This schism was also caused in part by immigration. Both Melanie Klein (who, though born in Vienna and becoming an analyst in Budapest, at this point mostly identified with Abraham and "Berlin values") and Anna Freud and her Viennese colleagues now found themselves in London. Klein, who had emigrated from Berlin in 1926, was so upset by the conflict that she accused Jones of doing "much harm to psychoanalysis" by inviting Freud and Anna to England (Grosskurth, 1986, p. 255)—a selfish expression in view of the circumstances of their emigration in 1938!

Training issues had an important role in these Controversial Discussions (King and Steiner, 1991)—especially issues of homogeneity and heterogeneity of the curriculum, indoctrination versus broader exposure, the power of training analysts to influence their analysands and turn them into disciples, and so forth. The compromise reached at the end of the discussions—which allowed for coexistence of the three faculty groups (followers of Anna Freud, of Melanie Klein, and the Middle Group) in a single institute — survives to this day but is not always implemented. As a notable example, though the agreement stipulated that all trainees receive one supervision from outside their group, this rule is honored only by the Independents (heirs to the Middle Group), who often seek one Kleinian supervision, and by the Contemporary [Anna] Freudians, who often seek one Independent supervision. The Kleinians, who became the most powerful group (Sorenson, 2000),[1] usually go only to Kleinian supervisors.

Although the fierce battle and near-split occurring from 1941 to 1945 was between the followers of Anna Freud and those of Melanie Klein, my particular interest is in the interaction between Klein and Winnicott, who were quite close at the time but later parted ways (Winnicott becoming a leader of the Independents). Their initial relationship as supervisor and supervisee led to radical differences in both treatment and training — differences that color many present-day positions regarding the place of authority in analytic practice and training.

In the history of training in the United States, a major theme was the conflict between the medical psychoanalytic establishment (which for many decades struggled for medical exclusivity, to the point of deceiving immigrant analysts regarding the legal requirements for the practice of analysis in the United States; Kirsner, 2000) and those who favored a more flexible professional foundation (including Freud, 1926; Ferenczi; and later generations of psychologists and social workers). The latter eventually won the battle, with the help of legal measures (Wallerstein, 1998) — a victory that may prove crucial for the future of psychoanalysis in the United States in view of the distancing of many psychiatrists from psychotherapeutic and analytic treatment in favor of psychopharmacology. But the question still remains whether psychologists and other nonmedical analysts, who finally gained full recognition, will uncritically join the more rigid

---

[1]Sorenson (2000) concluded that in psychoanalysis, as in religion, it pays to be a fundamentalist. I think there may be other ways to interpret the strengthening of the Kleinian group, but in any case my own preference is for training with which I can identify, even if it leaves me in a smaller group. I can appreciate Balint's (1948) pride in that Ferenczi's analysands (including Klein, Jones, and himself) each followed an individual path.

structures that the medical establishment developed or will help to transform them in more open-minded directions (Slavin, 1997). This question, again, depends to some extent on increased knowledge and awareness of the historical origins of training structures and supervisory styles and of their social and cultural implications.

The relational tradition—especially influential in the New York University Postdoctoral Program in Psychotherapy and Psychoanalysis in New York City (one of the first alternative training programs for psychologists) and in many of the new training programs affiliated with Division 39 of the American Psychological Association—has the potential to contribute to a more critical, innovative attitude to training and supervision. This tradition, however, is not immune from some of the risks of "party lines" and "school loyalties."

Orthodox and Heterodox Story Lines

Although relational psychoanalysis now has its journals, organizations, and conferences, I still hope that it will not evolve into a school in the traditional sense and that instead it will help mold a professional and intellectual climate free of the constraining impact of "schools" (Berman, 1997d). For many years we have become used to thinking of psychoanalytic theory as divided into "schools." Many textbooks have separate chapters on the interpersonal school (defined in older books as "neo-Freudian"), on ego psychology as a school, and, in newer versions, on self psychology, or on the Kleinian school.

Such "schools" have made positive contributions by allowing a multiplicity of voices, safeguarding against a repressive global uniformity, and offering analysts a friendly, facilitating environment of like-minded colleagues; but they have also produced inbred groups whose members espouse a single viewpoint (often that of a particular founding father or mother), created their own vocabulary, read mostly their own journals, and have become involved mostly in their own training programs.

Winnicott attempted to combat such separatism in his moving letters to Melanie Klein and Anna Freud, who demanded loyalty from their followers even though they all functioned within the seemingly unified British Psychoanalytic Society. In 1934, he wrote both of them:

> If we in the present try to set up rigid patterns we thereby create iconoclasts or claustrophobics (perhaps I am one of them) who can no more stand the falsity of a rigid system in psychology than they can tolerate it in religion.... I find the prospect of having to deal with the rigid groupings that would become automatically established at the death of either of yourselves one which appalls me [quoted in Rodman, 1987, pp. 72–73].

And to Klein he wrote, "You are the only one who can destroy this language called the Kleinian doctrine and Kleinism and all that with a constructive aim" (p. 35).

One expression of the partisan impact of school identification is in the way the history of psychoanalysis has been written. Many books and papers, the best known of which is Jones's Freud biography, express the "orthodox" story line regarding the development of psychoanalysis (Berman, 1983). In narratives following this line, Freud and Freud's thought are idealized, and all other figures are judged according to their supposed loyalty to Freud. Dissent is seen as barren and destructive, and ruthless ambition, pathologic narcissism, and juvenile rebelliousness are attributed to dissenters, who are often characterized as deviationists (for Jones, these are especially Ferenczi and Rank[2]).

Jones's judgments of Ferenczi shift dramatically. He is generous and appreciative when describing periods of close agreement between Freud and Ferenczi, reserved when disagreements appear, and vicious when they reach their peak. Jones (1957) stated his belief in theoretical loyalty as a criterion for mental health directly: "Rank ... and Ferenczi ... developed psychotic manifestations that revealed themselves, among other ways, in a turning

---

[2]I vividly recall my discomfort, at my first International Psychoanalytic Congress, on hearing International Psychoanalytic Association president Lebovici (1978) praise Abraham for warning Freud against Ferenczi and Rank. Lebovici enthusiastically quoted Abraham's definition of Rank's evolution as "a neurotic regression to the anal-sadistic stage" (p. 134).

away from Freud and his doctrines" (p. 47). I return in chapter 1 to the stormy debate aroused by these claims.

This "orthodox" story line of the history of psychoanalysis has a mirror image in the equally biased "heterodox" story line, which denigrates Freud and most of his followers while idealizing a few dissidents. This bias is prominent in Jungian and Adlerian literature but also in Thompson's (1950) *Psychoanalysis: Evolution and Development*. In spite of the all-encompassing book title, Thompson completely disregarded such authors such as Hartmann and Melanie Klein (major figures in American and British psychoanalysis at the time) in an effort to show that the only innovations in the psychoanalysis of that time were those propounded by Sullivan and his circle.

Both story lines encourage dogmatism and stand in the way of the integrative and dialectical view needed for a thoughtful critical perspective on the history of our profession. Such a perspective may enable us to recognize the fruitful contributions both of Freud and of his antagonists and to see what was valuable both in traditional views and in radical challenges. We may then gain a richer contemporary understanding of the treatment process and of the training process — transcending the polemics of the past.

Complex Individuals, Generative Dyads

Most psychoanalytic authors, being complex individuals, produce work characterized by inherent tensions and even inner contradictions rather than by the simple expression of a single-minded view. The best example is Freud, who was often torn between his positivistic upbringing (expressed in his attempt to create a general metapsychology) and his hermeneutic tendencies (his "literary" investment in figuring out the nuances of a person's life story); between his ambition to be accepted by the medical profession and his refusal to accept its concepts and rules; between his wish to develop a purely intrapsychic model (a "one-person psychology") and his frequent awareness of the impact of interpersonal and social processes ("two-person" and "multiple-person" psychologies); and between his hope of developing a standardized treatment technique (images of the analyst as a surgeon working in a sterile environment, as a mirror or a blank screen) and his personal style as a sociable, expressive, and usually flexible person, as evidenced by many episodes recounted by his patients (Momigliano, 1987; Roazen, 1995).

Among the many specific tensions evident in Freud's writings on analytic technique (Berman, 2002c), prominent is the conflict between two viewpoints on transference. One is his emphasis on recovering pathogenic memories and fantasies as a major goal (a remnant from the hypnotic and cathartic stages, as Ellman, 1991, showed), leading him to see transference as the "most powerful resistance," making "free associations fail . . . [being blocked by] an association which is concerned with the doctor himself" (Freud, 1912a, p. 101). At the other pole stands Freud's growing awareness of the crucial role of transference, because "it is impossible to destroy anyone *in absentia* or *in effigie*" (p. 108), and transference could become a vital "playground" facilitating "an intermediate region between illness and real life" (1914, p. 154). Another important tension resulted from the conflict between Freud's awareness of the damage caused by "any standpoint other than one of sympathetic[3] understanding" (1913, p. 140) and his conviction that, to be really cured, "the patient must be left with unfulfilled wishes in abundance" (1919, p. 164).

At different points in time, these tensions were resolved in various ways. In Freud's (1900) work with young Dora (Ida Bauer), there was no attention paid to their relationship — only an effort to interpret her unconscious as fast as possible (which apparently drove her away). In a postscript, probably added four or five years later, Freud (1905) regretted the omission: "I neglected the precaution of looking out for the first signs of transference" (p. 118). A few years later, he suggested a precondition for effective interpretation: "The patient . . . must have formed a sufficient attachment (transference) to the physician for his emotional relationship to him to make a fresh flight impossible" (1910c, p. 226). The relationship becomes crucial but only as a precondition to the real curative work of interpretation, and countertransference still remains in the shadow.

---

[3]A more accurate translation would be "empathic understanding" (Pigman, 1995).

When any relationship formed by Freud with one of his patients is studied in depth, however, its intersubjective complexity becomes apparent. Although Freud had a "negative . . . countertransference to countertransference" (Schafer, 1993, p. 85) and often avoided dealing with it, a study of Freud's (1905) relationship with Dora (an example I explored in detail; Berman, 2002a) reveals the omnipresence of Freud's powerful countertransference.

This countertransference, in the broadest sense of the term, has its sociocultural aspects, such as the conventional views of femininity typical of the period — the male as a bearer of knowledge and alone having the power to penetrate women and penetrate the text (Moi, 1981). These aspects exist side by side with such uniquely individual dimensions as the impact of Freud's childhood relationships with his mother and his nursemaid (Glenn, 1986); conscious levels, such as Freud's ambition to find support for his theoretical views; and unconscious levels, such as his struggle with feminine identifications and homosexual urges (Hertz, 1983).

The countertransference also includes such permanent character traits as Freud's tendency to come to authoritative conclusions (described by Marcus, 1975, as *hubris* or *chutzpa*) and involves specific reactions, such as his anger at Dora for depriving him of a full success. With his patient, Freud made concordant identifications (Racker, 1968) that led to some of the more empathic interpretations (supporting Dora's view that she was being used as a trade-off to allow her father's affair with Frau K) and complementary identifications with figures in her life, such as Herr K (Lacan, 1952), which eventually seemed to gain the upper hand. There are affective manifestations, such as open annoyance at Dora for turning down "attractive" Herr K, and cognitive manifestations, such as Freud's consistent errors regarding the time of the analysis (reported as 1899 rather than 1900—i.e., a period deeper into Freud's friendship with Fliess, marred by the latter's jealous wife, Ida) and errors regarding Dora's age (putting her older, which makes the sexual abuse by Herr K seem more trivial). We see a direct countertransference to young and attractive Dora and an indirect countertransference (Racker, 1968) influenced by Freud's relationships with Breuer (whose daughter was named Dora) or with Fliess (to whom Freud reported, proudly at first, his progress with Dora).

When Dora announced her wish to leave after only a few months, Freud practically gave up on her. He wondered, "Might I perhaps kept the girl under my treatment if I myself had . . . shown a warm personal interest in her . . . providing her with a substitute for the affection she longed for?" (Freud, 1905, p. 109). Freud answered his own question, "I have always avoided acting a part." But this strictness sharply contrasts with his work with Elizabeth von R, only eight years earlier, when he reported, "I was able to relieve her still more by taking a friendly interest in her present circumstances" (Breuer and Freud, 1895, p. 158); after termination, he went out of his way to attend a ball where he could see her "whirl past in a lively dance" (p. 160). Although one might argue that he treated Elizabeth before crystallizing his psychoanalytic technique, clear expressions of personal interest also appear in his later work with the Rat Man (Mahony, 1986). Clearly, countertransference had a part in his differing reactions.

For some decades, the inner tensions and contradictions in Freud's clinical model were covered up by a psychoanalytic establishment eager to present a standard theory (crystallized around a drive-defense model and ego psychology) and a standard technique (emphasizing abstinence, anonymity, and a pure use of interpretations). The fictitiousness of calling this technique *classical* was exposed by Lipton (1977), who in discussing Freud's (1909) Rat Man case pointed out that Freud never worked with such rigidity and that creating lists of rules is antianalytic, as it disregards the significance that any behavior of the analyst acquires for a particular analysand.

It could be argued that analytic practice today is closer to Freud's flexible practice than to his stricter recommendations. At the same time, Freud's tendency to put the more personal interactions "outside the borders" of psychoanalysis proper — and not to mention, for example, the meal he offered his patient Ernst Lanzer (the Rat Man) in the published case study, possibly because he did not consider it an aspect of the analysis itself (Lipton, 1977) — may have been costly, as it prevented his analytic scrutiny of his patients' reactions to such personal interactions (e.g., Lanzer's negative feelings after the meal; Mahony, 1986, pp. 120–125).

Another theoretician whose inner contradictions are prominent is Melanie Klein. Klein claimed all her life to be a drive theorist, but

her work focused on the subtle processes of object relations
(Greenberg and Mitchell, 1983, p. 146) and of affective experiences (Stein, 1990) and eventually helped displace drives from
their central role in psychoanalytic theorizing. She believed in an
intrapsychic world only marginally influenced by outside objects
(the fantasy about the parent is more critical than the personality
of the parent), yet her ideas created an excellent springboard for
exploration of interpersonal dyadic exchanges. (A major step was
Bion's reconsideration of projective identification as a powerful
influence on the projected-into individual.) Klein, like Freud, objected to an emphasis on countertransference, but colleagues inspired by her (Heimann, Winnicott, Racker) eventually turned
countertransference analysis into a cornerstone of psychoanalytic treatment.

A possible conclusion to be drawn from these realizations is
that we learn the most from exploration of the life and work of
any particular analyst by attempting to illuminate all the nuances of his or her interrelated personal and theoretical development. Psychoanalytic thinking is subjective by its fundamental
nature (Stolorow and Atwood, 1979; Baudry, 1998). I emphasize
the importance of historical and biographical knowledge because psychoanalysis often progresses through the contact, personal exchanges, dialogue, and conflicts between two or more
individuals. Theoretical innovations do not spring from the
mind of an isolated person ("immaculate conception") but usually evolve in the transitional space created within an intense,
lively, interactive dyad (an "impregnating intercourse").

Often, the dyad consists of therapist and patient: Breuer and
Bertha Pappenheim (Anna O) gave birth to the talking cure;
Freud and Fanny Moser (Emmy von N) to free association;
Ferenczi and Elizabeth Severn (RN) to mutual analysis (Fortune,
1993); and Bion and Samuel Beckett to the understanding of
primitive mental states (Simon, 1988).

In other instances, the dyad members are colleagues, often
friends, who turn into rivals, such as Freud and Jung (Kerr,
1993). Complete loyalty may make a dyad smooth and efficient,
but not creative. Watch Freud and Eitingon, a dyad that Zusman
(1988) portrayed as a prototype of the barrenness that may be
generated by strict hierarchical training of the kind Eitingon created at the Berlin Psychoanalytic Institute of the 1920s and 1930s

and that, as I mentioned, gradually became a worldwide model of inspiration.

The Complex Evolution of a Relational View

According to my understanding of the initial sources of the relational psychoanalytic viewpoint, two difficult but fertile generative dyads (Freud–Ferenczi and, later, Klein–Winnicott) had critical roles, and major issues of discipleship or training were played out dramatically in both. These two dyads have an important role in this book.

I view Ferenczi and Winnicott as major sources of inspiration for a relational psychoanalysis (and surely for my own development as an analyst), but I do not advocate total loyalty to either. Becoming "Winnicottian" or "Ferenczian" is foreign to the deep individualistic streak in the personality of both men, who never attempted to found their own "schools." Rather, I point to a desirable professional atmosphere in which analysts and therapists integrate their personal vision and unique language with a curiosity and knowledge about the ideas of past masters. Ferenczi and Winnicott were deeply inspired by the thinking of Freud and of Klein and by their profound insights into unconscious processes, but then both men integrated this inspiration into their own individual versions of psychoanalysis. It is significant to me that, for both, the intellectual and emotional outgrowth of an intense, conflictual, and fertile personal/professional relationship led to a great sensitivity to the relational dimension of human life.

I cannot list here all the authors, in addition to Ferenczi and Winnicott, who were influential in promoting a relational and intersubjective viewpoint; my selective discussion is based on the major influences in my own growth (Berman, 1997d). Different contemporary relational positions are based on various combinations of central influences out of a broad range of theoretical models.

Sullivan and Fairbairn made enormous contributions to the development of theoretical models that put the self–other relationship at center stage. Sullivan displaced drive theory with his creative interpersonal model and paved the way for our understanding that the intrapsychic is inherently interactive and relational. Fairbairn boldly challenged Freud's metapsychology by offering as an alternative an innovative object-relations model in which drive is object seeking and libidinality is the result of certain object relations rather than their antecedent.

Neither man, however, drew full conclusions from his theoretical insights when doing clinical work. Some of Sullivan's case examples (Kvarnes and Parloff, 1976) may be disappointing to read today, for they disclose his limited interest in transferential and countertransferential feelings. Sullivan responded to a patient's sexual wishes toward him not by any exploration but by a rational explanation: "I know I would enjoy it . . . but I am selling expert service and not having a good time" (Kvarnes and Parloff, 1976, p. 216). Sullivan's avoidance of working in the transference was discussed by Hirsch (1998); Fairbairn's analytic style was described by Guntrip (1975) as conservative.

Here I do not go into the complex story of the Fairbairn–Guntrip dyad (see Hughes, 1989), but I do credit Guntrip with being the first author to notice the affinity between British object-relations theories and the American interpersonal tradition and to point the way to their potential integration. Guntrip, and Winnicott's student, Laing, whose thinking was deeply relational, especially in *Self and Others* (1961), expressed reservations about using the old term *object*.

Object is better suited to Freud's model (where it is indeed an object, in the day-to-day connotation of "merely a sexual object") than to models in which the *other* has its own intrinsic value. We still have not managed to do away with *object* in our vocabulary, but the label *relational* at least pushes object out of our definition. Moreover, the emphasis on *subject,* implicit in speaking of intersubjective processes (Lazar, 2001), is an attempt to overcome some of the limitations of *object*. The interrelatedness of the terms *relational* and *intersubjective* has been variously understood, and the word *intersubjectivity* itself has many connotations (Aron, 1996a). For Stolorow, Atwood, and Brandchaft (1994), *intersubjective* has a global theoretical definition — a concept that can be applied to all that transpires in close relationships, including the analytic relationship. Other theoreticians, such as Benjamin (1995), have pointed to intersubjectivity not as a given but instead as a developmental or analytic goal signifying the full recognition of the other's subjectivity —

as distinct from using the other as an object. Owing to these differences, it would be misleading to see all analysts interested in issues of intersubjectivity as belonging to one uniform "school" or as advocating the same technique.

The differing formulations may be confusing. When Winnicott (1971) spoke of *object-relating* and *subjective objects* (colored by our needs and projections), and when Bollas (1987) spoke of *transformational objects,* they came close to aspects of Kohut's *selfobject.* When Winnicott (1971) spoke of *object use* and *objective objects*[4] (recognized for their separateness), he came closer to the current implications of the other as "subject." The paradox is that, when the child sees the mother as herself, free of the coloring of the child's subjectivity, this opens the door to the mother's own subjectivity. All these are different from the *object of libidinal desire,* as portrayed by Freud, and from Klein's *part object.* These are all different aspects of relating to the other.

Returning to developments in Britain, I mention only briefly Balint's disappointment that Winnicott did not comment on the similarity between Winnicott's ideas and those of Ferenczi, Balint's analyst and teacher. Balint wrote Winnicott, "You emphasized on more than one occasion that 'though — (I quote from memory) — Ferenczi and Dr. Balint have said all these many years ago, here I am not concerned with what they said'" (quoted in Rudnytsky, 1991, p. 86).

Another noteworthy point is the intriguing way in which Balint and Winnicott criticized each other's proneness to an idealized version of the analyst as a good object. Winnicott wrote Balint in 1960, "I become more definitely in disagreement with you when you use the word harmonious in description of the relationship which you call primary love. As soon as the word harmonious is used I feel I do know that a highly complex and sophisticated defense organization is at work" (Rodman, 1987, p. 128).

Balint (1969), after discussing the problems with classical and Kleinian techniques, devoted a chapter to the "hazards inherent in managing the regression." He doubted "whether the analyst

---

[4]The formulation *objective objects* as the most advanced objects points to Winnicott's belief in the value of objectivity — a topic explored in chapter 2.

can function as, or indeed actually be, a primary object" (p. 112) and warned that, in such corrective "grand experiments," which he related to Ferenczi and Winnicott, "something in the end slips through our fingers and we remain intrigued and disappointed" (p. 114). I think they were both right and saw in each other's work a risk that exists in many object-relations models—a risk that came up later in the context of Mitchell's (1988) critique of the image of the patient as a child.

Bion's contributions to a subtle understanding of intersubjective dynamics, especially in the analyst–analysand dyad and around issues of containment, are fascinating, but I agree with Aron (1996a) that the "empty container" may become a myth (joining the myth of the "blank screen"). The Sandlers' notion of transference as an invitation and of countertransference as role responsiveness (Sandler, 1976) and their formulation of the present unconscious, in which avoidance of shame is crucial (Sandler and Sandler, 1983), sensitize us to interpersonal nuances in the analytic here and now.

American psychoanalysis was dominated for some decades by Hartmannian ego psychology, which evolved into a rather rigid dogma (Kirsner, 2000). Interpersonal psychoanalysis coexisted with it in its secluded territory—mostly in New York City (at the William Alanson White Institute) and in Washington, DC—without much influence on the mainstream. One of the few exceptions is Searles's work on the border of the two trends— work that is another important springboard for a psychoanalytic model portraying the treatment process as involving a powerful mutual impact, including the patient's attempt to cure the analyst. Searles's early papers on countertransference were turned down by numerous journals (some editors wondered why he bothered readers with his personal problems!) and appeared only years later.

Mahler (with her separation-individuation paradigm), Loewald (through his notion of analysis as allowing a new object relationship), and then Kohut (with his vision of self psychology) all grew out of American mainstream psychoanalysis but transformed it in substantial ways that evoked considerable opposition to their creative ideas. Relational approaches have subsequently absorbed much of the their work, including the Kohutian emphasis on empathy and flexibility in analysis and on remaining "experience near." Still, Ghent (1989) pointed to the "one-person psychology" elements in Kohut's work, particularly in the selfobject concept, which "dramatically played down the focus on the real object, and did away with the need for a new beginning with a real object" (p. 190).

Clinically, there seems to be a contrast between the wish of some self psychologists for the analyst to become the needed selfobject for the patient and the more characteristic relational view that the understanding (and at times disclosure) of the countertransference is a better guarantee of authentic growth. This view implies that the analyst recognizes aggressive attitudes toward the patient as meaningful aspects of the developing relationship rather than tries to eliminate them in the name of remaining empathic (Berman, 2001a; I return to these issues in chapter 7). As for Mahler, her separation-individuation model was later creatively reformulated by Benjamin (1995), who offered mature mutual dependence as a substitute developmental goal for Mahler's total independence.

Simultaneously with the innovations of Mahler, Loewald, and Kohut, British object-relations emphases were being imported into American ego psychology by Kernberg and Modell. This importation was initially courageous, as both British theoreticians were boycotted or denigrated by the older generation of conservative American analysts, as evidenced by Rangell's (1974) hostile comments about Klein in his presidential speech to the International Psychoanalytic Association (IPA) and by the cold reception to Winnicott's work at the New York Psychoanalytic Institute, discussed in chapter 2.

The most direct beginning of a relational viewpoint was Greenberg and Mitchell's (1983) publication of *Object Relations in Psychoanalytic Theory*. Recent graduates of the William Alanson White Institute at the time, Greenberg and Mitchell transcended partisan identifications. In their contemporary classic, surveying the evolution of psychoanalysis, they identified two distinct traditions — a drive/structure emphasis (an intrapsychic libido-focused model prominent in Freud's metapsychology and in ego psychology) and a relational/structure trend that, expressed with many variations in the work of Sullivan, Fromm, Melanie Klein, Fairbairn, Winnicott, Kohut, and others, puts self–other relations in the forefront.

The revolutionary impact of Greenberg and Mitchell's book must be understood against the background of the history of American psychoanalysis. Whereas the Controversial Discussions in Britain culminated in an agreement enabling all three groups to coexist within the same institute, the parallel controversies in the United States in the early 1940s, though not necessarily expressing a deeper conceptual rift, culminated in a split and in the mutual dismissal, which I described earlier, between mainstream ego psychology and the interpersonal-cultural group.

Moreover, Sullivan apparently never read British literature, and he paid scant attention to fantasy, dreams, and unconscious internalization processes, while American interpersonal thinking was barely known in Britain. As mentioned, Guntrip (1973) first noticed the inherent affinities and potential complementarity between American interpersonal theory and British object relations models and was a guest lecturer at the White institute. Greenberg and Mitchell, coming out of the interpersonal school itself, challenged its claims for exclusivity, and many of their teachers at White (and later some of their colleagues at New York University; Drescher, 1994) condemned them as disloyal to the interpersonal tradition. In retrospect, I believe they served Sullivan's contribution much better with their inclusive approach—dialectically transcending both orthodoxy and heterodoxy—than it was served with the counterexclusion practiced by "pure" Sullivanians.

Moreover, Greenberg and Mitchell's book appeared at a time of growing dissatisfaction with classical metapsychology and its philosophical foundations—a dissatisfaction also expressed in the work of such traditionally trained authors as the Sandlers, Schafer, Gill, and others. With the notions of id, libido, and cathexis receding into the background in psychoanalytic discourse, one could notice a yearning for new "experience-near" conceptions that suited the growing clinical focus on analysands' self-development and intimate relations with others.

For many clinicians, Freud's traditional concepts seemed no longer to fit their daily concerns, and the emerging relational paradigm offered an opportunity to bridge the gap. Whereas Sullivan's original model, the "pure" interpersonal paradigm, had visible limitations in exploring inner experience, the new relational integration seemed more well rounded and richer.

The broad relational viewpoint was fully articulated by Mitchell (1988), who wanted to reach a selective critical integration of compatible sources while avoiding an orthodox single-theory approach or haphazard eclecticism. Mitchell spelled out his belief that humans are inherently structured in relational terms (Sullivan), form intense attachments because they crave relatedness (Fairbairn), and develop a self in the context of relatedness (Winnicott, Kohut). This view, he suggested, offers an alternative to the drive model and could be a new basis for the understanding of human sexuality as well. He also discussed the dangers of conceptualizing a patient primarily as a child or an infant (an aspect of the "developmental tilt") and the importance of conflict, which may be overlooked in developmental-arrest models.

The appearance of Mitchell's (1988) book, noteworthy for its scholarly investment and intellectual passion, was soon followed by developments that marked the coming of age of the relational viewpoint. One development was the creation of a relational orientation or track within the New York University Postdoctoral Program in Psychotherapy and Psychoanalysis, an alternative training setting for psychologists initiated by Bernie Kalinkowitz in the 1960s, at a time when psychologists were being excluded from the "official" (medical) psychoanalytic institutes in the United States. Historically, the program had been structured around two tracks, Freudian and interpersonal. Mitchell was invited to join the interpersonal faculty but soon found himself in constant conflict with colleagues who dismissed object relations theories (Drescher, 1994).

Eventually, Mitchell, Emmanuel Ghent, and Bernie Friedland established a third orientation, which became the most influential in the program (Aron, 1996a). It is meaningful that they chose not to start a new, independent institute (in the separatist "school" tradition) but rather to function within a highly heterogeneous and liberal program in which candidates are actively involved in decision making and can freely choose elective seminars and supervisors from among the options offered by three distinct theoretical orientations. The New York University program was the setting of my first analytic training, and its unique climate certainly had a role in the development of my views on training, as expressed in this book.

In recent years, several independent American psychoanalytic groups have joined the IPA, but the White institute and the New York University program have not. A major obstacle is their acceptance of three-sessions-per-week analysis (the IPA demands four). Consequently, many prominent relational theoreticians remain outside the IPA, reducing its breadth (Schachter, 1996). Paradoxically, this organizational separation has persisted even as influential authors within traditional American psychoanalysis (e.g., Jacobs, McLaughlin, Ogden, Poland, Renik) have developed relational and intersubjective notions of their own; departing radically from the image of the analyst as an impartial objective interpreter, these authors have portrayed interaction and enactment as unavoidable features of the analytic process.

Similarly, when in 1991 Mitchell and colleagues Aron, Bromberg, Ghent, and Harris established a new journal, *Psychoanalytic Dialogues: A Journal of Relational Perspectives,* they deliberately invited authors from various theoretical backgrounds and many countries, encouraged open debates, and allowed much space for commentaries on published papers and for authors' responses to such commentaries. Both the word *Dialogues* in the title of the journal and the plural word *Perspectives* in the subtitle signified the intention to create an arena for a lively interchange of ideas. The resulting open, communicative atmosphere must have had a role in the success of the journal and perhaps inspired similar endeavors in other journals and, later, Internet discussion networks. The breadth of the journal has made it clear that relational psychoanalysis is far from being a binding, definitive, single theory and that it is striving to be a stimulating and questioning force.

Although relational psychoanalysis was dealt a major blow by Mitchell's death in 2000 (Berman, 2001b), it remains a vital force. The relational orientation at New York University, *Psychoanalytic Dialogues,* and the new International Association for Relational Psychoanalysis and Psychotherapy, initiated by Mitchell during the last year of his life, continue to thrive.

Relevance of Cultural Context

Relational psychoanalysis, with its search for solutions for specific difficulties and limitations in the original psychoanalytic models of the human mind and of treatment, also reflects changes in the *Zeitgeist*.

The age of monolithic and totalistic grand theories seems to be over, and we are now less inclined than before to observe reality through the eyes of a single genius, be it Marx or Freud. Growing doubts about positivism make us reject the model of the impartial natural scientist in all areas of the social sciences and humanities. Our wish to be objective has given way to an interest in, and respect for, subjectivity. Postmodernist trends encourage the deconstruction of accepted postulates and expose many as simplified mythologies.

We have also become generally critical of omniscient authorities, be they political leaders, medical doctors, judges, or overconfident psychoanalysts. Biographies no longer gloss over the dark side of their protagonists' lives. Civil rights considerations make us respect medical patients' right to know their fate and allow patients to be active participants in deciding that fate. In the arts, the wish for a perfect final product gives way to works of art that disclose the dilemmas and processes of their creation—conflicting possible endings in a novel, abandoned lines left in a drawing. An analyst sharing with the patient her or his personal reactions, doubts, and confusions may fit in the present era more than a classical analyst offering a fully formed, definitive interpretation. Relational psychoanalysis, with its interest in mutuality and intersubjectivity, may be seen as an attempt to maintain and develop the richness and subtlety that have always characterized psychoanalysis—but in a more egalitarian, flexible atmosphere.

Renik (1999) expressed concern that, by relating change in analytic technique to the democratic or postmodern *Zeitgeist*, "we dismiss it as determined by political aims or academic fashion" (p. 523). I believe, however, that such connections are inevitable, whether or not we acknowledge them. We are all continually influenced by our cultural milieu. Indeed, the "evolution toward less self-importance and more candid self-exposure by analysts ... has been motivated by immediate, pragmatic considerations" (p. 523). Our capacity to become pragmatic rather than doctrinaire, however, has been strengthened by a certain cultural climate, and the analysands' capacity to benefit from our candid self-exposure has been equally increased by this same climate (Berman, 2001a).

A specific example of the impact of postmodern challenges is Mitchell's (1993) use of the postmodernist critique of the modernist concept of a unitary core self as he explored the notions of multiple versus singular selves and true versus false selves while noting the ambiguity of the notion of authenticity. Mitchell spoke of a "plural or manifold organization of self, patterned around different self and object images or representations, derived from different relational contexts. We are all composites of overlapping, multiple organizations and perspectives, and our experience is smoothed over by an illusory sense of continuity" (p. 104).

Such a conceptualization undermines a certain outgrowth of Winnicott's influence today—namely, the romantic notion of "uncovering the patient's true self" as a goal of psychoanalysis. More modest and relative analytic goals, better geared to unique and possibly transient cultural and individual needs, sound more convincing to our contemporary ears and more suitable for a secular, pragmatic, realistic psychoanalysis. Still, even these aims may be counterbalanced by a critical deconstructive tendency that exposes the limitations and inner contradictions of any goal and any technique—subverting potential idealizations. This climate may indeed explain the growing impact of Winnicott's work, in which paradoxes are not to be resolved.

Plan of This Book

In chapters 1 and 2, I explore the dynamics of two influential generative dyads—Freud–Ferenczi and, later, Klein–Winnicott. One of the sources of orthodoxy is the view of psychoanalysis as a "single-parent family" in which Freud is the sole parent. Such a view easily deteriorates to treating innovative scholars as "bastards" or traitors ("deviationists"). But a serious exploration of psychoanalytic theorizing, practice, and training in the past decades shows that much of it is remote from Freud's positions. My own belief is that contemporary psychoanalysis can be much better understood as a "two-parent family," as an outcome of the dialectical exchange between Freud and Ferenczi. Against this background, an exploration of their 25-year interaction and debate (the subject of chapter 1) is crucial. Their interaction is directly relevant to discipleship and individual uniqueness as central issues in training and even more specifically to the impact of a trainee's personal analysis on identification and rebellion in training.

Other major themes in contemporary relational thinking originated in the Klein–Winnicott relationship (a central focus of chapter 2), which began as a supervisory relationship but again turned into a lively debate lasting 25 years. Winnicott's rebellion, like Ferenczi's, raises the crucial issues of the analyst's autonomy and authenticity and of the vital need to safeguard them vis-à-vis authoritarian and institutional pressures. Winnicott's wish to acknowledge the impact of reality is therefore relevant both for the patient and for the trainee, who are influenced by gender, race, ethnicity, affluence or poverty, power relations, and many other "external" realities and their internal representation. These issues reverberate with my critique of contemporary Kleinian approaches, which still tend to deny the analyst's impact.

I have commented on the relevance of relational viewpoints for the way clinicians are educated. Many other aspects of the question are explored more fully in subsequent chapters. Emphasis on the personal and subjective nature of psychoanalytic and therapeutic identity—on one's need to discover one's unique clinical style based on one's personality and life experiences (a process that can be identified in the life work of Ferenczi and Winnicott in particular)—points to the impossibility of basing clinical training on the study of "technique" in its narrow sense. Moreover, idealization of a particular "proper analytic identity" may become persecutory—contributing to the growth of a painful chasm between a clinician's work and an idealized image of what is expected, or else to an attempt to mold oneself as the desirable New Person, and introducing the risky influence of "false analytic self" elements. In chapter 3, I explore these issues and summarize and further develop the critical tradition in studying analytic training—from Balint to contemporary views.

Are such persecutory (and infantilizing) aspects inherent in analytic and analytically oriented training, or can they be considerably reduced by certain changes in its structure and rules? There may be some truth in both answers, but the first tends to be used defensively to block changes in training. In chapter 4, I attempt to demonstrate the relevance of the second answer through a case study of numerous changes in psychoanalytic training in

Israel and of the complex and stormy group processes surrounding the introduction of these changes.

Personal analysis has been a central component of analytic training from its beginnings—to a great extent starting with Freud's analysis of Ferenczi. This context clearly demonstrates how illusory is the "blank screen" of the supposedly anonymous analyst. Exploration of a trainee's analysis unavoidably requires paying attention to the interaction of intrapsychic, intersubjective, and social processes, including the institutional context of the analysis. Analysis of trainees and, more generally, analysis of mental health professionals (in which analyst and analysand are also colleagues and part of an incestuous network) pose several unique quandaries. These quandaries are the subject of chapter 5.

The other universal component of dynamic clinical training is supervision. I believe that relational and intersubjective trends necessitate changes in the definition and style of analytic supervision—a focus on the many relationships that are always involved in the process, as I discuss in chapter 6. The connection between the Freud–Ferenczi debate and the issues of supervision was highlighted by Frawley-O'Dea and Sarnat (2001), who saw a "Ferenczian model of psychoanalytic supervision" (pp. 17–20) as the springboard for new supervisory approaches. Supervision becomes more personal and less guarded, making it more difficult at times but increasing the chances that supervisor and supervisee will form a fertile transitional space and become a generative dyad.

I conclude the book, in chapter 7, with a broad discussion of the future of analytic training and analytically oriented clinical training and of the ways in which training can be improved not only for educating clinicians to practice according to today's standards but also for helping and encouraging our trainees to meet creatively the yet unknown challenges of tomorrow. The goal of improving training makes understanding the social and cultural implications of psychoanalysis and psychotherapy a vital component in dynamic training programs, so that graduates can be attentive to the social context of their work now and in the future. The present theoretical diversity frees analysis from burdensome uniformity but may also be confusing and anxiety provoking. It requires a unique understanding of our theories in their historical and biographical contexts—as personal ways theorists found to

make sense of their experience—and integrating this understanding into our trainees' quests to figure out "who they are" as
persons and as therapists, and what theoretical directions and
styles of analytic work make sense to them as part of this genuine
identity.

1

Freud and Ferenczi: Their Generative Dyad as a Springboard for a Relational View of Treatment and Training

Nothing is more harmful to the analysis than a schoolmasterish, or even an authoritative, attitude on the physician's part. Anything we say to the patient should be put to him in the form of a tentative suggestion and not of a confidently held opinion, not only to avoid irritating him, but because there is always the possibility that we may be mistaken.

—Sándor Ferenczi
"The Elasticity of Psycho-Analytic Technique"

In this chapter, I explore the development of Sándor Ferenczi (1873–1933), as a person and as an analyst, against the background of his intense relationship with Sigmund Freud (1856–1939). Their interaction formed a lively generative dyad in which a strong mutual influence evolved, and their continual dialogue set the context of many current issues of psychoanalytic practice, training, and supervision.

Ferenczi was Freud's student, colleague, analysand (briefly), and close friend for 25 years—from their first meeting, mediated by Jung, in 1908, when Ferenczi was already a successful psychiatrist and therapist in Budapest at age 35 and Freud was 52, to 1933, the year of Ferenczi's untimely death from pernicious anemia at age 59 (Haynal, 1988; Stanton, 1991).

The history of their complex relationship has come to light only recently with the full publication of their intense correspondence (Brabant, Falzeder, and Giampieri-Deutsch, 1993; Falzeder and Brabant, 1996, 2000),[1] though a full biography of Ferenczi is

---

[1]Publication was delayed for many years, mostly because of Anna Freud's reluctance, but also because of Balint's concerns about uncovering the Elma affair, which I outline later here. The issue was discussed extensively in the correspondence between Balint and Elma (Berman, 2004).

still sorely missing. How interconnected their theoretical and clinical debates and their personal lives were has now become clear (Berman, 1996; Aron, 1998).

Ferenczi's work predating his meeting with Freud has also become better known recently, and his early papers highlight many of his lifelong concerns. Ferenczi (1899) wrote in his paper on spiritism, "I do believe that at the heart of these phenomena there is truth, even if it is a subjective truth rather than an objective truth" (p. 7). Subjective truth is a major theme in all of Ferenczi's work, and a clear thread can be identified between his early interest in "spiritualist" interpersonal influence and his later fascination with transference and countertransference. "Two Errors in Diagnosis" (Ferenczi, 1900) opens with, "There is an old saying that errors are at the root of most learning. But, in fact, we jealously guard the lessons that we draw from personal experience so that we can appear knowledgeable to our peers" (p. 9). This is Ferenczi's first allusion to the "professional hypocrisy" that preoccupied him toward the end of his life. And in "Love Within Science," Ferenczi (1901) stated, "It is useless to explain the attraction between men and women as merely a derivative of lust" (p. 13); indeed, the value of love and its place in treatment continued to concern him all his life (Lothane, 1998).

The First, Stormy Years of the Freud–Ferenczi Dialogue

The Freud–Ferenczi relationship and their discourse went through many complex stages, so that any concise summary of the emotional and theoretical position taken by each man is unavoidably oversimplified. Still, some continual themes are prominent. From their first letters, one notices the contrast between Freud's belief in the benefits of a firm hierarchical structure regulating the interaction between the sexes, between generations, and between patients and therapists (a structure in which boundaries are firm and knowledge is passed on or withheld wisely and cautiously) and Ferenczi's oppositional enthusiasm about equality, openness, and mutuality, about blurring boundaries, transcending hierarchies, and sharing knowledge freely (Aron, 1998). The two opposing stances come up first in the context of the men's differing images of their own friendship: Ferenczi wanted

Freud to be more open with him and fantasized becoming Freud's therapist to help him overcome his reserved position, which Freud preferred to maintain.

Ferenczi's very first letters seem to convey an idealizing transference, a touching search for a substitute father (Sándor's beloved father died when he was 15) and anxious concerns about potential rejection. The first letter starts with, "I am very grateful to you that you have declared yourself ready to receive me, unknown that I am" (Brabant et al., 1993, p. 1).

When writing his first major psychoanalytic paper, "Introjection and Transference," Ferenczi (1909), in a particularly telling letter, expressed a wish to avoid having Freud's work compared with his own and was concerned that his paper "loses its justification after the publication of your work" (p. 31). Freud reassured him, "I don't have the feeling of being the 'benefactor' towards you and others and thus do [not] tie to my actions the justified fears of which you speak" (p. 33). Ferenczi, always attentive to Freud's slips of the pen, confronted him (p. 35) with his omission of the word *not*, and Freud attributed this quintessential Freudian slip to a bad migraine (p. 36). In episodes such as this, Ferenczi's independence of mind can be seen to be emerging, even if cautiously.

The paper itself is most innovative and has never lost its justification, as Ferenczi feared. Portraying introjection of the other (a concept here created by Ferenczi) as a central building block in forming one's personality, the paper focuses on "the first 'object-love' and the first 'object-hate'" (Ferenczi, 1909, p. 42). It also outlines for the first time the process of gradual differentiation between inner and outer — a cornerstone in the subsequent work of Klein and others: "To the new-born child everything perceived by the senses appears unitary. . . . only later does he learn to distinguish from his ego the malicious things, forming an outer world, that do not obey his will" (p. 41).

Indeed, the most striking early example of the theoretical impact of the Freud–Ferenczi relationship is the way Freud accepted and used Ferenczi's original idea of introjection. However, though Ferenczi in this pioneering work conceptualized introjection as a basic universal phenomenon (paving the way for a view of object relations as fundamental to emotional life), Freud used the idea much more selectively and in specific instances (introjecting the lost person in mourning, superego formation, etc.) and never allowed object relations a central role in his model, on a par with drives.

In the same paper, there are other expressions of Ferenczi's unique beliefs about life—notably his warm description of the "large-hearted, impressionable, excitable neurotic . . . taking into his ego [introjecting] as large as possible a part of the outer world," contrasted with disdain for the projection-prone, "narrow-souled, suspicious paranoiac" who "expels from his ego the impulses that have become unpleasant" (pp. 40–41). Ferenczi seemed to be able to identify in himself this large-hearted, excitable quality, and his openness to the world often caused him much pain as well. In the second part of the paper, dealing with transference in hypnosis (hypnosis equated with suggestion and interpersonal influence, in the Bernheim tradition; Ferenczi identified with Bernheim more than Freud did [Aron, 1996b]), we learn much about Ferenczi's rich experience as a therapist and hear of his conceptualization of two paths of effective treatment—one based on fear ("father hypnosis") and the other on love ("mother hypnosis").

The Freud–Ferenczi correspondence goes on intensively. The men met often, spent summer holidays together, and traveled together, along with Jung, to the United States. In 1909, aboard the *George Washington*, the three men conducted a sort of "mutual analysis" of one another, and Jung was frustrated by Freud's reticence. The Freud–Jung bond had been marred by the first letters Freud received from Sabina Spielrein regarding her love affair with her therapist, Jung, and by Jung's initial deceitful denial (Kerr, 1993). The Freud–Jung friendship collapsed within the next four years—making Ferenczi an even more vital ally for Freud. But already every morning at Clark University, Freud had planned with Ferenczi the talk he was to give that day (Freud, 1910d, 1933).

Freud's and Ferenczi's differences in outlook regarding boundaries and openness colored their discussions of Ferenczi's complicated personal life, which centered on his intense relationships with two women—his loyal friend and lover, Gizella Pálos, who eventually became his wife, and her young, stormy, and attractive daughter, Elma. This is a drama in which Freud, whose own marriage to Martha was remote (Gay, 1988), was an active partner—always warning his younger friend about confiding too much in either woman. Freud also took sides— favoring the mother and disparaging the daughter.

Ferenczi first wrote Freud about Gizella in 1909. Sándor and Gizella had had a love affair since 1900 (Falzeder and Brabant, 1996, p. 141). By 1909, he was 36 years old and still single; she was 44, unhappily married, and the mother of two daughters, Elma (almost 22 years old) and Magda (20 years old). In 1909, Magda married Sándor's younger brother, Lajos. Ferenczi wrote Freud of his bond with Gizella, "The difficult and painful operation of producing complete candor in me and in my relationship with her is proceeding rapidly" (Brabant et al., 1993, p. 87). Ferenczi continued:

> The confession that I made to her, the superiority with which, after some reluctance, she correctly grasped the situation, and the truth which is possible between us makes it seem perhaps less possible for me to tie myself to another woman *in the long run,* even though I admitted to her and to myself having sexual desires towards other women and even reproached her for her age. Evidently I have *too much* in her: lover, friend, mother, and, in scientific matters, a pupil, i.e., the child [p. 88].

Ferenczi was "eagerly at work analyzing" his lover (p. 90), by which he probably meant their soul-searching conversations rather than a structured analysis. Freud had his doubts:

> It belongs to the ABC of our worldview that the sexual life of a man can be something different from that of a woman, and it is only a sign of respect when one does not conceal this from a woman. Whether the requirement of absolute truthfulness does not sin against the postulate of expediency and against the intentions of love I would not like to respond to in the negative without qualification, and I urge caution. Truth is only the absolute goal of science, but love is a goal of life [p. 122].

Later in the same letter, Freud, responding to Ferenczi's desire to cure people, suggested another lasting and fateful difference between them: "This need to help is lacking in me, and I now see why, because I did not lose anyone whom I loved in my early years" (p. 122).[2]

A few months later, Ferenczi mentioned Gizella's "concern for her unmarried daughter [Elma] and for the two-sided (partly communal) relationship" (p. 157). He still did not know how complicated this "commune" was going to become; at this point, it involved only the marriage of Magda and Lajos.

The most conflictual event between Freud and Ferenczi in the early years of their friendship was an incident during their joint vacation in Palermo in 1910—an incident alluded to in the correspondence and described more fully in Ferenczi's letter to Groddeck on Christmas Day 1921: "As a result, on our very first working evening together in Palermo, when he wanted to work with me on the famous paranoia text (Schreber), and started to dictate something, I jumped up in a sudden rebellious outburst, exclaiming that this was no working together, dictating to me" (Fortune, 2002, pp. 8–9).

After returning home, Ferenczi mentioned their difficulties in Palermo, and Freud responded in a reassuring but patronizing tone: "I think back about your company on the trip only with warm and pleasant feelings, although I often felt sorry for you because of your disappointment. . . . I would have wished for you to tear yourself away from the infantile role and take your place next to me as a companion with equal rights" (Brabant et al., 1993, p. 215). Freud assumed Ferenczi was disappointed because he was "quite an ordinary old gentleman," far from a "fantasy ideal," but Ferenczi disagreed, saying that the reason for his being inhibited and taciturn was quite different: "I was longing for personal, uninhibited, cheerful companionship with you . . . and I felt—perhaps unjustifiably—forced back into the infantile role" (p. 217). Ferenczi described his idea of

---

[2]Freud disregarded the fact that both he and Ferenczi lost a younger sibling in childhood. Years later, in a more sarcastic mood, Freud (1926) explained this difference in other terms: "I have no knowledge of having had any craving in my early childhood to help suffering humanity. My innate sadistic disposition was not a very strong one, so I had no need to develop this one of its derivatives" (p. 253).

companionship between two men who tell each other the truth *unrelentingly,* sacrificing all consideration. Just as in my relationship with Frau G. I strive for *absolute* mutual openness, in the same manner, ... I believed that this, apparently cruel but in the end only useful, clear-as-day openness, which conceals nothing, could be possible in [our] relations. . . . But what I forgot—in my egocentric blindness—was that these things didn't move you at all [p. 218].

Although Ferenczi accused himself of exaggerating and of being inconsiderate, he was clearly committed to mutual openness as a value—the same commitment that culminated with his method of mutual analysis two decades later.

Freud, referring to the traumatic ending of his close friendship with Fliess, answered, "I *no longer* have any need for that full opening of my personality" (p. 221). Ferenczi insisted, "I do not want to give up hope that you will . . . bring more sympathy to bear toward my 'ideal of honesty.' You know: I am an unimpeachable therapist" (p. 224). This fantasy of himself as Freud's therapist, though it went underground later, was central to Ferenczi's experience of their relationship.

The dilemmas regarding degrees of involvement and openness once again appeared around the question of relating to a woman, but this time Gizella's daughter, Elma. Planning a trip to Vienna with Gizella and Elma, Ferenczi asked Freud for permission "to ask [Freud's] advice in a rather difficult matter (marriage and love affair of that same daughter)" (p. 248). Freud surprised Ferenczi by diagnosing Elma as having a mild case of "dementia praecox" (probably the equivalent of a borderline diagnosis today), and this response had a "rather depressing effect" on Ferenczi (p. 253). Half a year later, Ferenczi reported that he was honoring Gizella's wish and had taken Elma into psychoanalytic treatment: "The effect is favorable. Of course, she has to talk much more about me than other patients do, but that is not turning out to be an absolute hindrance" (p. 296). Freud wished him success but warned, in line with his beliefs, "I fear that it will go well up to a certain point and then not at all. While you're at it, don't *sacrifice* too many of your secrets out of an excess of kindness" (p. 296).

Elma's analysis suffered a setback when a man she was interested in shot himself on her account. (In her July 5, 1966 letter to Balint, Elma erroneously attributed the beginning of her analysis to that event; Berman, 2004.) Ferenczi realized, "I wanted to commit a terrible act of violence. Dissatisfied with both parents [Freud and Gizella], I wanted to make myself independent!" He reported fantasies about marrying Elma—fantasies that he indicated had begun before the analysis; a talk with Gizella, however, led Ferenczi to conclude that his attraction to "young, pretty creatures" was only an attempt to mask his fixation on Gizella (p. 312).

In the same letter, Ferenczi dealt with his relationship with the "other transferential parent," Freud, and with Freud's attempt to avoid giving too much opportunity for his transference, his attempt to make himself independent in reaction, a "phase of my struggle for freedom" (p. 312). Freud responded by addressing Ferenczi "Dear son" (p. 314; he used to write "Dear colleague," then "Dear friend") and by disregarding the developments with Elma, which seemed deeply related to their relationship.

Ferenczi then reported, "I was not able to maintain the cool detachment of the analyst with regard to Elma, and I laid myself bare, which then led to a kind of closeness which I can no longer put forth as the benevolence of the physician or of the fatherly friend" (p. 318). Fifty-five years later, in her July 5, 1966 letter to Balint, Elma described the event: "Sándor got up from his chair behind me, sat on the sofa next to me and, considerably moved, kissed me all over and passionately told me how much he loved me" (Berman, 2004). She blamed herself: "I was a young girl with a fiery spirit. . . . I was an evil seducer, I was only thinking about myself and did not care about my victims. But perhaps I was not evil at all, only the slave of nature" (p. 514).

We must remember, of course, that in 1911, when this event took place, the ethical norms of psychoanalysis and psychotherapy were far from evolved. Actually, dramas such as this one (as well as Jung's entanglement with Sabina Spielrein), which led Freud (1915) to deal thoughtfully with the issues of transference-love, gradually contributed to the formation of sharper boundaries in psychoanalytic treatment (Gabbard and Lester, 1995). Still, such boundary violations were as likely to be destructive then as they are now, as I demonstrated in my study of Elma's subsequent life (Berman, 2004).

Ferenczi told Gizella what happened; she was "unstintingly kind and loving." He thought of his wish for a family, complicated by Gizella's age (Brabant et al., 1993, p. 318). Freud responded, "First break off treatment, come to Vienna for a few days . . . don't decide anything yet" (pp. 318–319). Two weeks later, Freud sent Ferenczi a letter for Gizella in which he interpreted Ferenczi rather reductionistically: "His homosexuality imperiously demands a child and . . . he carries within him revenge against his mother." Freud raised many doubts about Elma's character, the pace of the process, and the risk of building an alliance for life "on concealing the fact that the man has been her mother's lover in the fullest sense of the word" (p. 320). Elma apparently saw them as friends. A day later, Ferenczi wrote, "Marriage with Elma seems to be decided. What is still missing is the fatherly blessing." Freud succumbed: "Perhaps I have said more than was justified. . . . I will congratulate you wholeheartedly when you let me know that the time has come" (p. 322).

Two more weeks brought a reversal. Following on Elma's father's objections, "doubts crept into [her] mind," and her repetitive inability to wish without reservation came up. Ferenczi wrote, "The scales fell from my eyes. . . . I had to recognize that the issue here should be one not of marriage but of the treatment of an illness . . . she consented to go to Vienna and enter treatment with you" (p. 324). Ferenczi accepted Freud's view of Elma and turned her over to him. Freud agreed to analyze her, though he brought up all the complicating factors. He said that at first he thought Ferenczi's letter would announce the engagement and that he wanted to show "no sensitivity now that you neglect the sullen old man in favor of the charming young woman" (p. 324). Surprisingly, he claimed, with regard to Ferenczi's change of mind, "I have done nothing to bring that about" (p. 325).

The next stage in the correspondence involves Freud's detailed (and, by today's standards, highly unethical) reports to his friend about Elma's analysis. Freud fluctuated between attempting to "prepare" Elma for Sándor ("So wait, not without good expectations," p. 327) and providing him with more pessimistic notes ("She doesn't want to get into the experience with you. . . . I am cooling off noticeably again," p. 362). At the same time, Ferenczi was becoming more and more skeptical. Retreating from defiant rebellion against both "father" and "mother," he now wrote, "I would find sufficient compensation for the loss of family happiness in the understanding and loving company of Frau G. and in scientific intercourse with you" (p. 328). He visited Freud in Vienna, and both agreed to keep his visit secret from Elma. Ferenczi wrote, "Rarely has a visit with you given me such undisturbed intellectual and emotional satisfaction. . . . The fault on some other occasions (Palermo!) lay not in you, of course, but in me" (p. 350). "The fact is that the experiences that came about through Elma's analysis significantly diminished her value in my eyes. . . . You were right when, on my first trip to Vienna where I revealed to you my intention to marry, you called attention to the fact that you noticed the same defiant expression on my face when I refused to work with you in Palermo" (pp. 352–353).

With Elma back in Budapest, another problematic stage began. Gizella encouraged Sándor to marry her daughter after all and promised to remain his friend. He responded, "I made it clear to her that the possibility . . . depended on two conditions: Elma's suitability — and the fact that she becomes agreeable to *me*. (And on Elma's inclination as well, naturally)" (p. 365; the last sentence seems to be an afterthought). Ferenczi would examine Elma's suitability through a renewed analysis, and he also demanded that she "break off all relations . . . for the duration of the treatment. . . . She has to decide to speak with me freely and uninhibitedly, to admit all her resistances. If she doesn't do that, then I am firmly resolved to give her up" (p. 369). Freud followed the process with encouraging interest.

The two friends now seemed to have a joint Pygmalion fantasy. They shared a misogynist view, typical of their cultural milieu, that a woman is a dangerous seductress who must be tamed: "I am very glad that you have remained consistently firm against Elma and have thwarted her tricks," Freud wrote (p. 395).

While I was reading this part of the correspondence, my identification shifted completely to Elma. Freud was as unempathic to Elma as he was to Dora (Berman, 2002a). Ferenczi was attentive to Gizella's suffering but not at all to Elma's. I found myself amazed by the two men's lack of awareness of the cruelty of the experiment and of the hopeless double-bind created by making analytic openness the precondition for marriage with the analyst: "no talk of engagement as long as she doesn't commit herself to open (analytic) discourse" (Brabant et al., 1993, p. 374).

Ferenczi, quoting extensively from a letter from Elma, now allowed her a voice:

> I know quite certainly that you will not come to get me.
> And yet I have such a terrible anxiety about it. . . . Why subject myself to the danger that this test will exceed my strength? Do you wish that, perhaps? Or are you also afraid of it? Talk about yourself, for once; up to now you have been talking only about me! . . . Write to me once, one single time, honestly, the way one speaks to an adult, and tell me what you really feel [pp. 383–385].

This moving letter, the aging Elma's letters to Balint, and many additional sources led me to conclude that Ferenczi's counter-transference-love sensitized him to the depth of Elma's personality, whereas Freud mistook her adolescent turmoil for profound pathology and was blind to her wisdom and integrity.

Naturally, the experiment failed. Both the analysis and the relationship collapsed. Ferenczi wrote, "Giving up my (almost realized) fantasy with Elma and the analytic executioner's work with which I had to put this fantasy to death by myself still gives me considerable pain" (p. 396). Elma married and left for the United States; Sándor returned to Gizella, in spite of sexual difficulties. To the end of his life, Ferenczi resented Freud for his role in preventing him from having children (Dupont, 1994). Freud, though oblivious to his own active role, later told Ferenczi, "You, because of your infidelity to Elma, have inflicted a deep wound on her and have confused the possible future with demonic dexterity" (Falzeder and Brabant, 1996, p. 226).

At the end of 1912, a few months after separating from Elma, Ferenczi seemingly abandoned his egalitarian ideals and asked Freud to take him into analysis. Ferenczi wrote:

> Mutual analysis is nonsense, almost an impossibility [he was referring to Jung's experiment with Otto Gross; Kerr, 1993]. Everyone must be able to tolerate an authority over himself from whom he accepts analytic correction. . . . I, too, went through a period of rebellion against your "treatment." Now I have become insightful. . . . I am also a case in need of treatment [Brabant et al., 1993, pp. 449–450].

Ferenczi yearned for help and forgot for a while the fantasy of helping Freud, of becoming — in a more mutual climate — Freud's "unimpeachable therapist." But, as we shall see, this change was only temporary.

Analysis, Collaboration, Innovation

Ferenczi's analysis was delayed for almost two years by the ambivalence of both partners (Dupont, 1994). Freud expressed his "dearth of inclination to expose one of my indispensable helpers to the danger of personal estrangement brought about by the analysis" (Brabant et al., 1993, pp. 481–482); though Ferenczi naively reassured him that "my analysis could only improve relations between us" (p. 485), Ferenczi's own delays seemed to convey anxiety too. When the analysis finally materialized, it was quickly interrupted by World War I and by Ferenczi's service as an army physician.

Remaining brief and intermittent, the analysis eventually consisted of three periods — about two weeks in October 1914, three in June–July 1916, and two more in October 1916. Freud worked six days a week and part of the time accepted Ferenczi two hours a day. By today's standards, this analysis was ridiculously brief, but we must remember that many early analysts were not analyzed at all. As for the boundaries, today we may view with irony Freud's minimal attempts: "I will . . . reserve for you two hours a day. . . . I also hope to see much of you otherwise, and you should at least have one meal with us daily. Technique at least will require that nothing personal will be discussed outside the sessions" (Falzeder and Brabant, 1996, p. 130).

During the interruptions, Ferenczi's letters to Freud were intensely self-analytic — a trend about which Freud was ambivalent. The entire period, in and out of analysis, was colored by Freud's paternalistic insistence that Ferenczi marry Gizella, whom Freud admired. Because of this wish, Freud was worried about the use Ferenczi made of analytic scrutiny: "Analysis should enter in before or after an act and should not disturb one during it. . . . So, act now, as swiftly and decisively as possible, and refrain from analysis now " (p. 105). Ferenczi responded, "Better during than after a — perhaps useless — act" (p. 107).

After the second segment of analysis, Ferenczi said, "These three weeks were the decisive ones in my life and for my life." Still, his account was profoundly ambivalent: "I have become another person, one who is less interesting but more normal . . . something in me pities[3] the old, somewhat unsettled man, who was nonetheless capable of such great enthusiasm (and certainly often needlessly depressed)" (p. 132).

When Ferenczi still hesitated about marriage after the third period of analysis, Freud gave up: "Nothing will come out of it" (p. 153). Ferenczi, in what we might today call an intersubjective intuition, interpreted, "You wanted to free me from the suggestive influence of your earlier view . . . so that I can decide freely" (p. 154). In 1917, Ferenczi asked Freud to convince ambivalent Gizella to marry him. Eventually, Gizella filed for a divorce and married Sándor on March 1, 1919. Ferenczi's decision signifies his achieving stability but also sacrificing his yearnings for passion and fatherhood.

The period surrounding Ferenczi's marriage was stormy and fateful in other ways as well. After World War I, Hungary achieved independence. Governments, however, came and went. First there was a liberal regime, moderately friendly to psychoanalysis. Then, a communist regime supportive of psychoanalysis (unlike its Russian counterpart) appointed Ferenczi to the first psychoanalysis chair at a university. Later, an anti-Semitic, right-wing regime headed by Horty fired Ferenczi and closed the newly founded psychoanalytic institute in Budapest. Thus, though the International Psychoanalytic Congress was conducted in Budapest in September 1918 under favorable conditions, and the election of Ferenczi as IPA president suited the hopes of turning Budapest into a centerpiece of international psychoanalysis, in 1919 he resigned, owing to the tense political situation, and was replaced by Ernest Jones in London.

By then, Ferenczi had become a central figure in the psychoanalytic mainstream, while maintaining his continuing independence and originality — and the Freud–Ferenczi dialectic went on. I cannot follow it here fully, but I mention several points, in line with Ferenczi's (1919a, p. 184) advice against abstract generalizations.

---

[3]Dupont (1994) translated, "Regrets the loss of the man I was."

The paper that includes this advice, "On the Technique of Psycho-Analysis" (Ferenczi, 1919a), is itself a clear example of Ferenczi's individuality. The clinical detail in the paper is striking in its liveliness, and the paper features the richest discussion of countertransference of that period—surpassing anything Freud ever wrote on the topic. In the paper, Ferenczi fluctuated between authoritarian attitudes toward patients ("the patient's duty to relate everything . . . Under no circumstances may an exception be made to this rule"; p. 177) and bold intersubjective insights into "patients [who] are unmasking the doctor's unconscious" by identifying the analyst's countertransferential need to be "his patient's patron or knight" (p. 188). Ferenczi's is the first discussion ever of a therapist's rescue fantasies (in chapter 3, I explore the implications of this issue further) and the first consideration ever of the way countertransference influences transference—a possibility never raised by Freud. Ferenczi shared Freud's concerns about critical scrutiny and "Control of the Counter-Transference" (Ferenczi's subtitle)[4] but dialectically balanced them against the analyst's need for a "free play of association and fantasy, the full indulgence of *his own unconscious*" (p. 189).

Ferenczi's (1919b) second major paper in the same year, "Technical Difficulties in the Analysis of a Case of Hysteria," is bold in another way. Whereas it is traditional in its adherence to libido theory (the patient's continual subtle masturbation is interpreted in "economic model" terms, and the possibility that this masturbation might ward off depression, or strengthen a shaky sense of bodily existence, is never contemplated), its treatment method is far from traditional: the analyst becomes very active and uses commands and prohibitions in a struggle to find a way out of the blind alley in which he now finds the analysis.

This direction is very different from Freud's (1912–1915) recommended style in his technique papers, which he may have rarely followed himself, as Lynn and Vaillant (1998) documented. Still, Ferenczi (1919b) insisted that "we owe the prototype of this 'active technique' to Freud himself" (p. 196).

---

[4]This translation, however, is one-sided and may convey the translator's bias. The German word *Bewaltigung* could also be translated as "coping with" or "handling."

Indeed, Freud's paternalistic insistence on Sándor and Gizella's marriage may have been, as Hoffer (in Falzeder and Brabant, 1996, p. lxii) suggested, the inspiration for Ferenczi's own paternalistic active technique. He may have hinted at it when he spoke of the need for the "constraining to an already formed decision which has been postponed owing to resistance" (Ferenczi, 1921, p. 209). Freud (1919) also publicly supported Ferenczi's new ideas: "Developments in our therapy . . . will no doubt proceed along other lines; first and foremost, along the one which Ferenczi . . . has lately termed 'activity' on the part of the analyst" (pp. 161–162).

And yet it was Ferenczi who took the risk and presented the new radical method publicly — for which he was criticized, at times harshly (e.g., Glover, 1924). His readiness to undergo such censure must be related to his eagerness to find new paths to help the most difficult patients, for whom traditional psychoanalytic methods may prove to be insufficient. Although some of the new steps he recommended may remind us of systematic desensitization and other behavioral methods, his goal remained analytic — to free the associative process and reach deeper insight into the meaning of the symptoms, to make lasting change possible.

Also striking is Ferenczi's patient, nondefensive examination of the new method in a series of papers in which he considered the benefits and drawbacks of the approach according to clinical experience and kept modifying it. Ferenczi (1921) started contemplating contraindications, such as the need to discourage beginning analysts from active methods (they may lose the opportunity to learn fully the dynamics of the neuroses) and to avoid active techniques in the early stages of an analysis so as not to disturb the spontaneous unfolding of the transference (p. 208). In addition, he emphasized "the 'social' aspect of analytic therapy" (p. 216) and pointed the way to a two-person psychology. He also highlighted the importance of early preverbal experiences, which "cannot be simply remembered at all, but can only be reproduced by a re-living" (p. 217).

Ferenczi (1923) went further into the value of early experience. Children's "wish to become learned and to excel over 'the great' in wisdom and knowledge" is both a reversal of their vulnerability and an expression of a profound truth, as "the young

child is familiar with much knowledge . . . that later becomes buried by the force of repression" (p. 350). The patient–child analogy
initially expressing scorn ("Nervous patients are like children
and wish to be treated as such"; Ferenczi, 1919a, p. 186) gradually
changed in tone in Ferenczi's (1932) subsequent work ("Adults
are relative idiots. Children are all-knowing"; p. 154).

In "On Forced Fantasies" Ferenczi (1924a) suggested that pro-
posing potential fantasies to the repressed patient is another way
out of stalemates; he emphasized the child's right to sexual experience. He attributed an inability to fantasize freely in adulthood to people "who are such *well-brought-up* children that their
infantile-sexual instinctual impulses simply *have not the opportunity to get anchored in the world of reality* . . . children who really
have experienced nothing wilt hopelessly in the ever anti-sexual
atmosphere of educational ideals" (pp. 76–77).

Again, this is not far from Freud's (1908) view "that under the
domination of a civilized sexual morality the health and effi-
ciency of single individuals may be liable to impairment and that
ultimately . . . the cultural aim in view will be endangered as well"
(p. 181); and, again, Ferenczi was more down-to-earth and more
daring in his conclusions.

When expanding the discussion of contraindications to the active technique, Ferenczi (1925) became much more concerned
that activity may become a "disturbing or destroying agent of the
transference" (p. 219). Authoritarianism becomes a central danger, as injunctions and prohibitions "induce the physician forc-
ibly to thrust his will upon the patient in an all too true repetition
of the parent–child situation, or to permit the sadistic bearing of a
schoolmaster" (p. 220). Ferenczi presented the very opposite option now, as in this crisis: "I was only able to keep the patient by
making full acknowledgment of my mistake and after apparent
loss of regard letting him disport his triumph over me" (p. 220).
The self-critical, non-narcissistic position Ferenczi described vis-
à-vis his patient is also his position vis-à-vis his listeners and
readers.

Another aspect of this position echoes Ferenczi's (1909) dichotomy between the hysteric and the paranoid: "The last and
logically irrefutable word of the pure intellectuality of the ego on
the relationship to other objects is a solipsism which cannot
equate the reality of other living beings . . . and speaks of them as

more or less living phantoms or projections" (Ferenczi, 1925, p. 229). In contrast, bringing up emotions, transference, and love, he concluded that "knowledge of . . . the most important part of reality is not intellectual, but only to be obtained *experientially* as conviction. . . . I prefer to see in you who sit there before me and hear my words not ideas in my ego but real beings with whom I can identify myself" (p. 229). I view this as one of the sharpest early statements of a relational position in psychoanalysis.

Ferenczi's continuing dialogue with Freud was, in the early 1920s, part of a three-person drama also involving Otto Rank. Rank, initially Freud's young secretary and later one of the first nonmedical analysts, became Ferenczi's ally in the secret "committee" established to guard Freud's heritage. Ferenczi and Rank, who were personally close to Freud (Freud also encouraged them to befriend each other), often represented the more open and innovative line, in contrast to the conservative Berlin group (Abraham, Eitingon, Sachs), which usually had the support of Jones (Ferenczi's former analysand).

The book written jointly by Ferenczi and Rank (1924) is a radical call for a more experiential and less intellectual psychoanalysis, in contrast to the Berlin line. They warned that avoiding personal contact leads "to an unnatural elimination of all human factors in the analysis" (pp. 40–41), explored the subtle nuances of the transference–countertransference, and pointed out its mutual impact — the analyst "plays all possible roles for the unconscious of the patient" while a "kind of narcissistic counter transference . . . provokes the person being analyzed into pushing into the foreground certain things which flatter the analyst and . . . suppressing remarks and associations of an unpleasant nature" (p. 41).

While reading early drafts, Freud encouraged Ferenczi and Rank to develop their book; when the book appeared, however, Freud wrote Ferenczi, "I am not completely in agreement with your joint work, although there is much in it that I value" (Falzeder and Brabant, 2000, p. 119). Ferenczi was shocked: "For the first time since our acquaintance, which you soon elevated to friendship, I hear words of dissatisfaction from you. . . . [We strove] to avoid everything with which you might not agree" (p. 119). Freud expressed understandable concern: "As regards your effort to remain in harmony with me throughout, I value it highly as an expression of your friendship, but I find the goal neither necessary nor easily attainable. . . . Why shouldn't you have the right to try and see whether something doesn't go differently than I intended. If you make a mistake in doing so, then you will notice it sometime yourself, or I will take the liberty of telling you so" (p. 123).

Freud's cancer, discovered in 1923, left him vulnerable and pessimistic. He became concerned about the survival of his ideas and seemed to oscillate between a wish for his disciples to be creative and independent (as expressed in the quoted letter) and a fear that they will give up elements central to his theories. Rank (1924) intensely activated this conflict in his next, independent work, *The Trauma of Birth*, and Freud wavered between valuing its originality and resenting its avoidance of the Oedipus conflict. Rank wavered between loyalty and rebellion but eventually separated from Freud, lived in France and in the United States, and developed independent theories (Liberman, 1985). Thus, Ferenczi was forced to make a choice. He sided with Freud, to the point of disregarding Rank when he accidentally ran into him in a New York City train station — an act that hurt Rank deeply (Haynal, 2002, p. 105).

This development further influenced Ferenczi's critical approach to his active technique. A central element of this technique was the setting of a forced termination date — initially Rank's idea (related to his wish to shorten analytic treatment). Ferenczi (1925) noticed that this method "works brilliantly in particular cases; in others it misfires lamentably" (p. 222). But a fuller reversal came later, when authoritarian control of "dismissal" was replaced by careful attention to the patient's experience: "A truly cured patient frees himself from analysis slowly but surely; as long as he wishes to come to analysis, he should continue to do so" (Ferenczi, 1927, p. 85).

From his growing rejection of forceful authority, Ferenczi (1928) concluded, "We must content ourselves with interpreting the patient's concealed tendencies to action and supporting his feeble attempts to overcome the neurotic inhibitions . . . without pressing or even advising him. . . . It is the patient himself who must decide the timing of activity" (pp. 96–97). Eventually Ferenczi (1933) credited his patients with discovering the "aggressive features of my 'active therapy'" (p. 160).

Then, in the context of Freud and Ferenczi's harmonious relationship, Ferenczi's old fantasy reappeared: "I find it actually tragic that you, who endowed the world with psychoanalysis, find it so difficult to be . . . in a position to entrust yourself to anyone. If your heart ailments continue . . . I will come to you for a few months and place myself at your disposal as an analyst—naturally: if you don't throw me out" (Falzeder and Brabant, 2000, p. 250). Freud was thankful but not interested (p. 252). Ferenczi's eight-month stay in the United States, in 1926–1927, may be seen as the peak of his close collaboration with Freud. Ferenczi loyally represented Freud's views vis-à-vis the behaviorists (confronting Watson; p. 294), vis-à-vis Rank's influence, and vis-à-vis the attempt by the medical psychoanalytic establishment to block nonmedical analysts—a policy that outraged Freud (1926). Ferenczi defiantly trained and supervised American nonmedical analysts throughout his stay.

Growing Originality, Growing Tension

Within the next few years, Ferenczi's trust in the realistic side of patients' critical perceptions regarding their analysts solidified: "Every patient without exception notices the smallest peculiarities in the analyst's behavior, external appearance, or way of speaking, but without previous encouragement not one of them will tell him about them" (Ferenczi, 1928, p. 93). Encouraging an openly critical view went hand in hand with emphasizing that "every analytic statement should be put forward with . . . qualification . . . our confidence in our own theories should be only conditional, for in every case we may be presented with a resounding exception to the rule, or with the necessity of revising a hitherto accepted theory" (p. 94). Ferenczi reminded us that "one must never be ashamed unreservedly to confess one's own mistakes" (p. 95). Authority, earlier relied on, was now consistently deconstructed.

Although still paying tribute to Freud's drive theory, Ferenczi's interpretation of the drives became much more experience based. A combination of loyalty and rebellion was sharply expressed in the title of Ferenczi's (1929) paper, "The Unwelcome

Child and His Death Instinct." Ferenczi's somewhat strained effort to amalgamate Freud's drive theory ("death instinct") with his own emerging object relations theory ("unwelcome child") may be related to his rigid view that "scholars who do not a priori deny the possibility of 'many truths' about the same thing are probably people whose scientific morality has not developed into a unity" (Ferenczi, 1927, p. 78). This positivistic trend, in contrast to some of Ferenczi's other views, is also evident in his utopian belief[5] that, after analysts are thoroughly analyzed, the personal elements in their work "dwindle away," so that all "will inevitably come to the same objective conclusions . . . and will consequently adopt the same tactical and technical methods" (Ferenczi, 1928, p. 89).

We may interpret this yearning for objectivity and uniformity as "whistling in the dark," in view of the growing uniqueness of Ferenczi's analytic style and the loneliness it brought. Luckily, in reality, Ferenczi was far from giving up the very personal element in his own work. Moreover, the attempt to reconcile his and Freud's views was at times theoretically fruitful. For example, in concluding "The Unwelcome Child," which emphasizes early rejection by one's family as the deeper cause of much emotional pain and many symptoms (including sexual difficulties, which Freud explained quite differently), Ferenczi (1929) struggled with the gap between his new existential emphasis and Freud's oedipal model. Ferenczi suggested, "Often it is only the struggles of the Oedipus conflict and the demands of genitality which reveal the consequences of an aversion to life acquired at an early age" (p. 107). This way of thinking about the interaction of preoedipal and oedipal layers (parallel in some ways to Fairbairn's, 1954, later views) became, with time, quite influential.

The differences between Freud and Ferenczi gradually reemerged in these last few years of Ferenczi's life. A meaningful though subtle indication arose already in 1928, when Freud

---

[5]Elsewhere (Berman, 2003a), I discuss more fully the utopian aspects of Ferenczi's thought and their relation to the centrality of rescue fantasies in his life. Balint (1954) characterized the quoted passage as an "idealized, utopian description" (p. 161).

responded to a draft of Ferenczi's (1928) "The Elasticity of Psycho-Analytic Technique," which emphasizes tact and empathy as central analytic tools. Although empathy was a meaningful concept for Freud, he used it mostly in an intellectual sense, as a basis for deciphering and interpreting the other[6] (Pigman, 1995), but it was Ferenczi (1928) who introduced it in its contemporary emotional connotation, as used by Winnicott, Kohut, and others: "Only real empathy helps; the patient's sharp wits will easily detect any pose" (p. 95).

Freud, in a letter that Ferenczi quoted anonymously in the published version of his paper, praised the paper but expressed concern: "As true as what you say about 'tact' is, this admission seems to me to be all the more questionable in this form. All those who have no tact will see in this a justification of arbitrariness, i.e., of the subjective factor, i.e. of the influence of one's own unrestrained complexes" (Falzeder and Brabant, 2000, p. 332). Freud's fear of subjectivity is evident.

In his last series of daring papers, culminating with "Confusion of Tongues Between Adults and the Child," Ferenczi (1933) reformulated the analyst–patient relationship as interactive, portrayed the analyst as a potential source of repeated trauma, and outlined a revised analytic method focusing on tact, flexibility, elasticity, emotional availability, relaxation, and nurturance.

The patient–child equation, which, as I mentioned, has lost its condescending connotation and instead acquired empathic tones, serves as a rationale for more flexible and creative analytic work and for being more fully in touch with childhood experiences that emerge in analysis and with the childlike neediness of adult patients. These directions reappeared in paper after paper: "Through this indulgence the patient is permitted, properly speaking for the first time, to enjoy the irresponsibility of childhood, which is equivalent to the introduction of *positive* life-impulses and motives" (Ferenczi, 1929, p. 106). This is the direct springboard for the idea of a new beginning in analysis,

---

[6]Moreover, Strachey made empathy look even more marginal in Freud's work, as he often translated the German word *Einfühlung* in other ways, such as "sympathetic understanding" or "feeling our way into" (Pigman, 1995).

developed by Balint: "What such neurotics need is really to be adopted and to partake for the first time in their lives of the advantages of a normal nursery" (Ferenczi, 1930, p. 124).

As the formulations grew clearer, the tension with Freud increased. Ferenczi spoke of a "certain anxiety . . . about coming into conflict with you even in questions of the finest detail" (Falzeder and Brabant, 2000, p. 372). Freud was worried: "You have doubtless outwardly distanced yourself from me in the last few years. Inwardly, I hope, not so far as a step towards the creation of a new oppositional analysis might be expected from you, my paladin and secret Grand Vizier" (pp. 373–374). Ferenczi attempted to summarize his new emphasis in four points — a traumatic-hysterical basis for patients' problems; better therapeutic effects when this level is reached; the risk of overestimating fantasy and underestimating traumatic reality; and, in technique, "all too harsh measures must be relaxed" (p. 376).

Freud, in a conciliatory tone, reminded Ferenczi, "You passed over some jocular and tender things that I wrote" (p. 380). But Ferenczi's unhappiness extended now to his past analysis: "I was especially sorry that you did not comprehend and bring to abreaction . . . negative feelings and fantasies" (p. 382). He also highlighted more disagreements: "I do not, e.g., share your view that the process of healing is an unimportant procedure" (p. 383). Freud responded, "At the time we were by no means so sure that these [negative] reactions could be expected in every case." He also admitted, "My patience with neurotics runs out in analysis, and . . . in life I am inclined to intolerance towards them" (p. 386). He felt that Ferenczi had pressed him back into the role of the analyst, which Ferenczi denied: "I would no longer feel good in the one-sided role of the analysand. Do you consider such mutual openness impossible?" (p. 388).

A year later, Ferenczi was invited by the Vienna Psychoanalytic Society to be the keynote speaker at a celebration of Freud's 75th birthday. In opening his presentation, Ferenczi discussed his invitation in the context of his complex relations with Freud: "Over and over one hears irresponsible remarks about the intolerance, the 'orthodoxy' of our master. . . . I should like to throw into the scales your kind invitation to me as an argument against this notion. . . . I am fairly generally regarded as a restless spirit . . . the *enfant terrible* of psychoanalysis." Ferenczi mentioned the criticism of his ideas as well as Freud's own reservations but added that neither man "dream[ed] of suspending our collaboration because of these differences in method and in theory" (Ferenczi, 1931, pp. 126–127).

The paper itself, "Child Analysis in the Analysis of Adults," again testifies to the complexity of the Freud–Ferenczi dialogue. On one hand, the paper is a warm tribute to Anna Freud, and Ferenczi used her flexible methods of work with children as a model for potential work with adults. Although acknowledging Klein's work, too, Ferenczi clearly took a stand in the evolving struggle between the two—a struggle of great concern to Freud, who identified with his daughter and resented Jones for supporting Klein. At the same time, Ferenczi gently argued with Freud: "Freud is right . . . that it is a triumph for analysis when it succeeds in substituting recollection for acting out. But I think it is also valuable to secure important material in the shape of action" (p. 131). Here we find the starting point of the positive contemporary view of the place of enactment and of Winnicott's understanding of analysis as play.

The private correspondence, however, was more painful than what was conveyed in the public tribute. Ferenczi, saying he was immersed in his "work of purification," reassured Freud, "I am not (or only rarely) overstepping the bounds of normality" (Falzeder and Brabant, 2000, p. 417). Freud grew critical: "You are trying to press forward in all kinds of directions which to me seem to lead to no desirable end. . . . it could be a new, third puberty, after the completion of which you will probably have reached maturity" (p. 418). Ferenczi, offended, delayed his response and then finally wrote, "I definitely won't deny that subjective factors often significantly influence . . . me. In the past this has occasionally led to exaggerations . . . [but] these excursions into uncertainty also always were of significant use to me" (p. 419).

The tension reached a new peak when Freud heard Clara Thompson's account that she often kissed her analyst, Ferenczi, and in December 1931 Freud sent Ferenczi a scolding, sarcastic letter ("Why stop with a kiss? Certainly, one will achieve still more if one adds 'pawing,' which, after all, doesn't make any babies"). He reminded Ferenczi of past sexual games with patients (Elma?) and expressed hopelessness about influencing him because of his defiant self-assertion (pp. 422–423). Ferenczi, deeply hurt, answered, "'Youthful sins,' misdemeanors, when they have been overcome and analytically worked through, can even make one wiser and more careful. . . . I believe I am capable of creating a mild, passionless atmosphere" (p. 424). After this exchange, the correspondence dwindled. Freud urged a reluctant Ferenczi to become IPA president: "You should leave the island of dreams which you inhabit with your fatasy children and mix in with the struggle of men" (p. 433). Ferenczi protested Freud's use of "expressions like 'dream-life,' 'daydreams,' 'puberty crisis'" and expressed his feeling "that out of the relative confusion something useful will develop and has already developed" (p. 435).

Ferenczi's *Clinical Diary* and "Confusion of Tongues": The Break

Ferenczi apparently had given up on his dialogue with Freud as a springboard for creativity and felt forced to progress on his own. The result was Ferenczi's (1932) *Clinical Diary*, written between January and October 1932 and eventually published in the 1980s. Here I cannot summarize this rich and complex text, which deals with numerous clinical and theoretical issues (including trauma, ways of reacting to it, and splitting, in patients and in Ferenczi's own life), but I can say a few words about the light it sheds on the Ferenczi–Freud relationship and on the new stage in Ferenczi's technique—namely, mutual analysis, his most radical innovation.

With this new experiment, Ferenczi shifted his central therapeutic image from mothers and children to brothers and sisters. Parents are out of the picture. Analyst and analysand are now Hansel and Gretel, seeking hand in hand their lost path in a dark forest populated by abusive witches: "two equally terrified children who compare their experiences, and because of their common fate understand each other completely and instinctively try to comfort each other" (p. 56).

Mutual analysis can be seen as Ferenczi's return to his basic values and character style (Berman, 1995b), as evidenced in his early wish to practice mutual analysis with Freud. In a way, mutual analysis was also an attempt—after a long detour—to meet Elma's challenge to speak "honestly, the way one speaks to an

adult." At the same time, it was also his response to a clinical issue—the stalemate created when a vulnerable patient (in this
specific case, Elizabeth Severn,[7] called RN in the *Clinical Diary;*
Fortune, 1993) lost faith in the analyst because she experienced a
discrepancy between his conscious dedication and his unconscious hostility. Whereas the traditional response is to attribute
the patient's view to distorted displacements from past relationships or to arbitrary projections from the patient's own tormented inner world, Ferenczi raised a different possibility—
that the patient's experience may be a valid *perception,* and, if so,
that trust can be restored not by interpretation (which may be
correctly seen as defensive) but by acknowledgment and, furthermore, by the analyst's readiness to explore openly his countertransference with the analysand.

Mutual analysis evolved gradually. Ferenczi (1932) described
several stages in his work with Severn—catharsis; active therapy;
relaxation and consequent provocations; Ferenczi's gradual acknowledgment of negative and libidinous feelings; and Severn's
demand to analyze Ferenczi. "At first strong opposition on my
part; the patient may abuse the situation . . . analyze me instead of
herself. Surprisingly, it happened otherwise; the attitude
adopted by the analyst made it possible for the analysand to convey from then on . . . everything that had been formerly withheld"
(pp. 10–11).

---

[7]Severn, born in 1879 as Leota Brown, was an American who became a
self-proclaimed psychotherapist after undergoing theosophical treatment for one of numerous breakdowns. Severn suffered severe depressions and periods of confusion, at times became suicidal, and came to see
Ferenczi in Budapest as a last resort. She brought along four or five devoted American patients who continued therapy with her and helped
her finance her stay. Severn was in analysis from 1924 to 1932. Fortune
(1993) traced its various stages with the aid of the *Clinical Diary;* Ferenczi's papers, in which Severn's contributions are often acknowledged;
and more than 30 years of correspondence between Elizabeth and her
daughter Margaret. Many breakthroughs occurred in the analysis—
recollections of childhood abuse, mutual analysis, and so forth—but
Severn left Budapest in February 1933 traumatized by Ferenczi's severe
illness and by his inability to work through their termination. She published a book (Severn, 1933) and several articles, continued her practice
in London and New York, and died in 1959.

The *Clinical Diary* documents Ferenczi's thoughtful and self-critical attempt to integrate this new option into the psychoanalytic treatment method. Bold self-scrutiny and continual examination of our impact on our patients are the necessary counterbalance to authenticity; Ferenczi was capable of both. Ferenczi died before he could draw the final balance sheet of his new approach, as he had managed to do with his earlier active technique, but his diary testifies to his full awareness of the problems involved, side by side with his excitement about the new horizons he hoped to open for the therapeutic profession.

Here are a few of the difficulties Ferenczi identified regarding mutual analysis: "One cannot allow oneself to be analyzed by every patient!" (p. 27); it is difficult to end sessions after the analysand has been burdened with what the analyst has said (p. 29); there are problems with discretion (e.g., secrets of other analysands); does analysis turn into group analysis not carried out in a group? what to do with feelings that the patient cannot tolerate? (pp. 34–35); will projections and fears increase? what if the analysand asks to be paid for analyzing the analyst? (p. 46); what if an analysand in mutual analysis starts practicing mutual analysis with one of her or his patients? (p. 74). At times, Ferenczi considered accepting the "impossibility, even madness, of this whole idea and technique" (p. 74) or concluded that "mutual analysis: only a last resort! Proper analysis by a stranger, without any obligation, would be better" (p. 115).

For many years, Balint was reluctant to publish the *Clinical Diary*; he feared it would be misunderstood. When writing about Ferenczi's experiments, Balint (1967, 1969) did not hint in any way about the existence of an unpublished diary or about mutual analysis. Should we see Balint's caution, his avoidance of publishing or even quoting the *Clinical Diary*, as judicious and wise or as cowardly? To choose between the different views of Balint's behavior, we may need to pose an almost impossible question: Would earlier publication of the *Clinical Diary* have created an earlier "Ferenczi renaissance" and hastened changes in psychoanalysis? Or, to the contrary, would it have badly tarnished Ferenczi's name, as Balint feared, and pushed him even more into oblivion? Risking an answer may be foolhardy.

Some recent discussions of mutual analysis as a "boundary violation" seem to justify Balint's concerns (Berman, 1997b). Still, I believe that most contemporary readers understand this issue differently. Although Ferenczi's early entanglement with Elma was indeed an impulsive and destructive boundary violation in which the analyst lost control of his therapeutic task, mutual analysis — based on the egalitarian yearnings so prominent in Ferenczi's personality, which indeed had a certain role in his falling in love with Elma — is a much more thoughtful, deliberate, and controlled experiment, conducted under continual self-criticism.

I think of Ferenczi in this last stage of his life as a fearless soldier who threw himself on barbed wire so all his fellow soldiers could step on his body in order to cross a difficult and fortified border; the soldier may have been badly wounded, but his comrades reached a new territory that had previously been inaccessible.

The concrete technique of mutual analysis (patient and analyst alternating on the couch), as well as some other experimental methods used by Ferenczi during that period (e.g., no time limits for sessions, which, unlike Lacan's, tended to be long rather than short), may not be viable. Ferenczi may have been naive to assume that physical contact with patients can be purely nurturing and lack erotic significance. Balint (1969), who remained in contact with a few of Ferenczi's last patients after the analyst's death, came to realize some of Ferenczi's blind spots, such as his lack of discrimination between different patterns of regression. Aron (1996a) suggested that Ferenczi may have sabotaged mutuality by confusing it with symmetry, which is a different matter. This quandary (combining mutuality and asymmetry, the latter deriving from any analyst's ethical obligation) was also explored by Hoffer (1996), who suggested, "True analytic openness requires a professional relationship that is necessarily asymmetrical because both parties must be committed to the analysis of the analysand" (p. 113). Indeed, recent work on analytic self-disclosure (Berman, 2001a), though inspired by Ferenczi, presupposes different roles for analyst and analysand.

In the *Clinical Diary*, Ferenczi (1932) also tried to sort out his relationship with Freud:

I tend to think that originally Freud really did believe in analysis; he followed Breuer with enthusiasm, and worked passionately, devotedly, on the curing of neurotics. . . . He must have been first shaken and then disenchanted . . . [maybe by] the discovery that hysterics lie. . . . Since making this discovery Freud no longer loves his patients . . . he still remains attached to analysis intellectually, but not emotionally [p. 93].

Freud, he noted, adopted him "almost like his son" and turned him, as Freud had earlier turned Jung, into his "crown prince," but Freud could "tolerate my being a son only until the moment when I contradicted him" (pp. 184–185). Ferenczi also analyzed his motives for initially following Freud blindly: "membership in a distinguished group"; "the unruffled assurance that one knew better . . . finding of the causes of failure in the patient instead of partly in ourselves" (p. 185).

Ferenczi decided to prepare a paper for the International Psychoanalytic Congress planned for September 1932 in Wiesbaden. As Freud was too sick to attend, Ferenczi went to Vienna to read Freud the paper, "Confusion of Tongues" (Ferenczi, 1933). This meeting — their last one, as it turned out — was a total disaster. Freud was shocked, felt attacked by the paper, and saw it as a regression to his long-abandoned seduction theory (Blass and Simon, 1994). He advised Ferenczi to delay presenting the paper at least for a year. Ferenczi refused, and Freud avoided shaking hands on their parting. Ferenczi stumbled on the way out, and, though this may have been an early symptom of his deteriorating health, the emotional meaning of this moment is clear.

Indeed, in "Confusion of Tongues" Ferenzci (1933) was openly critical of Freud's advocacy of objectivity and aloofness[8] — which, he suggested, may become "professional hypocrisy" (p. 159) — though he was equally critical of the authoritarian side of his own active technique. Ferenczi reintroduced the fatefulness of family circumstances and trauma, which were central in Freud's early seduction model but were neglected after oedipal fantasy became the new cornerstone. I must emphasize, however, that Ferenczi's

---

[8]*Neutrality* is not a word used by Freud; it is Strachey's watered-down translation of Freud's *Indifferenz*, which can also be translated as "indifference."

highly original thinking at the time, intricately combining interpersonal and intrapsychic dynamics, was by no means a return to
Freud's seduction hypothesis (Aron and Harris, 1993, p. 4);
Freud's interpretation (Gay, 1988, pp. 583–584) was in this respect
erroneous. Regrettably, some contemporary authors repeat this
equation (Rachman, 1993, p. 90).

To make the difference clearer, allow me to highlight two central themes in the paper that have no parallels in Freud's early
work. On the interpersonal level, Ferenczi emphasized the family
dynamics (particularly the denial) that occur after the sexual
abuse of a child (sexual abuse, the central paradigm of trauma
here, complements the centrality of rejection in "The Unwelcome
Child," 1929): "Usually the relation to a second adult ... [such as]
the mother is not intimate enough for the child to find help there;
timid attempts towards this end are refused by her as nonsensi-
cal" (Ferenczi, 1933, p. 163). This attention paid to the crucial role
of the invalidation of the child's experience is a forerunner of later
models such as the "double-bind," Laing's (1961) notion of mystification, and much work in the family therapy tradition. It also explains why an analyst's refusal to validate the analysand's
perception is so damaging — a point Freud apparently missed.

Intrapsychically, Ferenczi offered a rich and intricate analysis
of the ways abuse is transformed inwardly by children, whose
anxiety

> compels them to subordinate themselves like automata to
> the will of the aggressor, to divine each one of his desires
> and to gratify these; completely oblivious of themselves
> they identify themselves with the aggressor ... he disap-
> pears as part of the external reality, and becomes intra- in-
> stead of extra-psychic [Ferenczi, 1933, p. 162].

This identification (Frankel, 2002) becomes a factor in the complex
splitting processes that now distort the child's entire personality — potentially creating dissociated precocious maturity and at
times evolving from fragmentation to atomization (Ferenczi, 1933,
p. 165). The relation of trauma and dissociation was recently de-
bated by Bromberg (1994) and by Davies and Frawley (1992, 1994).

Although the idea of "two languages" — the dichotomy between children's innocent tenderness and adults' frightening

passion — may belong to the utopian side of Ferenczi's thought (Berman, 2003a), much in "Confusion of Tongues" conveys a deep sensitivity to the life experiences of individuals. Ferenczi's conclusions regarding treatment focus on the analyst's sincerity and honesty, which can create a "confidence that establishes the contrast between the present and the unbearable traumatogenic past" (p. 160), but he avoided mentioning mutual analysis — a caution that was probably realistic.

Freud's negative view of "Confusion of Tongues" was shared by many analysts. Eitingon and others at first wanted to stop it from being presented in the Wiesbaden congress, and Jones prevented its publication in the *International Journal of Psycho-Analysis* for 16 years — an act deservedly called the "most regrettable editorial decision in the journal's history" (Berman, 1995b).

When Ferenczi wrote Freud again, he spoke of the "depth of the shock with which our conversation in Vienna before the Congress came to me." He described his rapidly deteriorating health and added, "You certainly know just as well as I do what a loss it means for both of us that my visit with you could transpire in such a way" (Falzeder and Brabant, 2000, pp. 443–444). Freud, clearly feeling abandoned too, answered, "I don't any longer believe that you will rectify yourself . . . you have been systematically turning away from me, probably developed a personal hostility" (p. 445). Haynal (2002) spoke of the tragic end of a love affair.

The *Clinical Diary* (Ferenczi, 1932) includes only three more pages, particularly painful, after this exchange with Freud:

> In my case the blood-crisis [pernicious anemia] arose when I realized that not only can I not rely on the protection of a "higher power" but *on the contrary* I shall be trampled under foot by this indifferent power as soon as I go my own way and not his . . . must I (if I can) create a new basis for my personality, if I have to abandon as false and untrustworthy the one I have had up to now? Is the choice here one between dying and "rearranging myself" — and this at the age of 59? On the other hand, is it worth it always to live the life (will) of another person — is such a life not almost death? [p. 212].

Dupont (1988) commented, "Ferenczi had to confront alone the choice between the love and support of a powerful father and his own self-fulfillment—a dilemma that in the end killed him" (p. xxvi).

Ferenczi became immobilized by his pernicious anemia and by the severe neurologic damage it caused. He could not walk and stopped seeing patients. But even from his deathbed he still wrote to Freud when the Nazis came to power in Germany in March 1933: "I advise you to make use of the time of the not yet immediately dangerously threatening situation and . . . to go to a more secure country, perhaps England" (Falzeder and Brabant, 2000, p. 447). Freud answered in a friendly tone, but blindly: "I am not considering leaving Vienna. I am not mobile enough . . . It is not certain that the Hitler regime will also overpower Austria . . . everyone believes that it will not reach the height of brutality here that it has in Germany" (p. 449). There are indications that Freud considered Ferenczi's concern to be an aspect of his delusions. Ferenczi congratulated Freud on his 77th birthday, and Gizella appended a note saying how heavy her heart was in view of his condition. Ferenczi died on May 22, 1933.

In writing an obituary for Ferenczi, Freud (1933) sharply distinguished among the different stages in the man's life. He mentioned their friendship fondly, praised Ferenczi's "contributions which have made all analysts his pupils" (p. 298), and noted that most of these contributions were made before Ferenczi reached 50. In the last paragraph, Freud added:

> After this peak in his achievements our friend slowly began to slide away from us . . . one problem alone absorbed his interest. The need to heal and to help became imperious. Probably he had set himself aims that to-day are not to be reached with our therapeutic means. From affective sources, imperfectly drained, he was persuaded that we could accomplish far more with our patients if we gave them enough of the love they had longed for in childhood [p. 299].

Four years later, Freud (1937) wrote about Ferenczi without mentioning the man's name, though many readers could guess his identity:

A certain man, who had himself practiced psychoanalysis with great success . . . made himself the subject of an
analysis by someone else whom he regarded as superior
to himself. This critical illumination of his own self had a
completely successful result. He married the woman he
loved and turned into a friend and teacher of his supposed
rivals. Many years passed in this way, in which his relations with his former analyst also remained unclouded.
But then, for no assignable external reason, trouble arose.
The man . . . became antagonistic to the analyst and re-
proached him for having failed to give him a complete
analysis. The analyst . . . should have given his attention to
the possibilities of a negative transference. The analyst defended himself by saying that, at the time of the analysis,
there was no sign of a negative transference . . . Furthermore, he added, not every good relation between an analyst and his subject during and after analysis was to be
regarded as a transference; there were also friendly relations which were based on reality and which proved to be
viable [pp. 221–222].

Comparison of this text with the story we traced through the
correspondence makes it clear that Freud "cut corners" — especially regarding the full success of the analysis and the circumstances of Sándor's marriage to Gizella — to justify his feeling that
the distancing came out of the blue. Freud's last paragraph is particularly defensive; in it, he mobilized his wise acknowledgment
of the possibility of realistic friendship to deny the mutual transferential conflict that had characterized the Freud–Ferenczi tie all
along.

Freud knew this. On May 23, 1919, Ferenczi wrote Freud,
"Since the moment in which you advised me against Elma, I have
had a resistance toward your own person" (Falzeder and
Brabant, 1996, p. 356). And, on February 27, 1922, Ferenczi wrote
Groddeck, "Prof. Freud . . . persists in his original view that the
crux of the matter is my hatred for *him*, because he stopped me . . .
from marrying the younger woman (now my stepdaughter).
Hence my murderous intentions toward him" (Fortune, 2002, p.
19; see also Haynal, 1988, p. 44).

The belated publication of "Confusion of Tongues" in English in 1949 and the appearance of *Final Contributions to the Problems and Methods of Psycho-Analysis* in 1955 signified a reintegration of late Ferenczi into psychoanalytic discourse. But Jones's (1957) biography of Freud blocked this process. Jones claimed bluntly, "Rank and Ferenczi . . . developed psychotic manifestations that revealed themselves in, among other ways, turning away from Freud and his doctrines" (p. 47). He suggested that Ferenczi's pernicious anemia "exacerbated his latent psychotic trends" (p. 188), manifested in "delusions about Freud's supposed hostility" and in "violent paranoiac and even homicidal outbursts" (p. 190).

These comments hurt all who knew Ferenczi personally. Elma wrote Balint, also on behalf of her sister Magda, on November 8, 1957:

It shocked us to read what Jones states about Sándor, namely that he died insane! As you know he was not insane! Even if Jones, and probably some other persons, cannot follow his last writings and do not agree with him, that certainly does not prove that Sándor was insane! It is horrible to make such a statement of a dead man, who cannot defend himself. Will somebody rectify it? Will something be written and done? Publicly, I mean [Berman, 2004].

Balint negotiated a public response with Jones and with Hoffer, editor of the *International Journal of Psycho-Analysis*. Balint told Elma, apologetically, "As a result of a compromise [it] had to be diplomatic," and explained, "That is a pity but what would the alternative have been? To start a public controversy with charges and counter charges, stirring up intimate details of Sándor's and the Professor's life, and so on" (January 28, 1958; Berman, 2004).

This last concern must be understood against the background of what Roazen (1998) described as an "implied threat on Jones's part" in Jones's December 16, 1957 letter to Balint: "Perhaps you might tell Elma and Magda that I was extremely careful to avoid dealing with Ferenczi's personal life, e.g., the way he treated Gisela [sic], his intimacy with her daughter, etc., but kept strictly to his relations with Freud" (p. 273).

In his published response, Balint (1958) said that Jones's alle-
gations could imply that Ferenczi's later writings "do not merit
proper attention." To prevent such a conclusion, Balint reported:

> I saw Ferenczi frequently once or twice almost every week —
> during his last illness. . . . Despite his progressive physical
> illness, mentally he was always clear and on several occa-
> sions discussed with me in detail his controversy with
> Freud, his various plans how to rewrite and enlarge his last
> Congress paper if he were ever able to take a pen in his
> hand again [p. 68].

Balint accepted Jones's description of Ferenczi's "touchiness and
an inordinate need to be loved and appreciated" and proposed
that Jones and he differ in their interpretation of the facts — a dis-
parity "caused, at any rate partly, by some subjective factor."
(Jones vetoed Balint's wish to mention that both of them were
Ferenczi's analysands.)

Fromm's (1970) view of this letter was harsh. Fromm pointed
to all the qualifiers and apologetic nuances and characterized
the text as a "tortuous and submissive letter" (p. 22). Fromm was
probably right that this letter "shows the intensity of the pressure which forbids any but the mildest criticism of one of the
leaders of the organization." One might add, however, that
Balint came to Britain as a refugee and depended on Jones's support for finding his place there. Moreover, we see Balint's attempts not to repeat Ferenczi's tragic fate and instead to express
his truth in a moderate way that will prevent intense conflict
and potential exorcism.

In a rejoinder to Balint's letter, Jones (1958) sympathized with
Balint (in a rather patronizing tone) but claimed that his own diagnosis "was based on the trustworthy evidence of an eye-wit-
ness" whereas Balint's impressions cannot contradict it "since it
is a characteristic of paranoid patients to mislead friends and relatives by exhibiting complete lucidity on most topics" (p. 68). Regarding Ferenczi's last writings, Jones merely recorded his
acquiescence "in the opinions expressed so firmly by Freud,
Eitingon, and everyone I knew in 1933 that they had been to some
extent influenced by subjective personal factors" (p. 68). Notice
the assumption that serious professional work (supposedly the

work of Freud or Jones) was not influenced at all by subjective personal factors — an assumption I strongly doubt. As for the reliable eyewitness, he has never been found, and there are many indications that Jones relied mostly on Freud's impressions (Bonomi, 1999) and possibly that he invented the eyewitness to justify those impressions (Haynal, 1994, p. 1279).

Ferenczi was never fully forgotten. The impact of his work spread through his analysands and students — Michael Balint, who became a central member of the British Independent group and eventually served as president of the British Psychoanalytic Society; Clara Thompson, a close friend of Sullivan and one of the founders of the American interpersonal tradition (she was encouraged by Sullivan to be analyzed by Ferenczi but returned with mixed experiences[9]; S. A. Shapiro, 1993); Frieda Fromm-Reichmann, Ferenczi's supervisee during her early work with his friend Groddeck (Hornstein, 2000, p. 450) and for whom Ferenczi was an inspiration in her work with psychotics; Margaret Mahler, through her growing impact on American ego psychology; and Paul Ornstein (formerly Balint's collaborator; Ornstein, 2002) and John Gedo, both of Hungarian background, who became close associates of Kohut when he formulated self psychology. Still, until the Ferenczi renaissance started in the 1980s with the publication of the *Clinical Diary* and with Haynal's (1988) pioneering book on technique, Ferenczi's full contribution was absent from the central psychoanalytic discourse.

Reviving the Broken Dialectic

Freud and his overly loyal followers failed to see that Ferenczi's last period had been enormously productive (Berman, 1999). This final, painful stage of the Freud–Ferenczi dialogue set the stage for new versions of a relational or an intersubjective psychoanalysis in which the relationship and the experience it provides are conceived as central therapeutic factors and interpretations can

---

[9]Thompson (1950) rejected in particular the idea of mutual analysis and warned that admitting mistakes by the analyst "should not degenerate into mutual analysis" (p. 187).

be used to deepen the relationship. For Freud, though, the relationship, when he came to value it, belatedly, was at most a prerequisite for allowing interpretations to be absorbed. In the numerous new models that have been developed in divergent theoretical contexts, the patient's experience of the analyst is taken as a potentially valid perception, and the analyst's personality and countertransference are seen as powerful influences on the analysand.

Hoffer (1993) suggested, "If Sigmund Freud was the father of psychoanalysis, Sándor Ferenczi was the mother . . . psychoanalysis lost its mother . . . [and] thus became a one-parent child" (p. 75). When I first quoted this moving metaphor, I felt obliged to add, "Now, it seems, mother is back for good" (Berman, 1996, p. 410). With time, however, I became concerned about some nuances of this image. Its two components, which we may wish to separate, are the two-parent aspect and the gender aspect.

Indeed, for a long time we have become accustomed to viewing psychoanalysis, and with it psychoanalytically oriented psychotherapy, as a single-parent family. Believing that we all sprang from Freud's head, as Athena sprang from the head of Zeus (an early, pre-Christian version of immaculate conception), makes many of our present concerns, ideas, and methods seem bastardly, rootless, representing mostly a negation. This indeed is the springboard allowing orthodox authors to describe as "deviations" any trends that differ from Freud's views.

On the other hand, if we reclaim Ferenczi as our missing initial "other voice," we can think of psychoanalytic thought and treatment as evolving from the dialogue of two voices—from the "intercourse" (both loving and conflictual, personally and theoretically) of the two parents, Freud and Ferenczi, as a true generative dyad. This idea allows us to find anew a freeing, dialectical view of our present professional world in which the Freud–Ferenczi dialogue is omnipresent (Berman, 1999).

These days, we all seem to be constantly negotiating our way between the inner world of fantasy (Freud) and the impact of family and environment (Ferenczi) as shaping personality; between drives and defenses (Freud) and self–object relations (Ferenczi) as central conceptions; between interpretation (Freud) and affective experience (Ferenczi) as our main therapeutic tools; and between viewing ourselves primarily as impartial observers

(Freud) and viewing ourselves primarily as involved in a mutual intersubjective process (Ferenczi).

We need our inner tie to both "parents" to be free to find our own individual paths within this dialectic. For this reason, I am personally critical of any attempt to develop a Ferenczian psychoanalysis or a Ferenczian treatment technique. Such attempts may lead to new heterodox story lines about our origins—which are likely to mimic the rigid, orthodox story line, only replacing the names of the idealized "good guys" with those of the denigrated "bad guys." New techniques may be as suffocating as "classical" technique; they may share with it the "illusion that there can be a technique that one needs only to apply 'correctly'" (Haynal, 1993, p. 62). To me, Ferenczi's legacy signifies a weariness with such limiting approaches, not development of yet another one.

In referring to father and mother, however, the gender component of the image is rather conventional. Ferenczi (1919a), discussing the "indulgent mother" and the "stern father" (p. 186), showed the intrusion of social stereotypes into original thinking—a phenomenon found also in the writings of Freud and other authors of the period. Earlier, Ferenczi (1909) set up a similar dichotomy in describing forms of transference in hypnotic treatment—"father hypnosis" and "mother hypnosis" —a differentiation that occupied him throughout his work. Still, he commented, "I lay no great stress on this distinction between parental and maternal hypnosis, for it happens often enough that the father and mother change their parts" (p. 59).

Even today, we often conventionally identify mother with primary caretaking and father with authority, with the Law; mother with holding and with supplying a protective shield, father with introducing reality testing and challenging a child to deal with reality; mother with affective attunement and empathy, father with verbalization and reason. However, we know that, in any child's development, these poles are not necessarily distributed by gender. There are "motherly" fathers, "fatherly" mothers, and parents who present unique and paradoxical combinations of traits and attitudes.

Moreover, in the lives and work of Freud and Ferenczi we find expressions of a nurturing, "motherly" Freud (who fed his hungry patient, Ernst Lanzer, the Rat Man) and of a strict, "fatherly"

Ferenczi (notably in the active technique, when he demanded that patients avoid symptomatic behaviors or do what their phobias prevented). An emphasis on Ferenczi's supposed femininity could be colored by sexist denigration,[10] as it was in Freud's responses to Ferenczi. After the Palermo clash, Freud wrote to Jung, "My travelling companion is a dear fellow, but dreamy in a disturbing kind of way. . . . He has been too passive and receptive, letting everything be done for him like a woman" (McGuire, 1974, p. 353).

Ferenczi often expressed skepticism about too sharply differentiating masculine and feminine identity. In *Thalassa* (1924b), he spoke of foreplay as "bringing about . . . an identification with the sexual partner . . . [serving] to efface the boundaries between the egos of the sexual partners" to reduce the experience of mutual threat (p. 17; Stanton, 1991). Ferenczi and Rank (1924, p. 41) reminded us that in the transference the analyst constantly alternates between the two parental images of father and mother.

At one point, Ferenczi (1931) emphasized the maternal role of the analyst: "The analyst's behavior is thus rather like that of an affectionate mother, who will not go to bed at night until she has talked over with the child all his current troubles . . . and has set them to rest" (p. 137). In the *Clinical Diary*, however, Ferenczi (1932) frowned on any set roles as potential poses covering up the analyst's conflictual and constantly fluctuating feelings. My preference in listening to Ferenczi's dialogue with Freud, as well as with his patients and readers, is not to typecast him in one binding role but rather to notice the multiple meanings and nuances of his personality and of the interactions created.

Still, the two-parent image is certainly relevant to the issue of dyadic and triadic dynamics, which is meaningful developmentally, irrespective of gender. Evolution from a dyadic bond to a triangular relatedness is liberating from constraining symbiosis,

---

[10]Winnicott was deeply offended when he was described as a "Madonna" in a 1966 article by Katherine Whitehorn in the *Observer* (Grosskurth, 1986, p. 233). Regarding Freud's misogyny, Ferenczi (1932) noted "the ease with which [Freud] sacrifices the interests of women in favor of male patients" and cast doubt on the "castration theory of femininity" (pp. 187–188).

dependence, and overidentification. Lacan, Mahler, and others, using various terminologies, have explored this developmental breakthrough. Having two meaningful parents, and feeling related to both, makes it clear to the child that he or she cannot be fully expected to be a "chip off the old block." No parent can be a perfect model, if the other is to be acknowledged too; no parent has an absolute claim on truth, when a second truth is evident nearby. If there are two origins, there can be a unique third option—a separate, autonomous self.

Let me add parenthetically that some people may be, consciously or unconsciously, fascinated with cloning. They are eager to become single parents—genetically (in their grandiose fantasy) or, if impractical, then at least socially and psychologically. Naturally, single-parent families of all varieties come into being for a multitude of reasons. Only in particular cases may we discover, through analytic scrutiny, a parent who cannot tolerate the partiality of joint parenthood. This wish for exclusive parenthood may at times be achieved secretly, even when the semblance of a two-parent family is maintained. For that man or woman, a narcissistic need for a replica—a desperate wish for total identity and control—takes the place of parenthood as an object relationship, with its unavoidable separateness.

But let me return to our professional history. Naturally, numerous other figures have strongly influenced our contemporary thought. But most of them knew Freud only marginally or not at all. In our internalized family representation, Klein, Winnicott, and Kohut are offspring; they and Freud are not on an equal generational footing. Ferenczi, though 17 years younger than Freud, is. The intense dialogue of these two men continued over a quarter of a century, and their exchanges were undoubtedly a springboard for innumerable theoretical and clinical innovations. The dialectical process was mutual: Freud and Ferenczi needed and influenced each other.

But during the last stage—the last years of Ferenczi's life, culminating with "Confusion of Tongues" (1933) and the *Clinical Diary* (1932)—Freud and Ferenczi's mutual influence was no longer possible. Freud completely rejected "Confusion of Tongues." He described it to Eitingon as stupid and inadequate (Gay, 1988, p. 583). This rejection signifies a worrisome ossification in Freud's thinking—a step into the defensive rigidity that was to stifle psychoanalytic theory and training for decades. Here the dialectic was visibly broken (Berman, 1999).

Turning opponents into madmen, as Jones (1957) did in discussing Rank and Ferenczi (p. 47), is one of the worst manifestations of that rigidity. It creates a make-believe split between "us, the sane" and "them, the crazy ones." Such a split signifies an abandonment of one of the most radical innovations of psychoanalysis, the awareness that "madness" resides in all of us and is a source of creativity and therapeutic power: "We are poor indeed if we are only sane" (Winnicott, 1945, p. 150). Acceptance of this subversive view leads us to acceptance of the possibility that the tormented, "mad" aspects in the emotional life of the greatest theoreticians paved the way for their brilliant insights; our knowledge of such sources in no way reduces the value of these insights.

Moreover, each analyst's capacity to develop a unique analytic self, based on genuine life experience and worldview, is endangered if stepping out of line is slandered as insanity. Such threats pave the way for developing a false analytic self — a danger I explore in chapter 3.

Against this background, I believe that, in the process of analytic training, we benefit from deidealizing (but not devaluing!) our "ancestors." Knowing the personal idiosyncrasies and flaws of Freud and Ferenczi, Jung, or Rank, as well as Klein and Kohut helps us to see them as fully human, which unavoidably means being both sane and "mad"; as struggling with the same personal and clinical dilemmas with which we all struggle; as having formed their theoretical and therapeutic models (brilliant, but necessarily limited) out of their unique life experiences. When we acknowledge these similarities, we realize that we too are destined to mold our analytic models from within and that we cannot use ready-mades. In relating to the theorists we find close to our heart, we can practice, in a way, a form of "mutual analysis" — use their insights to understand ourselves and use our own insights and analytic skills (with the added advantage of hindsight) to understand their lives and thinking better.

We can now see that Ferenczi was ahead of his time, and our generation finds him more understandable than his own did. We may also be better equipped to revive the broken dialectic — to integrate his contribution more fully into new psychoanalytic models and take full advantage of his genius while overcoming some of the inner contradictions and blind spots that contributed to the ultimately tragic quality of his life story.

The point is not to put aside Ferenczi's (or Freud's) personality and life when evaluating his ideas—as a conventional (nonanalytic) approach might indicate—but to use our growing knowledge of these personal aspects to understand his ideas better and to contemplate more richly his strengths and weaknesses.

To meet this challenge, we need to study Ferenczi's life and work patiently, wisely, in their historical and cultural context, and allow for their full complexity and paradoxicality—while avoiding, as much as we can, slipping into idealizations and devaluations. Such study has the best potential to enrich the Ferenczi renaissance, from which we can all benefit.

2

The Klein–Winnicott Relationship and the Debate on Inner and Outer Reality

Transitional space breaks down when either inner or outer reality begins to dominate the scene, just as conversation stops if one of the participants takes over.

— Adam Phillips, *Winnicott*

Let me turn to a second generative dyad, Melanie Klein and Winnicott, which in my view is another vital source of our present discourse. The two dyads I depict here are interconnected: Ferenczi was Klein's first analyst and initial mentor. However, she rarely gave him much credit, and she expressed more loyalty to Freud and to Abraham (her second analyst) than to Ferenczi. We do not know much about that first analysis. Grosskurth (1986) suggested that "her resistances were so strong that he was unable to penetrate her implacable defenses" (p. 72). Ferenczi's influence on Klein was examined by Stanton (1991), who contrasted Ferenczi's belief in the power of regenerative tendencies with Klein's emphasis that reparation is lifelong and cannot secure a permanent option on the "depressive position." Both complained about the same absence in their analyses — namely, their analysts' avoidance of negative transference (Ferenczi complained about Freud, Klein about Ferenczi). Was that lack a launching pad for their common interest in destructive drives — and for their divergent views about them?

Klein and Winnicott

Exactly as Freud and Ferenczi had done earlier, Klein and Winnicott maintained a complex relationship lasting a quarter of a century (Berman, 1997d). It started when Winnicott's first analyst,

Strachey, referred him to Klein for supervision in 1935 (Winnicott, 1962a) and ended with Klein's death in 1960. We do not have
their full correspondence, but a familiar picture emerges from
their papers and letters (Rodman, 1987) and from Grosskurth's
(1986) Klein biography. In this dyad, again the senior partner had
a fertile influence on the younger one, also valued him, and was
willing at some points to learn from him—but later, when the
younger partner became too independent, grew angry at him and
was unable to appreciate his original thought.

Thus, Klein was initially very happy when Winnicott confirmed some of her ideas through his vast pediatric practice. She
relied on his support when she could not return to London during
the war and was happy with his backing during the Controversial Discussions between her group and that of Anna Freud. I
wonder, however, if Klein saw all the implications of Winnicott's
brief but passionate contribution to these discussions on March
11, 1942.

Winnicott's speech that day followed one by Walter Schmid-
erberg, Klein's alienated son-in-law, who compared Klein to Jung
(as someone who had turned his back on Freud) and even to the
Mad Hatter from *Alice in Wonderland*.

Winnicott, in turn, focused on truth and fear of truth ("some
fear of truth is inevitable"; King and Steiner, 1991, p. 87), on the
constant changes in Freud's own views, and on his own belief
that "to continue his work is to continue to reach out into the unknown in order to gain more knowledge and understanding" (p.
88). Winnicott's central concern was the need for freedom of inquiry, of which he felt Anna Freud's followers were not tolerant.
Winnicott did not refer to the specific content of Klein's work but
strongly objected to "restricting our work to the study and application of psychoanalytic theory in the form in which it has crystallized out at any one point in history" (p. 89).

In other words, though Winnicott's contribution was pro-
Kleinian in the context of the time (Klein immediately rose to support it, emphasizing the danger that inhibition is the outgrowth
of fear that new hypotheses "may contradict accepted theory";
p. 90), it also expressed his need for his own freedom of inquiry—a
need that, within a decade, led to his estrangement from Klein.

Winnicott's original views were evident in another brief comment he made in the discussions (March 1, 1944). King and

Steiner (1991) reported, "Dr Winnicott did not think that a baby's first cries could be called sad. . . . He thought that there was only a baby–mother relationship as was contained in Dr Middlemore's title of her book *The Nursing Couple*" (p. 820).

It is intriguing that major personal issues were involved in the Klein–Winnicott encounter, just as they were in the one between Freud and Ferenczi. In the Freud–Ferenczi discourse, visions of a desirable male–female relationship were prominent: Should passion be a primary criterion? Should total openness be desired? The question of parenthood had a secondary role: Ferenczi's desperate wish for children, which had alienated him from older Gizella, was interpreted by Freud merely as a defense against latent homosexuality. Whereas Freud analyzed Elma and disliked her, Klein analyzed Clare, Winnicott's second wife (in analytic training at that time), who seemed to dislike Klein (Grosskurth, 1986, pp. 450–453). At one point, Winnicott had to mediate between them — after Clare stormed out of Melanie's office and refused to return following a 25-minute interpretation of her dream ("How dare you take my dream and serve it up to me?" she exclaimed). Worried and, again, attentive to the trainee's vulnerability, Winnicott advised his wife, "If you give it up, she'll never let you qualify" (p. 452). This event, however, happened late in their lives, whereas the first personal clash between Klein and Winnicott was about the nature of parenthood.

Although Winnicott, like Ferenczi, was childless (we do not know why, but the shaky mental condition of Winnicott's first wife, Alice Taylor, may have been relevant), he developed enormous sensitivity to the nuances of the parental position, and here he and Klein did not see eye to eye. "My trouble when I start to speak to Melanie about her statement of early infancy," Winnicott wrote Riviere, "is that I feel as if I were talking about colour to the colour-blind. She simply says that she has not forgotten the mother and the part the mother plays, but in fact I find that she has shown no evidence of understanding the part the mother plays at the very beginning" (Rodman, 1987, p. 96).[1]

---

[1]Aguayo (2002) argued that Klein's unpublished manuscript "Notes on Baby" (about her grandchild) shows Klein's sensitivity to the familial environment, but Aguayo did not sufficiently explain why this sensitivity is rarely evident in her published work.

According to Grosskurth (1986), Klein's mother, Libussa
Reizes, seems to have been a domineering, intrusive, and oppressive mother. Yet, Melanie described her in glowing terms (p. 459)
and may have deemphasized the role of mother in her theory as a
way to exonerate her mother (as well as herself vis-à-vis her own
children). She once told Clare Winnicott, "It's no good talking
about your mother.... We can't do anything about it now" (p. 451).

Klein had three children, and her postpartum depressions
had a role in her first seeking analysis. After becoming an analyst, she insisted on analyzing her own little children — and she
saw no problem in doing so.[2] She presented these analyses in
disguised form in her early work: Erich/Eric became "Fritz";
Hans (who later died under circumstances that aroused suspi-
cions of suicide) became "Felix"; and Melitta (eventually Klein's
theoretical and personal enemy) became "Lisa" (Grosskurth,
1986, pp. 95–96). Reading these case studies is disturbing.

Klein seemed utterly oblivious to her possible impact as a
unique, overwhelming "combined maternal/analytic object"
(Palgi-Hecker, 2003). Discussing "Fritz's" preoccupation with
the analysis ("He tries to make the analysis the business of life";
Klein, 1921, p. 50) and his developing a "marked distaste for
play ... [loss of] desire for the companionship of other children ...
signs of boredom in his mother's company . . . dislike for being
told stories by her" (pp. 28–29), she seemed to be completely unaware that these may have been his responses to her intrusiveness and to the way she made use of his play and of their verbal
communications. Instead of striving for empathic understanding, Klein tried to effect stricter separation of analysis and life
(forgetting that she had combined them) and demanded discipline: "I firmly discouraged his attempt to vent in any other way
something of the aggressiveness towards his parents and myself
revealed by the analysis, and demanded the usual standard of
manners . . . he very soon acquiesced" (pp. 50–51).

In analyzing Fritz's school phobia, Klein emphasized the
phallic significance of the trees on the way to school, his fear that

---

[2]Freud analyzed Anna, but she was an adult at the time and apparently made the request of him. This choice also arouses concern, but of a
different degree.

these trees would be cut off, and his fantasy that he would meet a witch on his way to school (Klein, 1923, pp. 94–95), but she never mentioned the boy's being an unwanted child, her depression during the pregnancy, his grandmother's death when he was an infant, his father's being drafted when the boy was three, his parents' separation when he was five, their subsequent emigration to Berlin, and the anti-Semitic harassment he experienced there.

Klein also seemed blind to the impact of her forcing "Felix" to give up his attachments to another boy and to an older girl — attachments she felt were threatening the analysis (and apparently her exclusive role as a domineering maternal/analytic object): "The transference proved strong enough for me to impose a temporary break in this relation ... This object choice served the purpose of a flight from the phantasies and wishes directed towards me" (Klein, 1925, p. 115).

Such was the background of Klein's request of Winnicott, in the 1930s, to analyze her son Erich under her supervision. Winnicott stubbornly refused, and she gave up the idea.[3] With the aid of her one-sided intrapsychic emphasis, Klein seemed to overlook the interpersonal dynamics involved and denied the destructive impact of a parent/analyst or a parent/supervisor. Meanwhile, Winnicott, with his deep interest in the influence of parenting, was painfully aware of the dangers such intrusiveness poses for a child's development — and for his own development as an autonomous analyst. Klein's consistent tendency to play down the influence of the mother's personality on the child, and that of the analyst's personality on the analysand, may be related to her need to avoid the destructive implications of her "primal sin" toward her children; in so doing, she erred both as mother and as analyst. We can see that, through their personal interactions with Freud and with Klein, Ferenczi and Winnicott became sensitized to the abuses of professional power. These abuses are, of course, a major training issue, to which I return later.

---

[3]Only to fulfill it years later, when Klein supervised Marion Milner — a candidate and apparently less assertive than Winnicott — in the analysis of Klein's grandson. "Milner was troubled about the scornful comments Klein made about her own son Eric [the patient's father] during the supervision" (Grosskurth, 1986, p. 396).

When Winnicott asked Klein to become his second analyst, she refused. Segal (2001, p. 404) suggested that her response was related to her hope that Winnicott would analyze Erich; Segal also suggested that Winnicott felt deeply rejected. Klein referred Winnicott to her disciple, Joan Riviere. Segal, who discussed the matter with Klein, said that Klein always felt guilty about her rejection of Winnicott and that years later she agreed to accept Clare into analysis "as a compensation." One of the reasons Klein gave Segal for her guilt, however, reveals her continued rejection of Winnicott and her patronizing attitude toward him: Apparently she saw her refusal to analyze him as a cause of his rejection of her work and therefore felt guilty because "his activities were quite a threat to analytic development in England" (p. 404)!

Many of the central themes of the Klein–Winnicott relationship reappear in Winnicott's moving November 17, 1952 letter to Klein (Rodman, 1987). In it, Winnicott verbalized his disappointment with her lack of reaction to his original work: "It is a creative gesture and I cannot make any relationship through this gesture except if someone come to meet me" (p. 34). Moreover, he expressed his concern that "some of the patients that go to 'Kleinian enthusiasts' for analysis are not really allowed to grow or to create in the analysis" (p. 37). Later in the letter, he bitterly hinted at the way his originality had been interpreted by Riviere, his second analyst.[4]

---

[4]The Riviere–Winnicott relationship has not been fully explored, but studying it in the context of what we now know of Riviere's complex experiences as an analysand — with Jones, Freud (Kris, 1994), and Klein — would be intriguing. It is striking that Jones was hurt by Riviere's hostility toward him; he complained to Freud that "her letters have become more intolerably dictatorial and harsher than ever" (Kris, 1994, p. 654); Freud spoke of her as "concentrated acid" but attempted "to be as kind to her as I can" (p. 653); Winnicott, years later, was deeply hurt by her public criticism of him during and after his analysis with her (Kahr, 1996, p. 62). Her supervisee, Milner, saw her as a "bully" (Grosskurth, 1986, p. 396) and recalled Riviere saying, "If you don't do what I say what's the good of your coming!" (Sayers, 2000, p. 64). Riviere's book reviews were characterized by Sayers (p. 55) as "eloquent but high-handedly dismissive" and "abrasive." Riviere's analysts, colleagues, readers, and analysands seem to have had somewhat similar experiences with

Winnicott jokingly paraphrased Riviere's reaction to him in another letter, to Padel: "You write a book on the environment and I'll turn you into a frog!" (p. 79). This experience may have been the background for Winnicott's (1947) comment: "Psychoanalytic research is perhaps always to some extent an attempt on the part of an analyst to carry the work of his own analysis further than the point to which his own analyst could get him" (p. 196).

Winnicott was reluctant to read Ferenczi, lest he discover that he had stolen ideas from him (Goldman, 1993, p. 5). Still, Winnicott's conclusion of his 1952 letter to Klein amazingly echoes some of Ferenczi's still unpublished letters to Freud: "This matter which I am discussing touches the very root of my personal difficulty so that what you see can always be dismissed as Winnicott's illness, but if you dismiss it in this way you may miss something which is in the end a positive contribution" (Rodman, 1987, p. 37).

Let me turn to the theoretical expressions of the growing controversy between Klein and Winnicott. Winnicott's early psychoanalytic work is predominantly Kleinian (Aguayo, 2002). A good example is his first psychoanalytic paper, presented when he was accepted as a member of the British Psychoanalytic Society. "The Manic Defense" (Winnicott, 1935) was strongly influenced by Klein's notion of the depressive position, but even in this paper there are indications of an original, less pathologizing, and more existentialist viewpoint: "What about living in a town like London with its noise that never ceases, and lights that are never extinguished? [It] illustrates the reassurance through reality against death inside, and a use of manic defense that can be normal" (p. 131).

In 1940, Winnicott was appointed training analyst and was counted by Klein as one of the five Kleinian training analysts (Kahr, 1996, p. 71). But even then "Klein had problems with him because he did not give her his contributions early enough for her or the group to vet them, and he had made a number of 'blunders,'" as she wrote to Susan Isaacs (King and Steiner, 1991, p. xxiv). The subsequent deterioration of their relationship

---

her—confirming the major impact of the analyst's personality. One may wonder why Klein referred Winnicott to Riviere, from among her several disciples and collaborators.

was dramatically expressed in Klein's objection to two of Winnicott's groundbreaking papers. "Hate in the Countertransference" (Winnicott, 1947) established the analyst–patient relationship as fertile ground for intersubjective exploration—contrary to Klein's avoidance of the analyst's emotional world. (Klein also begged Paula Heimann not to deliver her seminal paper on countertransference [Heimann, 1950] and insisted that countertransference is something that interferes with psychoanalysis; Grosskurth, 1986, p. 378.) Winnicott discussed patients who need more than interpretation, because the "analyst has to be the first in the patient's life to supply certain environmental essentials" (p. 198). The developmental model presented in the paper also contradicts Klein's views, as Winnicott suggested that the "mother hates the baby before the baby hates the mother" (p. 200).

The other paper Klein disliked was "Transitional Objects and Transitional Phenomena" (1951), in which Winnicott celebrated infants' creativity and explored mothers' capacity to allow it—contrary to Klein's image of reclusive and tormented infants. This paper was initially meant for a special *International Journal of Psycho-Analysis* issue celebrating Klein's 70th birthday. However, "Klein wanted [Winnicott] to revise the paper so that it more clearly incorporated her ideas. He refused; and with the manuscript under his arm, he sadly left the room" (Grosskurth, 1986, p. 398). This event marked the end of Winnicott's membership in the Kleinian group.

In the original, 1951 version of the paper, Winnicott used some Kleinian terms. For example, he referred to "*badness* [italics added] or failure" of the external object, which "indirectly leads to deadness or to a persecutory quality of internal object" (p. 237). Before publishing the paper in *Playing and Reality* (1971), he changed that formulation to "failure of the [external object] in some essential function" (p. 11). In using more cautious wording, he abandoned the notion of "bad objects."

After being rejected by Klein, Winnicott felt freer to criticize the dogmatic style of the Kleinian group. In 1952, he complained to Hanna Segal, "[Klein's theory] is seldom discussed because it is put forward aggressively and then defended in a way which can only be called paranoid" (Rodman, 1987, p. 26). In 1954, he wrote Money-Kyrle, "I think what irritated me was that I faintly detected in your attitude this matter of a party line, a matter to which I am allergic" (p. 79). In 1956, he wrote Riviere sarcastically, "The only thing that can happen is that those of us who like to support Melanie produce, as we could all do, clinical material or quotations from the Bible which support her theme" (p. 95).

When Winnicott (1962a) discussed Klein's contribution after her death, he changed his tone, became very generous, and warmly recalled their early joint work. But he also oversimplified history a bit: "I never had analysis by her, or by any of her analysands, so that I did not qualify to be one of her group of chosen Kleinians" (p. 173). Actually, Riviere had been Klein's analysand,[5] and for many years Winnicott had been part of the Kleinian group (maybe he preferred to forget the traumatic ending of that period). In the final, theoretical part of this personal paper, Winnicott credited Klein with numerous contributions — at times confusing her original terms (e.g., the depressive position) with his own changed emphasis ("a theory of the individual's attainment of a capacity for concern") — and ended with but a very short list of "*doubtful* contributions":

Retaining a use of the theory of the Life and Death Instincts,
An attempt to state infantile destructiveness in terms of
(a) heredity
(b) envy [p. 178].

This list seems to bypass many of the dyad's major differences, some of which emerged sharply in another paper from the same year, "The Aims of Psycho-Analytical Treatment" (Winnicott, 1962b). This concise paper begins powerfully:

In doing psycho-analysis I aim at:
Keeping alive
Keeping well
Keeping awake [p. 166].

---

[5]In the published paper, Winnicott mentioned his analysis with Riviere only in brackets — seemingly as an afterthought (Winnicott, 1962a, p. 176). When he first presented the paper, to the candidates of the Los Angeles Psychoanalytic Institute, he seemingly repressed that analysis and spoke only of Strachey as being his analyst.

A page later, Winnicott gave a major reason for making interpretations: "If I make none the patient gets the impression that I understand everything," and "it is axiomatic that the work of analysis is done by the patient" (p. 167).

Gradually, Winnicott's creative growth led to a theory of technique diametrically opposed to Klein's. In a letter to Klein, he rejected the assumption "that there is a jigsaw of which all the pieces exist; further work will only consist in the fitting together of the pieces" (Rodman, 1987, p. 35). Klein's view of interpretation as granting valid, deep knowledge is replaced in Winnicott's work, notably in *Playing and Reality* (1971), by a view of interpretation as an invitation to creative play and exploration; the Kleinian analyst as authoritative observer is replaced by the analyst as originator of a potential space in which meaning emerges jointly and may best be formulated by the patient. "Psychotherapy is done in the overlap of the two play areas, that of the patient and that of the therapist. If the therapist cannot play, then he is not suitable for the work" (p. 63).

These innovative emphases may be seen as an aspect of Winnicott's lifelong existential quest to discover the authentic, alive, and bodily and affectively connected experience in his own life and thinking and in those he treated (Goldman, 1993). In his quest, he approached psychoanalysis "from scratch," with a dread of official or dogmatic notions and avoiding metapsychology. "Winnicott loved standing classical ideas on their head! Where Freud saw psychoanalysis as a way of freeing people from illusions, Winnicott emphasized the freedom to create and enjoy illusions. Whereas classical technique centered on the value of interpretations, Winnicott pointed to the value of not interpreting" (Goldman, 1993, p. xxiii).

Winnicott's self-description in a 1953 letter to David Rapaport is revealing: "I am one of those people who feel compelled to work in my own way and to express myself in my own language first; by a struggle I sometimes come around to rewording what I am saying to bring it in line with other work, in which case I usually find that my own 'original' ideas were not so original" (Rodman, 1987, pp. 53–54). When Masud Khan urged Winnicott to read a book by Trilling, Winnicott "hid his face in his hand, paused, convulsed himself into visibility and said: 'It's no use, Masud, asking me to read anything! If it bores me I shall fall asleep in the middle of the first page, and if it interests me I will start re-writing it by the end of that page'" (Khan, 1975, p. xvi).

Goldman (1993), attempting to characterize Winnicott, conveyed a complex mixture of grandiosity and modesty. He quoted critical remarks about Winnicott's preference to see children irregularly rather than referring them ("as if he felt that an ounce of Winnicott is worth a pound of pedestrian psychotherapy"; p. 10) and about his insufficient concern with the formal structure of psychoanalysis as a safeguard against potential abuses. Indeed, the latter danger came up recently in discussions of Winnicott's analytic work with Khan and of the possible influence of their intense professional relationship on Winnicott's inability to help Khan overcome the abusive and self-destructive streak in his personality (Hopkins, 1998; Aguayo, 2002; Godley, 2002; Goldman, 2003).

When the Freuds moved to London in 1938, escaping the Nazis, Winnicott was the only British analyst who called at their new home to ask if they were all right, as Anna well remembered (Rodman, 1987, p. xix). This gesture stands in sharp contrast to Klein's self-centered rage at Jones for helping the Freuds to settle in Britain (Grosskurth, 1986, p. 255). Nevertheless, Winnicott's ambivalence toward Freud had a deep emotional foundation. In 1964, Winnicott wrote, "I was sane, and . . . through analysis and self-analysis I achieved some measure of insanity. Freud's flight to sanity could be something we psycho-analysts are trying to recover from" (p. 483). Goldman (1993) traced Winnicott's "efforts to re-create for himself, in a personal way, aspects of theory which he had imaginatively destroyed" (p. 133). "Winnicott was enormously devoted to Freud, but needed to defend his own sensitive imagination" (p. 138).

Winnicott, who often introduced and defended the value of subjectivity, was also ambivalent about it—consistent with the scientific ethos of his time. Paradoxically, Winnicott was invested in the value of objectivity. This investment, which may seem dated from a contemporary perspective, may be seen in his contribution to the Controversial Discussions, in his notion of "objective hatred" (Winnicott, 1947), and in the discussion of "objective objects." Its personal significance emerges in his 1956 letter to his former analyst, Riviere: "I want you to know that I do not accept what you and Melanie implied, namely that my concern about

Melanie's statement of the psychology of earliest infancy is based on subjective rather than objective factors" (Rodman, 1987, p. 97). In this respect, Racker's belief that the only possible objectivity in psychoanalysis is an awareness of subjectivity sounds closer to our contemporary views.

But Winnicott's concern about being dismissed owing to his subjectivity was not unfounded. The harsh initial reception to Winnicott's last major paper, "The Use of an Object and Relating Through Identifications" (in Winnicott, 1971), in which the object's surviving attempted destruction is seen as the path to full object use, brings to mind the initial reception of Ferenczi's (1933) last paper. In 1968, Freud and Klein were dead, but Winnicott's paper nevertheless received a destructive reaction from Freudian colleagues at the New York Psychoanalytic Institute.

Goldman (1993), quoting extensively from the minutes of that meeting, showed that none of the three discussants (Jacobson, Ritvo, Fine) appreciated (or understood?) the innovative thought in Winnicott's paper. Goldman quoted Ellman's testimony: "In the aftermath of the formal presentation, one participant noticed Winnicott to be visibly shaken and overheard him commenting that he now understood better why America was in Vietnam" (p. 210). Goldman rejected the myth that this reaction caused Winnicott's subsequent illnesses (Asian influenza, then pulmonary edema) and death a year later; Winnicott was already ill before the talk. But, indeed, he was deeply disappointed that he had failed to communicate something vital — that no one received his gesture.

On Inner and Outer Reality

The Klein–Winnicott dialectic, replicating and extending the Freud–Ferenczi dialectic, constitutes a crucial phase in the pendulum-like movement regarding the weight of external reality in our theorizing, particularly in our thinking about the way psychic reality is shaped in childhood. The place of the parents is central in Freud's seduction theory and is pushed aside in his later oedipal model, rediscovered by Ferenczi, deemphasized by Klein, and reemphasized by Winnicott and Kohut. Winnicott (1958) suggested, "In health the child's interest is directed both towards external reality and towards the inner world, and he has bridges between the one world and the other (dreams, play, etc.)" (p. 208).

Issues regarding the place of external reality in our understanding of adult mental life, and specifically of the treatment process, are naturally no less controversial (Berman, 1995a). The classical conception of transference — emphasizing displacement and (later) projection and treating the patient's perceptions of the analyst as mostly distortions — gave the reality of the analytic situation and the analyst's personality a marginal role in analysis. In this framework, "external" reality was viewed as a shallow layer mobilized for resistant rationalization—allowing defensive avoidance of deeper experiences and deflecting the analytic focus away from psychic reality. The "two realities," outer and inner, were seen as competing for our attention, and one of them needed to be pushed aside to allow the other space. Hurwitz (1986) provided a vivid example of this view: When he told his first analyst that the analyst's style may influence his (Hurwitz's) reactions to the analyst, the analyst insisted, "You'd respond the same way no matter who was in this chair." Hurwitz's later experience with another analyst firmly convinced Hurwitz otherwise.

It is ironic to recall that the image of the blank screen was developed by Freud in a reality in which many of his analysands were acquaintances and disciples (not to speak of his daughter Anna) for whom he was anything but anonymous. The defensive nature of the fantasy of being but a mirror is accentuated by this context; Freud never practiced according to his proclaimed principle of anonymity (Lynn and Vaillant, 1998).

Freud (1937) attempted to make room for this reality: "Not every good relation between an analyst and his subject during and after analysis was to be regarded as transference; there were also friendly relations which were based on reality and which proved to be viable" (p. 222). Our appreciation of this more flexible view may be marred, however, by understanding the context of Freud's comment. As I mentioned in chapter 1, this is actually Freud's defensive answer to Ferenczi's serious complaint that the negative transference was not sufficiently worked through in Ferenczi's analysis (Falzeder and Brabant, 2000, p. 382). We are reminded that both the belief in anonymity and the attention given to a realistic dimension can be used defensively.

Greenson's (1971) introduction of the concept of "'real' relationship" was a thoughtful attempt to correct the one-sided emphasis on transferential distortion. Yet, though acknowledging that "all object relationships consist of different admixtures and blendings of real and transference components" (p. 89), Greenson hastened to add that these ingredients "can and . . . should be separated from one another." In his examples, he seemed confident as to which perceptions of his patients are accurate and which are distorted.[6] Often, it seems, negative perceptions were portrayed as transferentially distorted, and positive perceptions were portrayed as part of the "real relationship."

Such divisions preclude more dialectical conceptions. Winnicott's (1971) hypothesis is indeed more dialectical. He believed that, after the object becomes real, "projective mechanisms assist in the act of *noticing what is there,* but they are not *the reason why the object is there*" (p. 106). Greenson's (1971) dichotomy may be one of several cases in which attempts to achieve breadth and flexibility in our theorizing are initially characterized by new dichotomies, which may eventually prove to be too rigid. I have in mind Balint's (1969) benign versus malignant regression, discussed by Ghent (1992); Eissler's (1953) parameters, which are contrasted with interpretations; Winnicott's differentiation of needs and wishes, challenged by Mitchell (1993); and Kohut's selfobjects as utterly distinct from objects (Ghent, 1989).

Merton Gill (1982) reintroduced the impact of the analyst's personality and behavior as a crucial determinant in shaping the analytic process, but now without any attempt to separate it sharply from the influence of the analysand's inner world. Transference encompasses all determinants; plausibility replaces accuracy as

---

[6]Hamilton (1993) reported a negative correlation between analysts' use of the term *real relationship* and their belief in the usefulness of countertransference responses. She attributed this empirical finding to the contrast between two implicit models of truth, "correspondence theory" (interpretations refer to something independent of the mind of the analyst) and "coherence theory." My own emphasis in explaining this research finding would be on the humility generated by giving serious attention to countertransference — as an antidote to an omniscient belief in knowing "what we really are."

an issue; and the analyst strives for the same open-mindedness and suspension of judgment expected of the analysand. This framework, I believe, can be fruitfully integrated with our current view of countertransference as ubiquitous. Likewise, it can be incorporated into the exploration of the analyst's subjectivity as another reality influencing the analysand's transference: "Transference is the expression of the patient's relations with the fantasied and real countertransference of the analyst" (Racker, 1968, p. 131).

Viewing the analysand's experience as constantly interweaving past and present, perception and fantasy, attempted objectivity and unavoidable subjectivity, makes the impact of "external" realities—the analyst's age, gender, character, appearance, health or illness, pregnancy, and other life events—crucial. We no longer attempt to put them outside the borders of the analytic exploration of transference (see Simon, 1993). To the contrary, the way such realities are processed and given significance becomes in itself an intriguing issue in analysis. What, for example, are the differences between the various permutations of the analyst's gender and the analysand's gender? And between the more numerous permutations of analyst's, analysand's, and supervisor's gender? And how are these influenced by differing sexual orientations of all participants? Similar questions were recently raised about similarities and differences in analyst's and analysand's race, ethnic identity, socioeconomic background, and the like (e.g., Basch-Kahre, 1984; Altman, 2000). The capacity to explore such external realities undefensively may be conceived as facilitating a greater acceptance of psychic reality rather than as competing with, and taking away from, the importance of psychic reality. Such openness can facilitate a "model that locates the psychological in the social and the social in the psychological" (Altman, 1997, p. 547).

In this context, the correlation between acceptance of inner reality and acceptance of outer reality seems central—with both considered aspects of the capacity to confront complex and at times painful reality on all levels. The capacity to bridge external reality (always colored by inner experiences) and psychic reality (always colored by actual events and persons), rather than experiencing them as competing opposites, is crucial to the formation of transitional space, that intermediate area of experiencing that, in Winnicott's (1971) view, facilitates flexibility, creativity, playfulness, and change.

Toward the end of his life, Freud became invested in the study of denial or disavowal as a mechanism for preventing full contact with external reality. He compared the impact of such disavowal (combined with the consequent splitting between recognized and disavowed aspects of external reality) with that of repression of aspects of the inner world and noted that "it is not always easy to decide in an individual instance with which of the two possibilities one is dealing. They have, however, the following important characteristic in common. Whatever the ego does in its efforts of defense . . . its success is never complete and unqualified . . . [and this] leads to psychical complications" (Freud, 1938, p. 204).

Freud's personal struggle against denial, expressed in his outrage at his physician's attempt to conceal his cancer from him (Gay, 1988), was a continuation of his struggle against repression in his self-analysis years before. On the other hand, when an analysand clings to concrete external details to avoid threatening affects or fantasies, it is doubtful that his or her understanding of external reality can be serious. And when another analysand floods the analyst with dreams to avoid painful issues in family life, or because of an "essential lack of true relation to external reality" (Winnicott, 1958, p. 152), it is doubtful that these dreams will lead to an in-depth understanding of the person's inner world: "Fantasy is only tolerable at full blast when objective[7] reality is appreciated well" (p. 153).

The challenge we face, therefore, is not to push aside external reality but to mobilize its understanding into the analytic process. It is not to deny our reality for the analysand — a hypocritical denial (Ferenczi, 1933) that may increase the analysand's defensiveness — but to take full responsibility for it. It is to avoid a shallow concrete representation of external reality in order to reintroduce it into the analytic dialogue at a deeper level, to make the analysis fuller and more integrative, to confront both the analysand's inner object world and her or his actual object relations and

---

[7]Again we notice Winnicott's admiration of objectivity, discussed earlier.

intersubjective patterns with significant others, including the analyst but not only the analyst (Berman, 2001a).

Later Repercussions of Klein's Blind Spots

Even with the considerable developments in Kleinian theory in recent years—which guarantee its place as a powerful source of inspiration in contemporary psychoanalytic thinking (Schafer, 1997)—some of Klein's blind spots that influenced the Klein–Winnicott drama are still present. The work of two eminent Kleinian authors, Horacio Etchegoyen from Argentina and Betty Joseph from Britain, is illustrative.

Etchegoyen's (1991) influential book, *The Fundamentals of Psychoanalytic Technique*, may be read as an attempt to work through his (often conflicted) feelings toward two major influences on his own professional development—Melanie Klein, his dominant theoretical inspiration, and Heinrich Racker, his first analyst and mentor.

Racker (1910–1961), a Polish-born Viennese who emigrated to Argentina in 1939, brilliantly integrated Freudian, Kleinian, and Fairbairnian ideas into a model of countertransference that is still useful. Although conceptually dated in some ways, Racker's (1968) study of analysis as an encounter between two three-dimensional individuals in a continual interplay of countertransference and transference (the latter also understood as counter-countertransference) has seldom been surpassed. It deserves being defined as one of the earliest expressions of an intersubjective view, even if the word is not mentioned.

Etchegoyen (1991), Racker's analysand and admirer, gave up this radical aspect of Racker's thought in his retreat to a conservative Kleinian "one-person psychology" in which the patient's pathology is confronted by the analyst's technique (Berman, 1994a).

Despite Klein's extensive influence on Racker, these two analysts differ in numerous ways; to label Racker a Kleinian is a mistake. One striking difference is Racker's favorite phenomenologic phrase, *paranoid-depressive anxiety*, which defies Klein's developmental paradigm in which paranoid and depressive experiences are sharply contrasted. There is also a global difference in conceptualizations of the analytic process. Klein's excitement with transference contrasts with her deep suspicion of countertransference, whereas for Racker the two aspects are complementary, inseparable, and of equal value. From Klein's hostile reaction to the parallel ideas of Heimann and Winnicott[8] (Grosskurth, 1986, pp. 378–379), we can easily infer that she would never have accepted Racker's (1968) notion that the transference is a reaction to the analyst's fantasized and real countertransference (p. 131). Neither did Etchegoyen (1991), who, discussing oedipal transference, added parenthetically, "I do not take account of the countertransference for reasons of simplicity and method . . .[it] does not change the nature of the phenomenon, although it complicates it" (p. 115).

Etchegoyen's definition of analytic material excludes "verbal acting-out," which is "what the patient does or says not in order to inform, but to influence or dominate the therapist" (p. 309). How can an analyst committed to unconscious processes dichotomize informing and influencing? This artificial dichotomy seems to serve Etchegoyen's consistent emphasis on the centrality of interpretation and insight as curative factors and his skepticism regarding the role of the analytic relationship and emotional experience per se. These are always relegated to where Freud had them — to the background, as preconditions (Freud spoke of "rapport," allowing the patient to accept interpretations).

Although Etchegoyen jokingly defined himself as a "fanatical Kleinian" (p. xxiv), he repeatedly emphasized his attention to reality and defensively argued against the critical view of "my friend Sandler" that "we Kleinians brush the reality aside" (p. 253). He

---

[8]Etchegoyen's (1991) critique of Winnicott's (1947) "Hate in the Countertransference" is interesting. He effectively used Waelder's principle of multiple function to show that "objective hate" is a simplification: "Then, if I am going to be truthful, as Winnicott asks me to be, I will have to tell him [the patient] that I hated him 'objectively' three years ago, not only for his insufferable behavior, but also because I got on badly with my wife at the time, I was worried about my financial situation, the *International Journal of Psycho-analysis* had rejected one of my articles . . . my class on countertransference was not turning out well and this caused conflict with Racker, my analyst, and with my friend Leon, and . . ." (p. 302).

explained, "The breadth of Klein's understanding of the transference exposes her disciples to seeing the transference too much
and neglecting reality; but the theory does not say reality does not
exist" (p. 254).

Theories, however, should be evaluated by their impact, not
only by their manifest, conscious content. Exempting Klein from
responsibility for her disciples is as superficial as claiming that
Marx had nothing to do with Lenin's and Stalin's authoritarianism. Etchegoyen's own work supplies many examples that support Sandler's claims more than his own. When criticizing a
colleague for attempting to interpret a patient's denial of her husband's apparent deceit, he added, "This position does not change
at all if the analyst were to have access to external (objective) reality, since that reality is not pertinent" (p. 323). I agree that we
should not seek external data, but I find it absurd to assume that
an analysis would not be influenced by the analyst's chance discovery that his patient's husband actually is having an affair (or
that he never had one and is deeply hurt by her unfounded suspicion). Such discoveries, difficult as they are to integrate or use,
irreversibly affect our countertransference and hypotheses and
probably behavior.

But the issue is even more crucial when we move from the
realities outside the consulting room to the realities of analysis
itself. Casement (1993) noticed a "selective blindness to his
[Etchegoyen's] own impact upon the analytic process," as in the
comment Etchegoyen made when discussing a therapy patient
who threw herself into his arms after he asked her to lie down on
his new couch, "It was not the setting but the Oedipus complex
that fed her desire" (p. 548). Etchegoyen (1991) rejected not only
the belief of Freud and Racker that transference is strengthened in
analysis (p. 93) but also Macalpine's view that the analytic setting
may infantilize patients (p. 544). Criticizing the Baranger model
of analysis as a bipersonal field, he quoted approvingly authors
who believe that "the analyst . . . abstains rigorously from offering any data" (p. 502), again steering away from considering the
analyst's unavoidable reality impact (see Aron, 1992, pp. 498–500).

Nowhere is this avoidance more dramatic than in Etchegoyen's thorough discussion of Klein's "first cases of analysis
(Fritz, Felix)" (p. 411). Etchegoyen praised the growing bold-
ness in Klein's interpretation of Fritz's negative oedipal feelings

("I told him that he imagined himself in his mamma's place and wished his papa might do with him what he does with her ... but he is afraid ... that if this stick — papa's wiwi — gets into his wiwi he will be hurt"; pp. 404–405). Later, he described approvingly how, in analyzing Felix, "Klein imposed on him certain prohibitions to ensure the continuity of analysis, since the boy's object choices were aimed at fleeing from the fantasies and desires directed at that moment to the analyst in the transference" (pp. 705–706). I find it difficult to believe that, when the book was published Etchegoyen was still unaware of Grosskurth's discovery that Fritz and Felix were Klein's own sons.[9] Avoidance of this part of the puzzle seems significant ("that reality is not pertinent"). By not coming to terms with this "primal sin" of Kleinian analysis, Etchegoyen bears the full burden of its ethical and conceptual impact.

Etchegoyen's commitment to Klein resulted in his losing the critical edge of Racker's thinking. When he concluded, "The fate of the analytic relation is defined by the psychopathology of the patient and the qualities of the analyst" (p. 56), making clear that by *qualities* he means professional competence, he seemed to regress fully to the "myth of the analytic situation" as an "interaction between a sick person and a healthy one," so powerfully denounced by Racker (1968, p. 132).

When casting doubt on Racker's differentiation between direct and indirect countertransference (the latter influenced by relating to others, e.g., supervisors), Etchegoyen (1991) suggested that a concern about the supervisor's view may be a displacement from a conflict with the patient. This may happen, but the strong emphasis on one direction of the parallel process again indicates avoidance of the reality context, a context so vivid in Racker's work — in this case, of the power structure of the analytic institute, a central topic of this book.

My other example is Joseph's (1993) paper, in which she described her ineffective eight-year analysis of "Dr. B." Before making my critical observations, I note that the place of relationship in Joseph's work is more central than it is in Etchegoyen's

---

[9]Parallel avoidance of the topic is evident in O'Shaughnessy's (1987) extensive critical review of Grosskurth's book.

book. I find enormously useful her way of transforming general Kleinian insights into minute observations of the here and now of the transference — into rich descriptions of how, at a particular moment in the session, the patient experiences himself or herself, the analyst, and the analytic relationship. I fully share Joseph's emphasis on striving to understand the total transferential situation (including its nonverbal layers and its impact on the analyst's emotions and actions) as well as her belief that only full experiencing can promote analytic progress.

Yet, in 1994, when I was asked to discuss Joseph's "non-resonance" paper, presented at a conference in Tel Aviv, I found myself concerned about one of its central aspects. Viewing resistance as a property of the patient alone may stop us, I believe, from seeing how it may result from a difficulty in the interactive dyad; speaking of a negative therapeutic reaction caused by the patient's ingrained problems may cloud its possible sources in an intersubjective disjunction (Stolorow, Atwood, and Ross, 1978). It worried me to discover that, though Joseph uses the word *non-resonance* in the title of her paper, the paper itself focuses exclusively on the pathology of a nonresonating patient, Dr. B. (Berman, 2002b).

Such a focus may imply taking our own role and technique for granted — avoiding the possibility that a patient's nonresonance in some way reflects either a difficulty we have in fully resonating with the patient or a mismatch in our mutual expectations of the treatment. If we approach each patient with deeply held beliefs about what constitutes effective analysis, what is real psychic change, what useful analytic interventions are, we risk not taking seriously enough the signals from our patient that he or she needs something else and finds our way of working unhelpful. These are the long-term consequences of retaining Klein's blind spots to the impact of both parents and analyst.

Joseph (1993) suggested that nonresonance "can be approached from two angles, that are, of course, connected: that of technique (are we failing to reach our patients because of faulty handling of the case?), or that of pathology [of the patient]" (p. 311). She implied that the analyst's part can be differentiated into either "proper technique" or "faulty handling." In the rest of her paper, only the patient's pathology is explored. This one-sidedness brings to mind Ferenczi's (1932) comment about Freud's way of "finding the causes of failure in the patient instead of partly in ourselves" (p. 185).

Joseph's line is again in striking contrast to Racker's (1968) view:

> The first distortion of truth in "the myth of the analytic situation" is that analysis is an interaction between a sick person and a healthy one. The truth is that it is an interaction between two personalities, in both of which the ego is under pressure from the id, the superego, and the external world; each personality has its internal and external dependences, anxieties and pathological defenses; each is also a child with his internal parents; and each of these whole personalities — that of the analysand and that of the analyst — responds to every event of the analytic situation [p. 132].

This view implies that we may be more effective if, rather than striving to crystallize a "correct technique," we keep listening for indications of the impact of each intervention and, when an intervention fails, we consider our possible contribution to its failure.

The equation unavoidably includes countertransference. When all manifestations of countertransference are interpreted as reactions to the patient's pathology, as they sometimes are in the Kleinian literature, that part of the puzzle may be said to be in sharp focus while other parts remain out of focus. Respecting her privacy and (unlike with Freud or Klein) having no biographical sources, I cannot discuss Joseph's specific countertransference to Dr. B, but I take it for granted that, though it is not mentioned, it had a role in molding their joint intersubjective field, which evolved into a *nonresonant field*.

Discussing Dr. B, Joseph (1993) stated, "Something always prevented any real deep contact between my interpretations and my patient's mind" (p. 317). She seemed confident that this "something" resides solely in the patient and would therefore appear in any analysis or analytic therapy with Dr. B. That may be so, but I find it risky to take it for granted. If Joseph's kind of interpreting, undoubtedly helpful to other of her patients, made Dr. B feel her "to be extremely insensitive, crude and forceful" (p. 318), I do not see this perception necessarily as a total distortion or as a

pure projection of his inner object world, and I do not see it as necessarily an "objective" and accurate assessment. It may be a complex amalgamation of perceptions and projections, a partial and
very subjective truth, which nevertheless testifies to the fact that
the analytic style of this particular analyst "rubs" this particular
patient the "wrong way."

When Joseph showed Dr. B how much he expected to be
treated badly by her, he responded "as if [she] had said something disturbing or had not realized what [she] had done, and he
would need to defend himself further" (p. 318). I am convinced
this reaction reflected his inner object world, but I suggest that it
may also be influenced by his realistic awareness that his analyst
considered his defensiveness as totally determined by his intrapsychic pathology and did not give any weight to the possibility
that she may have inadvertently strengthened his "fears of being
humiliated, criticized, made to feel guilty" (p. 318). This vicious
circle may have had a role in his tendency to have a "minor explo-
sion of anger, irritation or some other feeling" (p. 318) in response
to interpretations.

This viewpoint led me to interpret one of Dr. B's dreams, reported by Joseph, as follows. In the dream, the analysand, while
working as a doctor, pushes a man through a doorway and
down the stairs; then, realizing that the man is crippled, Dr. B
feels awful. Although Dr. B refers to himself directly, I wonder if
this dream could also be a reproach against the analyst, the
"doctor" who treats him roughly and without the compassion
he feels entitled to as an emotional cripple. This would be an example of transference expressed in a disguised way through
identification with the experienced attributes of the analyst
(M. M. Gill, 1982).

Joseph (1993) did indeed pursue this line of thought. She discussed the owl image in Dr. B's second dream, about an owl
squirting liquid at the dreamer and then sucking bubbles of air
into the water in a tank: "Is it partly myself seen not really as a
wise person, but seen in a narcissistic light? Is this partly a me
with whom he is identified?" (p. 322). Discussing the squirting of
the liquid, which could be either milk or urine, Joseph wondered,
"Can this also be understood as an identification with an analyst
who is felt to squirt analytic theories at him, in place of real
understanding?" (p. 322).

This courageous thought can perhaps be extended to the final part of the dream, in which "the owl seemed to suck bubbles of air into the water, and take them down, bubble by bubble, to its home, a kind of cardboard box at the bottom of the tank, so it had an independent place and supplied itself with air" (p. 321). This scene can be considered a cruel caricature of the analyst's meticulous interpretations, gradually accumulated and used to fortify a self-contained and isolated world of meanings, enjoyed by the analyst but depriving the patient of the fresh air he yearns.

We are not told whether this aspect of the possible meaning of the dream came up in the sessions.[10] There is no acknowledgment that the patient's complaints may hold a grain of truth — which in my view may have been needed to enable the analytic dyad to move out of the impasse. Moreover, such an acknowledgment may need to be expressed in active terms as well — for example, in the analyst's attempt to avoid the kinds of interventions that irritate the patient, to try a different style or focus of interpretations, maybe to refrain from giving interpretations altogether, to maintain a patient and empathic atmosphere, and to await the time when the patient can make his own interpretations.

We witnessed exactly this kind of flexible search for a more effective technique in Ferenczi's work, and it is evident in Winnicott's work as well. The tendency among Kleinian analysts not even to consider alternative options points to the potential risks inherent in any analytic model should we take its accuracy and usefulness for granted.

---

[10]Bringing it up, though, may still be seen as accusatory — that is, experienced as if the analyst were protesting a gross and unfounded distortion, proving the patient's pathology: "I give you good milk, and you spoil it and turn it into urine."

3

Psychoanalytic Training and the Utopian Fantasy of the New Person

It is a paradox of Freudian psychoanalysis that, whilst consistently struggling against illusion, it somehow activates it.

— Janine Chasseguet-Smirgel and
Béla Grunberger, *Freud or Reich?*

This chapter provides a critical evaluation of traditional psychoanalytic training. My specific focus is on the dangers of the utopian dimension in this training and particularly of the utopian New Person fantasy often identifiable in the more ambitious rationales of analytic education (Berman, 2000c). I attempt to relate these aspects to the frequent tendency toward idealization of analysis and analytic training, to potential persecutory aspects, and, in particular, to the "analytic false self" components that may emerge within a new analyst's identity.

The current worldwide model of psychoanalytic training is based on the structure of the Berlin Institute, established in 1920 by Eitingon, with Abraham's support. As I have mentioned, Ferenczi's earlier attempt to start a psychoanalytic institute took place in Budapest in 1919 but was short-lived owing to political upheavals in Hungary. In view of Ferenczi's strong antiauthoritarian views, it is fascinating to speculate what the style of worldwide training would be today if his institute had retained its seniority. In any event, the "Eitingon model" became dominant, and Eitingon actively tried to spread it throughout the psychoanalytic world (Schröter, 2002). Despite steady criticism since the 1940s, changes in this model have been slow and tentative.

A Critical Tradition

The critical tradition on which most proposals for reform are based spans more than half a century. Historically, the debate on

the damaging aspects of training was opened in London by
Balint, Ferenczi's disciple. Balint had already made some brief
critical comments about training (e.g., about assigning an analyst
or a supervisor to the candidate) during the Controversial Discussions (King and Steiner, 1991, p. 886), but in the paper he presented in 1947 these are richly elaborated. In Ferenczi's spirit,
Balint (1948) clearly outlined the need for a critical view avoiding
denial and strove to explain the "curse of strifes which seem to
adhere inevitably to our training organizations" (p. 167).

Balint's central concern was that candidates were "far too respectful to their training analysts" and developed "submissiveness to dogmatic and authoritarian treatment without much
protest" (p. 167). The secessions of Adler and Jung, Balint suggested, made Freud believe "that the new generation should learn
to renounce part of their self-assertion and independence, to be educated to discipline and self-discipline and to accept an authority
with the right and duty of instructing and warning" (p. 170).

Bernfeld (1962), a Viennese who settled in California, attributed much of the rigidity of the Eitingon model to the "Prussian
spirit which rather flourished among the founders of the Berlin
Institute" and to the anxiety aroused by Freud's cancer and the
imminent threat of his loss, which his colleagues dealt with by
"establishing a solid dam against heterodoxy" (p. 467). The result
was the introduction of rigid selection and the subjection of new-
comers to a "coercive, long drawn-out trial period of authoritarian training" (p. 467). Traditional training, Bernfeld suggested,
"distorts some of the most valuable features of psychoanalysis"
(p. 458); "institutionalization does not encourage thinking" (p.
468), he added. Although his radical paper was delivered in 1952,
it was published, by his colleague Rudolf Ekstein, a decade later.
Not by coincidence did the critique of the Berlin-based Eitingon
model initially come from colleagues whose origins were in Vienna and in Budapest (though Balint trained for some years in
Berlin before returning to Budapest).

Similar issues were raised by the Hungarian-born American
analyst Thomas Szasz. Szasz (1958) contrasted the revolutionary
stage of psychoanalysis with the institutional stage. In the former, the antiauthoritarian spirit of free exploration was also manifested in the option allowing anyone interested to join; in the
latter, selection and compulsory requirements led to conformity

and lessened creativity. Szasz expressed a wish for a "psycho-analytic education which will promote learning rather than teaching, or scientific inquiry rather than indoctrination" (p. 607).

Limentani (1974) described psychotic elements in the group countertransference reactions of psychoanalytic faculty to candidates. Rustin (1985) studied the tension in psychoanalysis between intimacy and self-exposure, on one hand, and formal regulation and institutionalization, on the other. He concluded, "Orthodox forms of analysis and also supervision require a structured inequality of relationships. The more orthodox the analytic practice, the more hierarchical the organizations through which it takes place" (p. 151). Bruzzone et al. (1985) described their painful experiences of regression and persecution during their analytic training in Chile. They attributed these intense feelings to unconscious dynamics (including splitting, projection, and envy) but also identified reality influences, such as their exclusion from activities of the local society, dismissal of colleagues from training, and "what we think was projective counter-identification on the part of the teachers" (p. 413).

Some of the harshest criticisms of traditional training have come from IPA leaders—Waldemar Zusman of Rio de Janeiro and André Lussier of Montreal (both IPA vice-presidents) and Otto Kernberg (IPA president, 1997–2001).

Zusman (1988) coined the term *Eitingon syndrome*, which he described as the basis of sectarianism, religiosity, and abuse of power in psychoanalytic institutes. Lussier (1991; see Wallerstein, 1993) highlighted the inherent contrast between the goal of encouraging candidates to search for the truth and the rigid setup of rules and rituals. Lussier called for safeguarding the privacy of a candidate's personal analysis and advocated avoiding any regulation of that analysis by the institute, except for the requirement that the analyst be reasonably experienced (e.g., practicing at least five years after having been graduated).

Kernberg (1986) began his involvement in the debate by expressing concern about indoctrination, about uncritical discussion of Freud, and about the reluctance of teachers to present their clinical work. Although our expected models for psychoanalytic education would seem to be either the art academy or the university college, he suggested that in reality our institutes are closer to technical trade schools, in which defined skills are taught without

encouraging creativity, or to monasteries or religious retreats
founded on faith (p. 810). More recently, Kernberg published
both a humoristic study, "Thirty Methods to Destroy the Creativity of Psychoanalytic Candidates" (1996), and a comprehensive
critique of psychoanalytic education (2000). With few exceptions,
his work is convincing, and it points the way to potential constructive changes.

The Paradoxes of Rescue and Utopia

Let me turn now to my specific hypothesis regarding the utopian dimension. The literature on utopian thinking has been
characterized in recent years by a tension between a positive
view, of utopia as an expression of hope and optimism and a
springboard for constructive social change, and a negative
view, of utopia as a source of illusory promises, fanaticism, and
even bloodshed. Although this chapter leans toward the second
emphasis, the dialectics between these two viewpoints should
not be oversimplified. Utopianism may be a vital motivating
force behind any attempt to improve human life, yet its risks are
considerable too.

In my view, utopian visions are a generalized form of individual rescue fantasies. The history of our thinking about rescue fantasies teaches us something about the potential of professional
and intellectual traditions to imagine themselves immune from
the blind spots they observe in the outside world. When Freud
(1910a) first discussed the phenomenon of the rescue fantasy, he
attributed it to certain male patients whose emotional life centered on the rescue of "fallen women." His interpretation was
along oedipal lines: The woman is unconsciously seen as mother,
and her rescue from sexual exploitation signifies having her for
oneself, in defiance of the oedipal father.

Reik, Stekel, and other early analysts pursued this line of
thought and supplied intriguing clinical and literary examples
(Berman, 2003a). Abraham (1922) added fantasies of rescuing the
father and interpreted them as a reaction formation to murderous
oedipal wishes. But none of these prominent authors seemed to
have contemplated the possibility that rescue fantasies may be
relevant to our own profession.

The roots of this insight, like the roots of our understanding of many other aspects of countertransference, appear in Ferenczi's work, though he did not use the term directly in this context. Ferenczi (1919a) described situations in which the "doctor has unconsciously made himself his patient's patron or knight" (p. 188). The context of this insight is important, too. As I mentioned in chapter 1, Ferenczi discussed accusations or even legal proceedings against therapists or "wild" analysts. In these cases,

> the patients are simply unmasking the doctor's unconscious. The enthusiastic doctor who wants to "sweep away" his patient in his zeal to cure and elucidate the case does not observe the little and big indications of fixation to the patient, male or female, but they [the patients] are only too aware of it, and interpret the underlying tendency quite correctly without guessing that the doctor himself was ignorant of it [p. 188].

That is a central example of Ferenczi's awareness that countertransference may mold the transference—that countertransference is not merely *counter*transference at all.

Although Ferenczi cautiously pinpointed nonanalytic therapists or "wild" analysts as being vulnerable to unconscious rescue fantasies, one can easily understand that well-trained analysts may be at risk too. In this he once again foresaw the future of our professional discourse. Almost half a century passed before this future came into being. Phyllis Greenacre (1971), in a paper initially published in 1966, first directly applied the concept of rescue fantasies to analysts (without any awareness of Ferenczi's insights—one more indication of the way Ferenczi's work was silenced for decades).

Greenacre portrayed the rescue fantasy of an overzealous analyst as an expression of the analyst's self-image as a substitute parent. "In such rescue operations the analyst's aggression may be allocated to those relatives or therapists who have previously been in contact with the patient and are, in fact or in fantasy, contributors to his disturbances. The analyst then becomes the savior through whom the analysand is to be launched" (p. 760). In recent years, much attention has been paid to the rescue fantasies of analysts, therapists, and especially child therapists (Esman, 1987), in line with the growing tendency of contemporary psychoanalytic writers to focus on the analyst's emotional world and counter-transference. The explanatory focus has shifted from the oedipal triangle emphasized by Freud and Abraham to the earliest ties to the mother, to experiences of loss and restitution, to a reparation of damage caused by aggression, to the need to save a depressed or helpless parent, to the rescue of oneself as projected onto the other.

Of course, one may ask if there can be psychoanalysis—if there can be "helping professions" in general—without a rescue fantasy. My answer is mixed. Yes, a rescue fantasy may be a nec-essary—or at least a very common—motivating force, and yet it may become a hindrance, because in some ways it conflicts with effective professional help.

We can list a few major differences between the state of mind dominated by an unmitigated rescue fantasy and an attitude in which this fantasy is sublimated into a realistic therapeutic frame of reference:

1. *Omnipotence.* Within a rescue fantasy, we can single-handedly change a patient's life from misery to bliss—enable a patient to be reborn. Realistic help may require more modest goals.

2. *Self-idealization and romanticization.* The rescue fantasy por-trays the therapist as an altruistic, pure-hearted, gallant knight and may block our awareness of our limitations, our more self-centered motives for doing therapy, and our conflicts about this taxing and difficult work.

3. *Demonization of a guilty party.* The patient's parents, for ex-ample, may be portrayed as highly destructive without our tak-ing into account the patient's own contribution to the disturbed patterns of the parent–child relationship—splitting between good and bad, guilty and innocent. This blind spot may block the analyst's awareness of the common pitfall of being lured un-consciously into the very same disturbed patterns the patient undergoes.

Because of these and related factors, the unmitigated rescue fantasy may blind us to the great complexity of the treatment pro-cess, to the ambivalence of both parties, and to the potential para-doxical results of the encounter. Being rescued, for example, may be experienced as humiliating and may leave the rescued person wishing to escape the relationship, as John Fowles (1969) showed in the novel *The French Lieutenant's Woman.*

The paradoxes of rescue are well portrayed in the myth of Orpheus and Eurydice. Orpheus rescues his beloved from hell by virtue of his courage and rhetorical power but ends up sending her back to hell by virtue of his forbidden look (wish to know? lack of trust? anxiety?). What seems at one point an omnipotent victory eventually leads to a much more fragile (i.e., human) outcome.

This issue is prominent in Hitchcock's film *Vertigo* (Berman, 1997a). Although the protagonist, Scottie, is a detective, his emotional world bears unmistakable similarities to that of an analyst dominated by a rescue fantasy. In the first part of the film, he believes he is valiantly rescuing the mysterious heroine, Madeline, from an obscure metaphysical, psychological, or perhaps criminal fate. His devotion and willingness for self-sacrifice are impressive, as is his identification with her. Only much later in the film do we realize that Scottie's naive, romanticized view of love and rescue has led to disaster. Actually, all along he has been as lonely and as helpless as the woman he tried to help. The understanding he reached was so partial that it blinded him to the larger, deeper truth behind the mystery. Indeed, he was duped by a villain. In his desperate attempt to free himself from the deception, however, he finds himself becoming as cruel and reckless as that villain. Eventually, Scottie's attempted rescue and his search for truth destroy the woman he loves and who loves him. The knight becomes the dragon.

That sharp division between valiant knight, helpless, victimized beauty, and horrible beastly dragon is the hallmark of the rescue fantasy. When we come to our senses, we discover that all partners in this drama are human and therefore more like one another than meets the eye. "Rescuer" may be as helpless as his "beauty" and as aggressive and intrusive as the "beast." Identities shift here easily, and all figures can be understood as externalizing an inner drama.

Some of the same issues are relevant to utopian thought as a generalized rescue fantasy toward humanity. Social rescue fantasies may backfire in ways parallel to the paradoxical impact of personal rescue attempts. This realization may lead us to a much more sober evaluation of attempts to improve our emotional life by various versions of "preventive mental health." Radical psychological experiments seem to have something in common with the enthusiastic scientific projects of improving life through building dams, rechanneling rivers, and spreading pesticides — all of which prove to be naive owing to their disregard of their own subtle destructive impact on natural ecology. The historian Talmon (1952) spoke in this context of the "curse on salvationist creeds: to be born out of the noblest impulses of man, and to degenerate into weapons of tyranny" (p. 253).

Utopian vision may indeed be the motivating force behind any attempt to improve human life, and in its lack pessimistic conservatism and stagnation may take over. As Mannheim suggested, "Without Utopia, humanity would lose its will to create history, sinking into either self-pity or complacency" (Turner, 1991, p. xlviii). But utopianism is different from realistic social innovation (in spite of common emotional roots), along the same dimensions listed before, differentiating unmitigated rescue fantasies from realistic therapeutic help — omnipotence, self-idealization, romanticization, demonization of a guilty enemy (projection of evil), and blindness to the complexity of social and psychological processes and to the paradoxical and unforeseen results of radical changes.

Several characteristics of the "utopian state of mind" (Berman, 1994b) may contribute to its risks. Its emphasis on desiderata, and constant comparisons with a valuable end-state, may interfere with the full appreciation of the complexities and inner contradictions of existing reality. Its splitting between evil (present) and good (yearned for) may imply blindness to the inherently paradoxical and conflictual nature of human existence. Its seriousness, strictness, and moralism may push aside humor and irony, often necessary preconditions for a "live-and-let-live" flexibility. Attributing emotional needs to condemned sources (evil, sinfulness, greed, materialism, narcissism, etc.) may prevent tolerance of the unavoidable imperfection of individuals and rationalize a judgmental and persecutory attitude toward them. Believing that goals sanctify means, one may forget how means mold outcomes. In structural terms, a utopian state of mind is dominated by a perfectionistic ego ideal and a rigid superego, at the expense of ego and id alike.

Talmon (1952) stated:

Like a psychoanalyst who cures by making the patient
aware of his subconscious, the social analyst may be able to
attack the human urge which calls totalitarian democracy
into existence, namely the longing for a final resolution of
all contradictions and conflicts into a state of total harmony. It is a harsh, but none the less necessary task to drive
home the truth that human society and human life can
never reach a state of repose [pp. 254–255].

The historian's conclusion is echoed in the psychoanalytic voice
of Chasseguet-Smirgel and Grunberger (1986):

Once it is purged of evil, be it represented in the form of
the Jews, private property, capitalism, patriarchal society, character and muscular armor, or any other projected
object [one could add here the primal scene or child
abuse – E. B.], the purified ego can exist without conflict,
man can be united with God. In *Aden Arabie*, Paul Nizan
says: when man shall be whole and free he will no longer
dream at night. In other words he believes that all desires
will be fulfilled. Psychoanalysis, however, maintains that
human incompleteness, and thus human desire, will
never disappear. Humanity is destined to dream from
here to eternity [p. 213].

The New Person

Many of the risky attributes of utopianism are prominent in a
component present in most utopian visions – namely, the fantasy
of the *New Person*. (*New Man* is the term that often has been used,
but, as it usually implies males and females alike, *New Person* is
more accurate.) This fantasy of the improved, purified individual
has numerous versions in the history of humanity. Its early
sources appear in Christianity: "Lay from you that old man,
which is corrupt through the deceivable lusts, and be ye renewed
in the spirit of your minds, and put on that new man, which after
the image of God is shapen in righteousness and true holiness"

(St. Paul, Epistle to the Ephesians, *Tyndale's New Testament*, 1989, p. 285). Similar visions appear in most religions and are accentuated in notions of salvation and in monastic aspirations for pure spirituality, versus the follies of the "lower world." A saint, in religion, is the ultimate New Person.

More secular versions may be identified in chivalry, in strict boarding schools, or in military education in which the message may be, "Basic training will make a man out of you." Here gender is significant, as it is in the hope of radical feminism for a New Woman, assertive and dedicated to sisterhood while liberated from the corrupting influences of patriarchal society. Elsewhere (Berman, 2000a), I discuss our contemporary fantasy of the New Sexual Person.

A New Person fantasy was powerfully present in the literature of the French Revolution and later became prominent in Communism as the New Soviet Person, hailed by propaganda and literature as free of bourgeois individualism and fully dedicated to the building of a just society, to the point of heroic self-sacrifice (Bauer, 1952). The fantasy was central, in a more individualistic, Nietzschean version, in German neoromantic modernism (Peled, 2002) and was then transformed into the harsh Nazi ethos of the pure Aryan *Übermensch,* purged of Semitic and other foreign and decadent contaminations.

A New Person vision can be identified in national liberation movements as an outgrowth of an ideology equating liberation from an external oppressor with liberation from internalized aspects of oppression (Fanon, 1963). In Zionism, for example, it went through many variations (Peled, 2002, pp. 26–27) but is most prominently expressed in the contrasting fantasy images of the New Israeli (healthy, physical, powerful) and the Diaspora Jew (neurotic, inhibited, easily victimized — all introjected anti-Semitic stereotypes; p. 13).

A more specific Israeli example is the early kibbutz movement and its pioneering ethos (Berman, 1988a). The fantasy of the New Communal Person in that milieu portrayed the genuine kibbutz member as fully dedicated to group goals while casting aside any personal needs. Communal upbringing in the kibbutz, rationalized along psychoanalytic lines (avoiding the primal scene, the Oedipus complex, etc.), aimed to rear an improved New Person. In the long run, unfortunately, this system proved to be quite costly in its emotional price—reducing these children's capacity for emotional expression and for intimacy (Bettelheim, 1969; Berman, 1988a). But, when belief in the system was at its peak, a kibbutz member who insisted on some private concern (e.g., studying an area not seen as useful for the kibbutz or creating an intense intimate involvement with her or his children) was often harshly condemned as a selfish individualist, was required to make public self-criticism, was humiliated in community meetings, and at times was pushed out.

Such traumatizing dramas, as well as their equivalents in various religious, political, and social movements, portray a major danger of radical utopianism: The perfectionistic quest to mold a New Person may legitimize the harassment of actual persons seen as flawed, as failing to achieve the new identity, as representing the worthless past that must be eradicated. Peled (2002) traced these dynamics to the French Revolution and spoke of the "tension between a liberating rhetoric of a utopian vision, presenting the liberation of the individual as the goal of revolution, and the oppressive practice turning the individual into means to establish the ideal collective" (p. 20).

Such authoritarian dynamics are not necessarily dependent on adherence to a strong charismatic leader, though such leaders may have a role (Berman, 1982). The main source of pressure is often a cohesive peer group united by a rigid and self-righteous devotion to common ego ideals and exercising shared control of its members. In communal upbringing in the kibbutz, for example, a new kind of harsh conventional superego may evolve that is less related to internalized parental figures and more to the internalized peer group (Berman, 1988a).

Our "Special Kind of Superego" and Common Idealizations

Is the issue of a New Person fantasy relevant to psychoanalysis? I believe it may offer us a useful context for critical examination of some pitfalls in analytic training (Berman, 2000c). These pitfalls were first highlighted by Balint (1948), who saw that candidates were influenced by an atmosphere creating "submissiveness to dogmatic and authoritarian treatment without much protest."

Balint said that the system, contrary to its conscious aim of developing a strong critical ego, necessarily led to a "weakening of these ego functions and to the formation and strengthening of a special kind of super-ego" (p. 167).[1]

I suggest that this "special kind of super-ego" is related to our tendency to envision the "real analyst" as a purified New Person and that such an expectation (conscious or unconscious) may contribute — through a complex interaction of intrapsychic forces and group dynamics — to the emergence of oppressive, hypercritical elements in the atmosphere of some psychoanalytic institutes and clinical training programs.

Several idealizations that at times appear in psychoanalytic thinking may potentially form a "utopian state of mind" regarding psychoanalysis. I do not refer here to utopian psychoanalytic visions of universal social change (Berman, 1993) but to our daily thinking about ourselves, our analysands, and our trainees.

Actually, the notion of idealization arouses in psychoanalysis the same dialectical tensions I referred to when discussing utopia. My use of the term *idealization* here emphasizes the dangers of idealization, in line with Kleinian conceptions, for example; it is less related to the study of the value of idealization for development, as highlighted by Kohut and others. One reason may be that I am dealing here with the dynamics of adult professional life and with group and institutional phenomena. I may view more hopefully the spontaneous development of idealization in an individual analysis, but this is to my mind another issue altogether.

"Idealization processes and an ambience of persecution are practically universal in psychoanalytic institutes," Kernberg (1986, p. 815) suggested. Let me list more specifically a few of our potential idealizations and explore the ways in which they can contribute to persecutory experiences in training.

The skeptical and deconstructive trend of current postmodern thinking is helpful only in identifying such possible idealizations

---

[1]Balint presented his paper to the British Psychoanalytic Society in November 1947. In February of that year, Winnicott (1947) had presented "Hate in the Countertransference." For me, these two papers have a lot in common. They both deidealize the analyst — deconstructing our fantasy images of selfless helper and benign dedicated educator.

in our conceptions. Naturally, every idea or ideal (including my own) may be perfectionistically idealized. Moreover, pointing to the dangers of idealizing certain notions does not, of course, negate the potentially valuable contribution of these same notions when used more cautiously and modestly.

Analyzability

Balint (1969, p. 101), Bachrach (1983), and others have pointed to the theoretical biases and omniscient elements in the idea of analyzability as a trait of the patient. This idea relies on a presumed capacity to predict objectively complex dynamic processes, casts aside the impact of countertransference, and leaves no room for intersubjectivity or mutual influences in treatment. This "one-person psychology" construct may therefore blind us to the possibility that a person not analyzable by one analyst could be analyzable by another analyst with a different approach or a different personality. Moreover, the traditional criteria for analyzability "clearly favor the relatively highly sophisticated patient, thus introducing a bias against many lower-class people" (Altman, 1993, p. 34) — contributing to a "stratification of patients according to 'ego strength' that often mirrors stereotypes based on class, ethnicity or race" (p. 33).

An uncritical view of analyzability may lead a candidate — who, in most institutes I know, often treats analysands with severe personality disorders — to the equation: "my patient is not really analyzable, what I do with this difficult patient therefore cannot be real analysis, and this experience does not prepare me properly to be a real analyst."

Correct Technique

Kernberg (1986) spoke of the "unrealistic idealization of psychoanalytic technique" in psychoanalytic institutes (p. 801). The belief in a standard technique that has clear, steady rules and that offers an analyst the answer to any dilemma cannot be found in Freud. To the contrary, Freud (1912b) wrote, "I must however make it clear that what I am asserting is that this technique is the only one suited to my individuality; I do not venture to deny that a physician quite differently constituted might find himself driven to adopt a different attitude to his patients and to the task before him" (p. 111).

Haynal (1993), speaking of the era of Freud and Ferenczi, suggested, "Analysts then were aware that it is always a matter of experimentation.... from the moment when we spoke of classical technique, we entered a phase of illusion, the illusion that there can be a technique that one needs only to learn and apply 'correctly'" (p. 62). This critique is in line with Lipton's (1977) observation that the so-called classical technique developed after Freud's death and that its strict rules do not fit Freud's actual practice; Roazen's (1995) extensive research on Freud's patients corroborates Lipton's view.

I believe that our current multiplicity of psychoanalytic models, as well as our growing awareness of the weight of subjective experiences in the analyst and of intersubjective processes in the analytic dyad, reduces even more the chances for standardization of technique along universally useful lines. The uniqueness of analysands challenges us to mold our technique anew in each analysis — using the subtle nuances of our own experience (countertransference, empathy, intuition) as guidelines. This means that the inner freedom and creativity of the analyst are crucial. Bergmann (1997, pp. 79–80) traced this view back to the work of Theodor Reik and to Reik's critique of the strict technique advocated by Wilhelm Reich.

On the other hand, an expectation to practice a correct technique may arouse a fear that we are straying from it (e.g., using a "parameter," a tool considered inferior to and less desirable than an interpretation). Such a judgmental focus may inhibit a candidate (and any analyst) from paying full attention to the actual impact of each intervention and how it is experienced by the analysand in the context of his or her inner reality (e.g., is our thoughtful interpretation experienced as a helpful effort to understand — or maybe as a seduction, a humiliation, a disapproval, a compliment?). Our actual impact can be understood through patient, empathic listening and through careful reliance on trial identifications and on our internalized "working model" of the unique patient (Greenson, 1960), not through referring to a generalized list of "do's" and "don'ts."

A strong emphasis on the "correctness" of technique may contribute to an illusion of knowing in advance both what helps and what sabotages clinical effectiveness and training.

Being Fully Analyzed

Our early literature is strongly influenced by this idealized fantasy, which Balint (1954) called *supertherapy* (p. 158). Ferenczi (1927) predicted "an almost unlimited inner freedom" (p. 81) to the lucky ones, and Freeman Sharpe (1937) said, "The 'analysed' person will experience only rarely if at all 'anxiety' dreams" (p. 197). The attribution of incomplete analysis was used to attack psychoanalytic opponents (including Anna Freud, to her father's dismay; Bergmann, 1997, p. 77). Freud (1937), expressing his doubts about attaining "absolute psychical normality" to the point where "no further changes would be expected to take place," spoke sarcastically of the way analysts say, "when they are deploring or excusing the recognized imperfections of some fellow-mortal: 'His analysis was not finished' or 'he was never analysed to the end'" (p. 219). The anxiety such attitudes arouse may still influence some trainees and analysts who feel, lamentably, "not fully analyzed."

Structural Change

Structural change, a more serious theoretical formulation, may evolve at times into an alternative version of the "definitive analysis" fantasy. The idealization of structural change was sharply criticized by Werman (1989), who argued that the idea of structural change "has outlived whatever usefulness it might ever have had" (p. 120) and pointed to the lack of any evidence of a substantial difference between the desired structural change and the disparaged clinical change. Yet the lack of structural change may often come up in informal discussions in which the analysis a trainee or a colleague has undergone or the analyses he or she conducts are disqualified. Many analysts, I suspect, are in doubt whether "real" structural change has occurred in their own training analysis and in their analysands.

Wallerstein (1986) reported the results of an extensive follow-up study on 42 patients referred after thorough evaluation
either for analysis or for therapy. The results, after years of treatment, proved to be very remote from the initial assumptions:

> In regard to the distinctions . . . between the so-called struc-
> tural change presumably based on the interpretive resolu-
> tion of unconscious intrapsychic conflicts, and "behavioral
> changes" . . . I question strongly the continued usefulness of
> this effort to link the kind of change achieved so tightly to
> the intervention mode. . . . Effective conflict resolution
> turned out not to be necessary to therapeutic change . . . a
> substantial range of changes were brought about via the
> more supportive psychotherapeutic modes and techniques
> . . . and these changes were (in many cases) quite indistin-
> guishable from the changes brought about by typically ex-
> pressive-analytic (interpretive, insight-producing) means
> [Wallerstein, 1989, pp. 586–587].

Differentiation of Psychoanalysis from Psychotherapy

Wallerstein's findings point to the relevance of this issue to the
debate about differentiating psychoanalysis from psychotherapy — in itself a valuable endeavor. There may be various ways to
conceptualize their similarities and dissimilarities (Wallerstein,
1989; Kernberg, 1999). Undoubtedly, broader theoretical debates
have a role here: Classical views of analysis emphasizing abstinence, anonymity, and neutrality make the dissimilarity more
prominent, whereas relational views emphasizing interaction
and enactment in the analytic dyad portray it as resembling the
therapeutic dyad.

We should note, however, that those positions accentuating
the differences and downplaying the commonalities (an issue to
which I return in chapter 7) have powerful implications for psychoanalytic training:

1. Many beginning candidates are nowadays experienced,
psychoanalytically oriented therapists. If we think of psychoanalysis and psychotherapy as mostly dissimilar, we may be

prone to view these trainees as total beginners whose past experience is irrelevant or even a hindrance (causing confusion). This view may, in more extreme cases, rationalize infantilizing, authoritarian training rules and contribute to the contrast between candidates' maturity in the "outside" professional world and their regression to being "passive, infantile, rigid" at the institute (Bruzzone et al., 1985, p. 411). On the other hand, if we conceptualize analysis and analytically oriented therapy as fairly close, we may be prone to view many of our trainees as experienced younger colleagues seeking additional, more advanced training. This view should encourage us to base our training model not on child-rearing images (e.g., if faculty and candidates are close, this is an "incestuous family") but on adult education models (Szasz, 1958) and to turn candidates into active partners in shaping their training.

2. A common criticism of analysts and candidates is that what they do is really just psychotherapy. A candidate exposed to such comments from supervisors or teachers may become obsessed with proving that this is not the case and as a result may become rigid and unresponsive to a patient's developmental needs or else less than honest in reporting what actually goes on in analytic sessions.

Objective Screening

Many institutes develop a thorough selection process during which a penetrating examination of an applicant's personality is attempted. Early generations of psychoanalysts never underwent any such screening but nevertheless proved to be enormously creative and productive. Not one of the early group of outstanding analysts—people like Abraham, Ferenczi, Rank, Jones, Klein, Anna Freud, Sullivan—was ever admitted by a psychoanalytic institute or went through its training.

Looking at the lists of criteria developed by some admissions committees, and thinking of what we know now about the personalities and private lives of our pioneers (thanks to relentless biographical research), we may wonder what the chances of passing such hurdles would have been for those brilliant early contributors.

Szasz (1958) attributed strict selection criteria to the growing power position of psychoanalysis, in contrast to its earlier stage, when it was revolutionary and powerless and welcomed any interested professional. "With the increasing acquisition of power on the part of the analytic group . . . those aspiring to become analysts were pushed into an increasingly powerless situation" (p. 600). Bernfeld (1962) attributed the introduction of rigid selection criteria to the anxiety produced by Freud's cancer and threatened loss. Bernfeld concluded, "Irrational motives of xenophobia . . . introduced melancholy traits into our training" (p. 467).

Just as with the issue of analyzability, an interest in intersubjectivity requires a reformulation of the dynamics of the interview process. The attempt to evaluate applicants objectively is usually serious and sincere, but it often implies downplaying possible personal sources of countertransference reactions in interviewers. An applicant's behavior during the interview is mostly attributed to intrapsychic processes, while the interviewer's impact, as well as the dyadic pattern evolving in the interaction, remains in shadow. This approach may also disregard the weight of personal values and of diverging visions of what constitutes good analysis. Finally, strict selection may indicate at times a disbelief in the possibility that undergoing an analysis can help an applicant overcome some personal difficulties and limitations unearthed during screening (a point raised by Alexander in the 1920s; Schröter, 2002, p. 888).

Admission interviews vary. Some are an exciting learning experience, an opportunity for a thoughtful exchange about one's life and work; others are predictable, dry, and uninspiring; and some, unfortunately, may be destructive. An experience of tactless intrusiveness, or of haughty, premature interpretation (perhaps implying, "I understand you better than your own analyst"), or of severe judgment may haunt an applicant for years. Of course, some such perceptions may be projections related to heightened anxiety, but the convergence of similar stories about certain interviewers points to the possibility that the power position of an interviewer can be abused.

A severe selection process, in which most applicants are turned down, may contribute to hostility toward psychoanalysis in the professional community, especially when there is only one institute in that city or country. What may be less visible, however, is the impact of such a process on those admitted. A candidate whose good friends, who may be very successful professionals, were turned down may develop survivor guilt. Such guilt, in turn, may contribute to the common fear that "sooner or later they will find out my admission was an error."

Thorough Evaluation of Candidates

Evaluation during training is, of course, unavoidable as well as an ethical obligation of the institute. A strong emphasis on unidirectional evaluation may easily degenerate, however, to a pattern characteristic of monasteries or religious retreats, in which mentors "focus on the limitations, shortcomings, mistakes, and inadequacies" of the student, while their own personality remains shrouded in secrecy (Kernberg, 1986, p. 810). "Candidates are subject to a process of judgment which is necessarily experienced as a judgement of themselves as persons" (Rustin, 1985, p. 152). Constant evaluation of candidates and "emphasis on how 'sick' the students are" (Szasz, 1958, p. 604) are major sources of the "paranoid atmosphere that often pervades psychoanalytic institutes and its devastating effect on the 'quality of life' in psychoanalytic education" (Kernberg, 1986, p. 803). Keeping candidates' progression slow and cumbersome is the first method listed by Kernberg (1996) among his "Thirty Methods to Destroy the Creativity of Psychoanalytic Candidates" (p. 1032). Discouraging rebellious candidates and stimulating them to resign is another method (p. 1035).

When a candidate is pushed out or dismissed from training, that action influences all other candidates (Bruzzone et al., 1985, p. 412). The impact is diminished if there is consensus about the candidate's inadequacy and if even other candidates informally express a feeling of "What is this person doing here?" The impact is enormous when a candidate is controversial, appreciated by some but seen negatively by others. The existence of problematic sides in each of us makes a controversial candidate into an identification figure, and dismissal can easily arouse the fantasy concern, "Could this happen to me as well?" Similar anxieties are aroused by deliberations (which often leak out and become public knowledge) regarding possible dismissal of a candidate, even when the eventual outcome is that the candidate continues with training.

How does a strong emphasis on evaluation influence supervision? I further explore this issue in chapter 6, but let me outline it here. There is a basic difference between the inherent critical-evaluative element in any honest supervisory intervention (enthusiasm or concern about what happens in the analysis discussed, attention to blind spots, ideas about possible improvements) and the evaluative reporting to education committees and similar authorities. The former, in my experience, may be painful but in the long run promotes growth. Within the live relationship in the supervisory dyad, just as in the effective analytic dyad, narcissistic vulnerability to criticism can usually be contained and worked through. In most cases, the supervisor's caring and trust in the trainee's potential create a background of safety that puts possible insults in perspective. These can be discussed and resolved, especially if the supervisor avoids assuming an omniscient position and is willing to admit blind spots or blunders when relevant.

In contrast, reporting to higher authorities generates intense anxiety but rarely promotes improvement. Committees, with all their good and serious intentions, can do very little to help resolve the deeper difficulties of candidates.

Paradoxically, existence of an elaborate evaluation system may allow a supervisor to avoid the stressful moment of expressing criticism within supervision. Kernberg (1996) sarcastically advised supervisors not to be outspoken and explicit with supervisees, because indirect communication of criticism better reinforces paranoid attitudes (p. 1037). The candidate lives in a "fool's paradise" until reaching the overwhelming moment of hearing from the director of training about misgivings that some unidentified faculty members have about his or her work. This is a formula for a defensive, anxious confrontation from which the trainee is not likely to learn much, while the chance for effective learning within the supervisory dyad has been missed.

Evaluation flourishing at the expense of learning itself may be an example of Szasz's (1958) observation that, though we learn how much our effectiveness increases when we relinquish our position of power vis-à-vis a patient, the "'power' which was repressed from analytic therapy returns and luxuriates in analytic training" (p. 608).

Training Analyst as Superior Analyst

Although many authors now agree with Ferenczi and Rank (1924) that the "correct didactic analysis is one that does not in the least differ from the curative treatment" (p. 60), the image of the training analyst as a superior analyst is still prominent in the literature, and much has been written about the outstanding qualities of training analysts. Such descriptions are very appealing, but I have some doubts whether they fit the way any of us are described in informal conversations among colleagues or trainees.

Moreover, though the goal is to make sure that candidates benefit from high-quality analysis and supervision, appointment of training analysts seems very often influenced by transferences, political alliances, charisma, visibility, personal popularity, rumors, and other factors not necessarily related to quality per se. "Discretion, secrecy and uncertainty about what is required to become a training analyst, how these decisions are made, where and by whom" are listed by Kernberg (1996, p. 1039) as widespread phenomena sabotaging the creativity of faculty members and subsequently of candidates.

The belief that training analysts can be chosen as the best according to objective standards again seems to disregard intersubjective emotional reality. This is one of my few disagreements with Kernberg (2000). Experience shows that views about most analysts vary, and even senior colleagues may be admired by some and criticized by others. Variations in theoretical approach and in preferences for different analytic styles seem to influence such gaps, in addition to purely personal likes and dislikes, which are easily rationalized and intellectualized.

In this respect, "objectively choosing the best analysts as training analysts" may be equivalent to "objectively choosing the best applicants to be admitted as candidates"; both beliefs convey disregard for the subjective and intersubjective nature of all interpersonal perceptions and attitudes. Moreover, as each of us is likely to have in mind a "private list" of analysts we genuinely respect (and to whom we would refer a family member or a close friend), and these lists all cannot be identical with the "official list" of training analysts, the forced idealization of an official list may inadvertently lead to an actual devaluation.

The training analyst category itself has been criticized by several authors. Bernfeld (1962) wrote, "We possess no way by which we can rationally rank our membership into Good, Very Good, and The Best Analysts. . . . By singling out a few members . . . implying that they are the best analysts, we confuse fantasy and magic with reality factors . . . [and] disturb perceptibly the transference in the personal analysis" (p. 481). Lussier (1991; see Wallerstein, 1993) also felt that having a separate class of training analysts is destructive:

> Can the science of psychoanalysis, by definition, admit, without inner inconsistencies, of two classes of analysts: The High Priests and the ordinary ones? For the unconscious phantasy formation of any candidate, the fact of being analysed by a member of the select group cannot but feed the unconscious belief in a special magic power, the phallic power, with which his "special" analyst has been invested. . . . What a fertile ground for idealization, unconscious magical participation to a special power through identification, a pathogenic transferential relation that can hardly be analysed [Lussier, 1991, p. 16].

A Brazilian analyst, Luiz Meyer, created quite a stir at the 2001 IPA Conference of Training Analysts when he described becoming a training analyst as a pursuit of status and power and discussed training analysis as stimulating narcissistic gratification, fostering an atmosphere with paranoiac qualities, and creating a tyranny veiled in academic clothing. In his subsequent paper, Meyer (2003) further elaborated his devastating deconstruction of the "official" training analysis as a fetish and as an ideologic structure, and he suggested that "every discriminated category of analyses should be abolished" (p. 1257).

Outlining the history of training analysts and institutes, Zusman (1988) spoke of the Eitingon syndrome. Eitingon treated Freud's work as sacrosanct and organized the Berlin Institute accordingly. "The Committee" running the psychoanalytic movement acquired the characteristics of a sect or a secret society (a process described by numerous scholars, notably Roazen, 1975; Weisz, 1975), and these were transmitted to all institutes, training committees, and local societies. "The Eitingon syndrome is a transference phenomenon defined by the transposition of a petrified bipersonal relationship (Eitingon/Freud) to the institutional level, where it then multiplies by 'regenerating' the original pair in each training analyst and his or her candidate" (Zusman, 1988, p. 361). This observation parallels Benjamin's (1997) comment, "The seduction by knowledge as power remained the unanalyzed transference in the geneology of analytic training, the unconscious basis of authority that leads us back to our ideal father" (pp. 792–793).

The intrusion of institute dynamics into a candidate's personal analysis, most prominent in institutes that still practice reporting in spite of the arguments against it (Kairys, 1964), provoked Kernberg's (1986) critique of the "hypocrisy and dishonest manipulation" involved in the "dramatic contradiction between hiding one's personality in order not to influence the candidate's analysis while actually influencing the candidate's progression behind his back" (p. 817).

But the issue is not limited to reporting. Another intense intrusion may occur when a candidate is admitted while already in analysis with an analyst who is not a training analyst. Some institutes require termination of the ongoing analysis and initiation of a new one with a training analyst irrespective of the feelings of either trainee or original analyst. To me, this procedure suggests that the idealization of training analysts has led us to lose our respect for the integrity, continuity, and natural course of the analytic process. Consequently, we present a negative role model to our trainees. A second analysis is usually a blessing (even when the first one was conducted by a senior training analyst), but our analytic knowledge indicates it should be chosen and timed by the analysand rather than forced by administrators.

The Allure and Price of a False Analytic Self

Undoubtedly, we all strive to achieve the best therapeutic results in our analyses and to reach the highest possible standards in training psychoanalysts and psychotherapists. My criticism is not meant to undermine this goal. To the contrary, I am suggesting that perfectionism, unrealistic idealizations, and a rigid and persecutory atmosphere may lower quality in spite of the honest wish to raise it.

Our fantasy wish may be to find the really suitable professionals, assign to them analyzable patients with whom they can practice correct technique until structural change is achieved, let only carefully chosen training analysts analyze them, and evaluate our trainees continually to guarantee good results. But this wish involves risky utopian elements and therefore may backfire.

This fantasy wish may stray too far from our clinical experience and from our life experience (Berman, 2000c). In reality we know that all of us, analysts in all stages of professional growth, have our personal and professional strengths and weaknesses; that we all do well with some patients and poorly with others (and rarely can predict this in advance); that at all levels of the professional hierarchy there are colleagues we respect and colleagues we have doubts about (and we rarely all agree on such judgments); that good analytic work is creative, individualistic, and never standard (an analysis "does not naturally . . . proceed from A to B. Its course is something else — more like the course of a neurosis or a love affair"; Lewin and Ross, 1960, p. 52); and that all analytic successes are partial and never preclude the need for additional treatment in the future.

Lussier (1991) spoke of the contrast between the goal of encouraging a candidate to search iconoclastically for the truth about himself and his reality and the tendency to constrain him in a rigid setup of strict rules and rituals. Another way of describing this contrast is to speak about varying proportions between divergent components in developing one's analytic self — aspects that develop from within, through an individuation process, through critical absorption and processing that allows the future analyst to discover what kind of analyst he or she wishes to be and genuinely can become, and aspects determined from without, shaped through fulfilling expectations, influenced too heavily by an aspect of one's personality that we might call a false analytic self.

The analytic false self differs, of course, from the earlier and more comprehensive False Self formation described by Winnicott (1960), but they may have some commonalities. Here, too, a person "gets seduced into a compliance, and a compliant False Self reacts to environmental demands . . . and by means of introjections even attains a show of being real" (p. 146). Just as the "child may grow to be just like mother, nurse, aunt, brother, or whoever at the time dominates the scene," so the acquiescing trainee may strive to be just like the training analysts who dominate the scene.

I suspect that many seeming successes to mold purified New Persons (in a religious, political, or national context) are variations of the False Self phenomenon, and we may encounter a similar danger. The allure of belonging, of being accepted, of being liked by our seniors is considerable and may have the upper hand in many instances.

Klauber (1983) said, "For many years the younger psychoanalyst functions — or at any rate I functioned — in part with an analytical false self" (p. 46). Eisold (1994, p. 788), who quoted Klauber, implied that such a situation is an unavoidable reaction to the loneliness of the analyst's work. Although I do not dismiss this universal factor, my feeling is that the analytic false self phenomenon is at least strongly reinforced by the impingements suffered during the training process. "Authoritarianism breeds discontent, fosters dishonesty, engenders dissolution" (Ross, 1999, p. 76).

Szasz (1958) quoted Fenichel, "Clearly human beings have only two ways of facing a power which restricts them: revolt, or else a (more or less illusory) participation . . . the fantasy . . . that they are already one with authority" (Fenichel, 1939, p. 158). Arlow (1972, p. 562) also suggested that candidates may be propelled by anxiety to identify with the aggressor (cf. Frankel, 2002) and to "remodel" themselves in the image of the ideal of the community. Orgel (2002), describing similar phenomena in discussing analysand-candidates who mimic their analysts (p. 437), cited Gaddini's (1984) comments about imitation as a path toward "magically becoming the object." Orgel warned, however, that imitation may turn into a caricature, with a "quality of mockery toward, and even triumph over, the analyst" (p. 438).

Balint (1948) dealt with similar issues when he spoke of an atmosphere "strongly reminiscent of the primitive initiation ceremonies," which aim "to force the candidate to identify himself with his initiator, to introject the initiator and his ideals,

and to build up from these identifications a strong superego" — accounting for the candidate's submission to authoritarian treatment (p. 167). Ross (1999, p. 70) spoke of a "disavowed sadomasochistic stance."

Zusman (1988) quoted Zimmerman and Messias, who discussed the final paper (case presentation) required by many institutes. They compared presenting this paper to an African tribe's
initiation rite in which the novice imitates the patron in correctly
roaring like a lion. Knowing how to roar like a lion, they suggested, means delivering a paper that represents exactly the mark
of approval of the group of training analysts to talk and write in
exactly the way demanded by the group wielding power. The
lion roar becomes a formula, a standardized way of behaving,
interpreting, and dealing with the patient.

Indeed, in my experience, the final case presentation is rarely
a genuinely free expression of the graduate's personal views and
analytic style. Spence (1998) spoke of a "concordance" among numerous such reports that may stem from "conscious and preconscious narrative smoothing" owing to "each candidate's need to
appear normative" (p. 643). In informal conversations, one can
hear comments about choosing a case that will not cause trouble,
about censoring interventions that may be seen as nonanalytic
(fitting a psychotherapy rather than an analysis), about writing a
theoretical discussion that will be liked by its readers, even if it
has little to do with the candidate's thinking while conducting the
analysis. The result is often a "well-ironed" case, with an orderly
inner structure (the analysis seems to follow too neatly the developmental stages of Mahler or Klein, etc.), an impressive fit
between associations and interpretations, an unobjectionable
countertransference (concern or confusion, yes; sexual arousal
or hate, no), and a moderately optimistic conclusion.

One may wonder, though, if this "ironing" really is an indication of a false analytic self or is a deliberate, conscious decision
that has little to do with the candidate's inner world. Although I
have no doubt that conscious considerations of survival have a
role (especially when the paper is subjected to numerous revisions and corrections and when final approval depends on a secret vote; Kernberg, 1996, p. 1033), I do not feel the answer is
clear-cut.

If I compare my experiences as a candidate (and later as a teacher and training analyst at a psychoanalytic institute) with my experiences as a student (and later as a professor at a university), I notice a meaningful difference. The university arouses less awe, identification, and idealization, and this makes differentiation and individuation easier. A clinical psychology student with psychoanalytic interests, required to submit an empirical research thesis, often sees it as a chore alien to his or her genuine goals but seldom is confused about the difference between the research standards and his or her views as a dynamic therapist. On the other hand, a candidate adjusting a case report (or an actual intervention in the session) to the expectations of the institute often becomes much more confused about what is deep-rooted and what is forced, what is genuine and what is a pretense, what is "mine" and what is "theirs."

Parenthetically, I add that the same comparison helps me to notice the quasi-religious elements in psychoanalytic training (cf. Bergmann, 1997, p. 83). At a university (which, of course, has many problems of its own, as Sorenson, 2000, wisely reminded us in his plea to avoid its idealization), no one raises an eyebrow when a talented junior faculty member is asked to undertake an important administrative role or when a promising graduate student teaches undergraduates only five years younger. At an institute, the possibility that a nontraining analyst will analyze a candidate or that a brilliant advanced candidate will give a seminar to beginning candidates arouses an anxiety reaction that seems to signify the breaking of a taboo.

Long-Term Impact

Another indication of the depth of the inhibiting influences of traditional training is that they do not easily evaporate after graduation. Klauber (1983) wrote, "It took me a good ten years of full-time psychoanalytic practice to feel myself a psychoanalyst" (p. 46). Orgel (2002) said that, "in committee meetings, one frequently 'hears' his or her own analyst's voice in the opinions expressed by present and former analysands" (p. 428). Rustin (1985) suggested that the public life of the analytic community is

inevitably "influenced by the pressures of the more primitive loyalties and claims on loyalty which arise from the particular relationships in which analysts are trained" (p. 145). Ross (1999)
added, "At almost every stage of their progression, candidates
and younger analysts found themselves subject to pathologizing
interpretations and to severe rites of passage in the manifest form
of successive certifications of competence" (p. 66)

Dulchin and Segal (1982), in a thorough sociological study of
the life of a psychoanalytic institute, showed how the informal
"leakage" of information, originating in personal analyses of candidates and members, as well as of their relatives and friends, influences all participants in the system and often inhibits them out
of fear of a damaging exposure. One senior faculty member became much more open in a research interview after finding out
that the interviewer was not in analysis (p. 32). Candidates and
analysts admit being conflicted about referring their spouses for
analysis, as doing so might intrude on their privacy and indirectly influence their present and future status in the institute.
"The analytic process involved all the junior Institute members in
a form of reporting on one another to their senior members" (p. 36).

In other words, impingements of the training period leave
their lasting mark and are also later reactivated in the relationships within the psychoanalytic community. "During training,
obviously, candidates are closely scrutinized and evaluated; after
becoming fully fledged analysts, this scrutiny becomes more subtle, but no less important, as selections are made to key teaching,
supervisory and administrative roles" (Eisold, 1994, p. 790). Such
scrutiny may snowball in some institutes and psychoanalytic societies until these places become haunted by the demons of ruthless perfectionistic judgment, turning at times into character
assassination. In such settings, *narcissism* and other diagnostic
terms may perform the same function that *sin* and *vice* perform in
fundamentalist milieus and *bourgeois individualism* performs in
utopian socialist groups.

The important point raised by Rustin (1985) is relevant at all
stages of the professional ladder, from applicant to training analyst: "Where 'interpretations' become utilized in everyday life to
control individuals or groups, they are often experienced as inva-
sions of privacy, and inhibit instead of supporting the development of individual autonomy" (p. 147).

Lussier (1991) described a pattern mirroring itself: "While . . . senior candidates, even the best ones, experience severe castration anxiety if they dare to voice their opinion . . . many training analysts reveal the same anxiety when they avoid the risk of being criticized by colleagues in front of their analysands, a narcissistic blow" (pp. 5–6). Faculty and trainees become inhibited by each other as part of a vicious circle that perpetuates itself from generation to generation.

Individual autonomy is crucial in psychoanalysis—a profession in which the analyst's personality is the major tool, a discipline that teaches us constantly about the illusory nature of all generalized conventional truths not reached through genuine personal experience. Our clinical effectiveness and our theoretical potency alike are dependent on flexibility, creativity, and a capacity to use ourselves fully to observe emotional reality freshly, in ourselves and in the other, and to become attentive to our own blind spots and the rigidities that stand in our way. Increasing such capacities is a primary goal of psychoanalytic training, and the factors that hinder them must be of great concern to us.

Bernfeld (1962) suggested that writing regulations and enforcing them "take the life out of psychoanalysis" (p. 479). Our choice, however, is not between rigid structure and anarchy (Wallerstein, 1993). A stable, containing structure need not be formalistic and impersonal. Unique individual needs of trainees can potentially be legitimized (as crucial elements to be taken into account and accommodated by the structure) rather than stigmatized (as a rebellious defiance subverting it and needing to be suppressed).

I am aware, of course, that my own thinking also runs the risk of arousing a utopian perfectionistic idealization of its own—that of painless psychoanalytic training, of a completely relaxed free institute. This perfection can never be achieved. Paranoid anxieties are ubiquitous. Learning new skills unavoidably arouses feelings of impotence and helplessness. Criticism may always be experienced as hurtful, but without criticism there is no growth. Psychoanalytic training can never be all fun and pleasure.

And yet, differences of degree and proportion are at times very important. Having graduated two different institutes (first the New York University Postdoctoral Program, then the Israel Psychoanalytic Institute) and having taught in more than one, I can attest to significant variations. The atmosphere of an institute may shape the balance between anxiety and excitement, between gradually increased confidence and a sense of being castrated, between a desperate, defensive reliance on a false analytic self (the fantasized Real Analyst as a variation of the utopian New Person) and a better potential for developing an intrinsic analytic identity unique to each of us.

In this respect, an exclusive focus on individual dynamics (conveyed in referring all difficulties "back to the couch"; Kernberg, 1996, p. 1038) can be defensively abused to deny institutional dynamics and group processes. A personal analysis is naturally geared toward an individual-biographical emphasis. At worst, it may be abused to deny group dynamics; at best, it can acknowledge them without being able to influence them directly. Open forums for group discussion of candidates and faculty, at times jointly conducted, may be more helpful than individual couches in resolving training issues. However, effective running of such forums requires group training and experience. Moreover, the attempt to establish them may arouse fears and then attempts to block their development.

Psychoanalysis can be seen as a theory about the possibilities and limits of psychic change. It has also been applied to the study of potential change in institutions and organizations and of the stumbling blocks along the way toward such change. It can be self-critically applied to our training structures to allow for a new understanding of inherent difficulties. This understanding can be useful in contemplating reasonable and realistic reforms in our own institutions and in working through the anxieties and resistances any such reforms are likely to generate.

In many national, religious, and social movements, a gap tends to develop between ideals and the structures created to implement them. This gap may have developed in our movement as well. Reaching a better understanding of individual and group regressive processes at our institutes and clinical training programs may be an impetus for making changes in the structure and climate of psychoanalytic and psychodynamic clinical training and may result in a better fit between institutional forms of training and its substantial goals of individual growth.

4

Detoxifying the Toxic Effects of Psychoanalytic Training: A Case Study

In my opinion a superabundance of regulations and prohibitions injures the authority of the law . . . Moreover, it does not mean one is quite an anarchist if one is prepared to realize that laws and regulations cannot from their origin claim to possess the attribute of being sacred and untransgressable.

—Sigmund Freud
"The Question of Lay Analysis"

The question that I pose in this chapter and study through the test case of Israeli psychoanalysis is whether training based on the "Eitingon model" can be transformed from within—whether its toxic effects, such as paranoia and infantilization, can be detoxified.

Today, with the serious attempt to reexamine all aspects of psychoanalytic theory and technique, a candid and critical reappraisal of traditional training and a consideration of alternative models become urgent tasks. In a rapidly changing world in which democratic values have a crucial role, the quality of psychoanalysis, its status, and its continued professional appeal may depend on far-reaching innovation in training and may be damaged by an authoritarian and overly hierarchical training method that encourages elitism and isolation.

Controversial Discussions in Israel, 1992–1996

How can a traditional psychoanalytic institute be transformed from within? What are the implications of such a change process? Here I describe attempts to overcome some of the drawbacks of

123

the traditional training structure, disagreements about the gains and risks involved in these attempts, and the complex processes they triggered. These efforts at the Israel Psychoanalytic Society (IPS) began with a stormy period of intense internal debates between 1992 and 1996, and I open my discussion by reviewing that crucial period (Berman, 1998).

In some ways, these debates in Israel parallel the Controversial Discussions that transpired in the British Psychoanalytic Society between 1941 and 1945 (King and Steiner, 1991). However, whereas the British discussions covered all areas of psychoanalysis (metapsychology, development, technique, training, etc.), the debates in Israel focused specifically on the structure and atmosphere of training. Still, more general issues were present in the background, insofar as opinions about training are necessarily influenced by views on other matters.

These background issues (I have alluded to a few already) include: Is psychoanalytic technique basically a clear method that has solid rules and that needs to be transmitted and taught by knowledgeable "expert" teachers, or is it to a considerable extent reinvented in each analysis and therefore strongly dependent on the candidate's inner freedom and creativity? Can analytic skills be judged objectively, which would allow for authoritative evaluation of candidates (which ones are fit to become analysts) and analysts (which ones are fit to become training analysts), or are such judgments frequently based on subjective feelings and intersubjective processes (transference–countertransference) and on personal values (diverging visions of what is good psychoanalysis) and therefore inherently open to controversy? How similar or dissimilar are psychoanalysis and psychoanalytically oriented psychotherapy, and, therefore, may an experienced dynamic therapist be deemed an advanced trainee when coming to train as an analyst, or else is his or her past experience irrelevant or even a hindrance?

As the history of the Israeli debates provides an instructive picture of the difficulties to be faced in any attempt to make substantial changes in traditional psychoanalytic training, this history is, I believe, of broader interest. Both my active participation in these debates and the short time that has elapsed since they took place do not allow me a detached perspective, so here I have decided to use as many existing documents (e.g., official protocols of IPS business meetings) as possible to try to present a factual account of the proceedings, and I have attempted to avoid interpreting or evaluating the different positions involved, beyond their manifest content. Still, my views have unavoidably influenced my descriptions of the course of events, and I remain open to the possibility that other participants in the debates may have different perspectives.

Before going into the specific content and sequence of the debates, I give a condensed picture of the history and structure of psychoanalytic training in Israel—drawing on and updating an official account[1] submitted by the IPS to the IPA (Litman, 1994).

Eitingon established the Israel Psychoanalytic Institute (IPI) in the autumn of 1934, shortly after his emigration from Germany, and naturally modeled it after the Berlin Institute (Gumbel, 1965; Winnick, 1977; Moses, 1992). The original members of the IPI — officially the Eitingon Institute, though this title is rarely mentioned now — were all emigré analysts from Europe. Since its founding, the IPI has operated as the training vehicle for its parent, the IPS, which itself was formed August 3, 1933 (initially as the Palestine Psychoanalytic Society) and which has been part of the IPA ever since. The IPI is governed by a training committee elected by the IPS. The separate position of institute director was abolished in 1991, and, since then, all members' involvement in policymaking has increased. The IPI is located in Jerusalem, but about half of its seminars and other educational activities are conducted in Tel Aviv, in the area where most members and candidates now reside (the percentage of Jerusalem people has steadily decreased). Candidates commute to seminars that are out of their area, and supervision and training analyses take place all around the country.

In early 2004, the IPS had about 140 members and the IPI about 100 candidates. Throughout the years, the IPI has been a highly demanding training center. Originally classical in orientation, the theoretical and clinical perspectives of the institute have broadened over time, and the ideas of Klein, Winnicott, Bion, Kohut, and relational psychoanalysis have influenced its faculty members.

---

[1]I participated in preparing this account.

Candidates are admitted after thorough evaluation from a pool of highly qualified mental health professionals. During the 1980s and early 1990s, 25 to 35 percent of the applicants were admitted biannually (i.e., a class of 10 to 15 candidates from among 40 to 50 applicants). Most of those admitted are clinical psychologists; a few are psychiatrists and social workers. With 10 to 25 years of experience in dynamic psychotherapy, they start training at the IPI in their late 30s and 40s. In the past, the first two years of study consisted of introductory theoretical courses, and a positively evaluated candidate began conducting supervised analyses in the third year. The candidate has always been required to conduct three such analyses, four sessions per week each, under the supervision of three training analysts, once a week with each. Only analyses that continue for at least two years are counted, but most are much longer. The candidate submits a written report on one of these analyses (after being recommended by all three supervisors) and concludes it with a theoretical discussion. When the report is approved by the Training Committee, often after editing and other modification, the candidate is invited to discuss the case in an open meeting and respond to questions and criticisms in the final step toward graduation.

During training, candidates are also required to undergo a personal analysis of four sessions a week. Although the formal requirement is for at least 500 hours, most candidates stay in analysis at least five years and at times undergo two analyses. On average, candidates graduate from the IPI and becomes associate members after eight or nine years of training, though some take longer. For many years, associate members who wanted to become full members had to present a theoretical paper to the IPS. Society members discussed the paper and the member's credentials as a psychoanalyst and as a contributor to the IPS and voted by secret ballot on acceptance, which required a two-thirds majority.

Toward the end of the 1980s, democratic reform began in the IPS and its institute. An effort was made to allow a much larger proportion of the membership to become actively involved in decision making and administration. Many members came to feel that too many functions had become concentrated in the Training Committee. Henceforth, responsibility for admissions was shifted to an Admissions Committee with a membership that does not overlap with that of the Training Committee. (Both committees include older and younger members, and both have a rotating membership, so many members are involved over time.) Responsibility for recommending new training analysts was moved to another new committee. This new committee made recommendations after examining potential training analysts' professional credentials (minimum credentials are full membership, five years of membership, and continual analytic practice of at least three analyses) and competence; if the committee was satisfied with a candidate, it submitted his or her name for a vote by secret ballot by all members (acceptance, again, required a two-thirds majority). This reform was effective and led to the selection of several new training analysts — after many years during which there had been no more than a dozen training analysts throughout Israel (Berman, 1998).

Nevertheless, in the atmosphere of the more open discussions that began developing at IPS meetings, members of the new committee for screening training analysts reported great difficulty in objectively evaluating the quality of potential nominees. Gradually becoming clearer was the fact that such evaluation was conducted in the absence of actual knowledge regarding a member's analytic skills and was often influenced (as I point out in chapter 3) by transference feelings, charisma, visibility, personal popularity, political alliances, and so forth. This realization eventually led to a radical change, to be described shortly.

Another major bone of contention arose with the changing of the composition of the candidate pool. Beginning in the late 1980s, fewer psychiatrists have been applying to the IPI — a result partly explained by the strong biological trend in Israeli psychiatry. In earlier decades, psychiatrists had made up the majority of candidates (though psychologists had also been admitted, initially as child analysts). Even in the early 1990s, the IPS was still composed almost equally of psychiatrists and psychologists. Since then, however, the proportion of medically trained members has been rapidly decreasing (a few have quit, after being inactive for some years). Today, about 80 percent of candidates are clinical psychologists, and the other 20 percent are social workers and psychiatrists (only these three professions are admitted).

Typically, psychologists are admitted after having established themselves firmly as psychoanalytically oriented psychotherapists and at times as teachers and supervisors in the field. Often, candidates are graduates of advanced psychotherapy programs, are knowledgeable in psychoanalytic theory, and are well acquainted with the psychoanalytic community. Being mature professionals, they tend to be critical, often in realistic and sharp-sighted ways. Many of them have persuasively argued that their discomfort with feeling infantilized, and their protest against rules that at times they see as rigid, ought not to be interpreted away as mere transferential distortion or oedipal acting-out.

Moreover, many recent candidates have come to the IPI while already undergoing a personal analysis. Although this analysis has been helpful in terms of the candidates' maturity as trainees, it has also intensified the problem that, though most of their analysts were experienced colleagues with good reputations, many were not training analysts. At this juncture, the traditional demand — that the prospective trainee interrupt his or her ongoing analysis and start a new one with an official training analyst — has aroused much pain and anger among candidates and members alike, especially among those whose analysands were "taken away." Many have complained that this practice conveys lack of respect for the integrity and natural course of the analytic process and poses a negative model for trainees. This complaint has been reinforced by the awareness that such a policy is not universal: "If the candidate is in analysis with a non-training analyst, he will, in some institutes, be required to transfer to a training analyst. In others every effort will be made to allow the candidate to remain with his analyst" (Sandler, 1982, p. 394).

Within the IPS, criticism regarding the antianalytic implications of interrupting analyses led to a two-thirds majority vote (as required for bylaw changes), in May 1992, in favor of a resolution I introduced to allow the Training Committee to "grant waivers" — the option to recognize, ad hoc, any ongoing analysis with an IPS member as fulfilling the training requirement. At the June 1992 business meeting, however, many belated objections to the change were raised — one in particular being that it would erode the status of training analysts. In addition, the Training Committee expressed an unwillingness to evaluate individual cases. The debate was heated, and the two camps that formed were clearly distinguishable — those who considered a firm structure to be the first priority (the "traditionalists") and those who put more emphasis on flexibility and individual consideration (the "reformists"). Eventually, a slim majority voted to suspend implementation of the May resolution, pending further discussion. This discussion, which occurred over the next three and a half years, continued to be stormy.

The tensions evoked by this issue were explored more fully when yet another phase of democratization was initiated—one focusing on the functioning of the IPS itself. Only then did members' feelings about the society and about the subjective experience of being members come to the surface. Among the experiences related by members were difficulties in speaking openly at meetings, anxiety regarding harsh criticism, the sense (among office holders) of being unappreciated, alienation (among younger members), and feelings that the IPS functioned too much by routine and that it had much difficulty with new initiatives. An attempt was made to alleviate these difficulties by gathering all members in a "town meeting" in which small groups could have informal discussions.

During these discussions, some members traced difficulties in their attitudes toward the society to persecutory experiences during their training. These reports of difficulties and persecutory experiences, and candidates' wishes to be involved in discussions, led to having a second town meeting, attended jointly by members and candidates. Small group discussions revealed a deep sense of alienation and distance among many candidates— an experience shared by some younger members. On the other hand, the invitation to speak openly and the discovery of experiences shared by members and candidates aroused cautious optimism regarding the possibility of a new beginning. Maybe, many wondered, the atmosphere in the institute would become less authoritarian and less paranoid. Perhaps candidates *could* be treated as younger colleagues rather than as schoolchildren, even as the goals of training continued to be the most sophisticated scholarship and the sharpest analytic skills.

The issue of interrupting ongoing analyses of incoming candidates reached the agenda again early in 1994. IPS members decided to devote three consecutive meetings to the topic, including a meeting for small group discussions and, finally, a business meeting for voting.

Around the same time, I presented to the society "Psychoanalytic Training: Dynamics, Social Processes, Pathology" (Berman, 1994b), a paper in which I explored the history of the critical discussion about psychoanalytic training, as outlined and further developed in the present book. I discussed some of the pathogenic influences of the hierarchical traditional institute, idealization of the training analyst, infantilization of the candidate, encouragement of regressive and paranoid fantasies, and the potential contradiction between the creative individualistic nature of psychoanalysis and the typical training process. I suggested that these contradictions can be resolved only by changing the structure and climate of training. Specifically, I called for admission of a higher percentage of applicants to our institute, as in preceding years numerous highly talented professionals had been turned down. Further, I pled for devoting less time and energy to demoralizing discussions about the adequacy of candidates and more to the improvement of teaching; for allowing candidates more freedom in choosing their analysts (limiting them only by objective criteria of experience); for avoiding interruption of ongoing analyses; and for making candidates more active partners in shaping their training.

In retrospect, that paper may have exerted some influence on the vote at the April 1994 meeting. I reintroduced my "waiver" resolution, but another colleague, Raanan Kulka, proposed a more comprehensive and radical change — removing the personal analysis of candidates from the list of functions exclusive to training analysts. In addition to eliminating the need to interrupt analyses, this would give the candidate full responsibility for choosing an analyst. Experience indicates, Kulka suggested, that candidates are very careful in choosing analysts — as the candidates themselves are most affected by the outcome. They are eager to have the most profound analytic experience, and they look for experienced and serious analysts irrespective of formal requirements.

Kulka's more comprehensive reform won a large majority of the votes and was accepted (31 members were in favor, 10 were opposed, and 4 abstained). The resolution read, "Each candidate must undergo a personal analysis while going through training in the Institute. The analysis will be conducted by a qualified analyst who is a member of the Society." Spontaneous applause, unusual in the society, followed the announcement of the results. In the brief discussion that ensued, some members expressed great satisfaction, and others gave vent to grave concerns about the quality of future training. In most cases, members' reactions were in line with their past positions — another indication of the partisanship of the two camps within the IPS.

The months after this resolution were particularly stormy. Members alarmed by the change sought to mobilize help from abroad by suggesting that the new policy was incompatible with IPA regulations. Members supporting the change saw no such incompatibility and cited the variability in training structures at various institutes recognized by the IPA. Furthermore, supporters emphasized that the new policy did not eliminate training analysts; training analysts were still supervising candidates and chairing the Training Committee.

Inquiries made of leading IPA members, by both camps, revealed a complex picture:

1. The structure of training per se is not part of the binding bylaws of the IPA. (Eitingon's attempt to establish a powerful International Training Committee with worldwide jurisdiction met with much opposition in the IPA and was given up after 1938; Balint, 1948, p. 168.)

2. Several IPA leaders, notably Horacio Etchegoyen (then president), Joseph Sandler (past president), and Charles Hanly (vice-president), strongly supported the traditional training structure and were particularly unhappy about the possibility of candidates undergoing analysis with inexperienced junior analysts. Other leaders, including past and present vice-presidents, viewed changes in training structure more favorably.

3. IPA bylaws sanction all training structures of component societies established up until 1975 (including, e.g., the Swiss Psychoanalytic Society, which has no training analysts, and the French Psychoanalytic Association, which legitimizes analysis of candidates with any analyst) but since then require international consultation before making changes in training policy.

4. A change in IPA bylaws — transforming the rule of consultation into a rule of formal approval — did not apply in the case of the IPS, as the IPA mail ballot on changing its bylaws was

completed only on May 31, 1994, after the IPS resolution had been passed and reported.

The unresolved issues and tensions came up again at a June 1994 meeting. For the first time, the division within the IPS was formally recognized—three training analysts representing the main viewpoints were invited to open the discussion.

Yecheskiel Cohen, past president of the IPS, represented the moderate middle group. He expressed reservations about both the traditional conservatism of the society and the risk associated with changes that are defiant and too radical. He disagreed with the April resolution but maintained that it was legal and legitimate, subject to change only by due process. He was also in favor of thorough discussions with the IPA before any further decisions are reached.

Shmuel Erlich, then chairperson of the Training Committee, expressed the traditionalist view. According to Erlich, the April vote took place in an overly emotional atmosphere of "rebellion or revolution," was influenced by the lecture preceding it, was conducted with insufficient understanding of its international implications, and was therefore invalid. Erlich reiterated the view that training analyses are a key element in training and are a unique kind of analysis (because of the different significance of termination) and therefore should be conducted only by analysts chosen on merit by the society. Candidates in analysis with other analysts on admission always have the option of postponing their training if they do not want to interrupt that analysis. Stratification and hierarchy are unavoidable, and the attempt to undo them is not democratic but perverse—leading to erosion of generational boundaries in the analytic family and sabotage of individuation and growth.

Raanan Kulka, expressing the reformist position, emphasized that IPA bylaws already recognize the possibility of changes in component societies' training policies and that the consultation process is meant to contain such changes and not prevent them. Maintenance of the *status quo ante,* or of uniformity between different countries and cultures, does not necessarily serve psychoanalysis. In Kulka's view, the change approved in April was the natural result of a deep-reaching development occurring within the IPS, and the attempt to present this change as impulsive was misleading.

The ensuing debate, which involved members' continued disagreement as to preferred policy, also showed their deep emotional investment in their positions. A consensus was reached to hold discussions with the IPA, to delay implementing the April resolution, and to reconvene for further discussion.

In July 1994, IPS president Shalom Litman submitted a detailed memorandum to the IPA. He described the history of the debate and ended with a plea:

> The resolution approved by our Society results . . . from a process of rejuvenation which is very vital to us. This process has considerably increased the morale and sense of identification of many members, who feel now as active partners in reshaping the Society and Institute to fit changing times and values, rather than as passive (and often alienated) recipients of immovable and binding structures. This sensitive process, crucial for the future of psychoanalysis in our country, should not be disrupted. To guarantee our vitality and integrity, we must find our own path. We may enter blind alleys on our way, but we feel confident that we will correct any errors by seriously monitoring the results of any policy we adopt, without idealizing it.
>
> Our belonging to the international psychoanalytic community, and to the IPA, is enormously important to all of us. The IPA has always been a collaborative democratic organization, attempting to increase unity and communication among analysts around the world, while respecting differences resulting from local traditions, cultural uniqueness and social processes. In such a mutually respectful partnership, we believe, a serious attempt can be made to learn from each other's experience.
>
> Our own internal debates are not over. Members who opposed the April resolution hope to convince the Society to change it. Many of the members who supported it are interested in formulating more moderate versions which would take into account the concerns raised by the critics, both within the Society and in the international community.

> We will be grateful for ideas and suggestions regarding
> various solutions and their implications. We hope that our
> own concerns and needs will also be taken seriously, and
> our autonomy respected [Litman, 1994, pp. 7–8].

The autonomy of the IPS has indeed been respected, and the IPS resolution has not been criticized by any official body of the IPA. The only direct response came in the form of a personal letter (dated August 17, 1994) from the IPA president (Etchegoyen) to the IPS president: "I hope you will be able to resolve, in a way satisfactory to all, the changes in the Society, in accordance with the standards of the IPA. The idea that *all* analysts in the Society could conduct analyses of candidates is not acceptable, and . . . should be rejected." Etchegoyen's emphasis on the word *all* seemed to leave the door open to compromise.

The next year, the president of IPS met with some of its past presidents, and they issued a statement supporting changes – in the direction of democratization and of seeking ways to lessen infantilization of candidates – while maintaining the status of the training analyst. I myself made many consultations with leading analysts in various countries, and I reported my findings to the membership. I learned more about the considerable worldwide variation in training structures. Whereas most English-speaking institutes maintain the traditional structure, most French-speaking institutes have revised it in an attempt to minimize interference in the analysis of candidates. (This has often been the long-term outcome of debates begun in the 1950s and 1960s by Lacan; Roudinesco, 1990.) Although the language of international communication for most analysts in Israel is English rather than French, we found ourselves aligned with the French-speaking analytic world in this matter.

The Paris Psychoanalytical Society, the largest such society in France, decided in April 1994 to follow the smaller French Association in allowing candidates analysis with any analyst they choose. Objections were raised within the society and within the IPA, and a compromise was reached. The resultant training regulations now state that training should include a "psychoanalysis which is recommended to be undertaken with a Training Member," but that statement is later qualified: "The Training Committee evaluates the candidacies of all individuals having undertaken analysis with a Member of the Paris Society, provided that the analysis had begun when the analyst was already a member" (Paris Psychoanalytical Society, 1994, articles 2/1 and 3/1).

Back in Israel, in June 1995, IPS members discussed and voted on the appointment of new training analysts. The tension was great, and animosities, expressed in members' reactions to the screening committee's informal poll conducted in preparation for the vote, clearly created a persecutory atmosphere paralleling that of the candidates in training. "The demon of intrusive and ruthless judgments, which we unleashed at the candidates, now gnaws at our own feet," someone remarked.

At the July 1995 meeting, many members expressed open disgust with the hostile and judgmental atmosphere generated by a determination to discuss people's "merit." They then voiced their desire to simplify the appointment of training analysts. The yearning for change was also manifested in the widespread call for resolution of internal conflicts by a reasonable compromise — one that "no one will be happy with but all could live with" in order to overcome the perpetual tension and even the danger of an eventual split. Although few members changed their opinions, most seemed more willing to accommodate opposing viewpoints. A decision was made to create a special task force of about a dozen members representing all viewpoints and to charge it with seeking a compromise. The task force, chaired by IPS president-elect Abigail Golomb, eventually agreed on recommendations that were then approved with slight changes and massive support at the January 1996 business meeting of the IPS (40 to 46 members were in favor of various articles, 3 to 5 were opposed, and 2 abstained). The task force compromise consisted of three points (Berman, 1998):

1. Candidates are expected to undergo analysis and supervision with training analysts.

2. The procedure for becoming a training analyst is to be made easier. All existing requirements are to be maintained (full membership; five years of membership; continual analytic practice of at least three analyses, four times a week; interest in psychoanalysis; activity in the IPS; and ethical conduct), but the plenary personal discussion and secret vote on each new training

analyst are to be abolished. The IPS board is to approve all members who meet all criteria one month after their names have been circulated and members have had an opportunity to raise objections.

3. Candidates who begin training while already in analysis with a member who is not a training analyst are expected to switch to a training analyst within two years, before seeing their first analysand. If they want to continue with their present analyst so as not to interrupt the analytic process, they may apply to the Training Committee for special permission. (The task force recommended establishing a separate "Waiver Committee" to deal with such requests, but attendees at the business meeting instead preferred that a subcommittee of the Training Committee be established. The Training Committee accepted this responsibility.)

The hope was that this compromise would be effective in a way reminiscent of the famous 1946 "ladies' agreement" between Anna Freud, Melanie Klein, and British Psychoanalytic Society president Sylvia Payne — an agreement that enabled the society to resolve its near-split during its Controversial Discussions (King and Steiner, 1991, pp. 906–908).

The international community reacted positively to the compromise. Former IPA vice-president Hanly wrote, "I congratulate you and your colleagues on the solution that you have found. . . . By drawing on the specific strengths of your Society, you have resolved a very divisive issue [. . .] finding a creative compromise to resolve a difficult situation" (Hanly, personal communication, 1996).

The sequence of events described here seems to prove that change can be implemented in traditional psychoanalytic institutes. A process of patiently searching for pragmatic compromises acceptable to most members can result in meaningful innovation even when opinions are divided, and this process need not have a catastrophic impact on the entire superstructure. The international psychoanalytic community is today quite heterogeneous, and even the IPA can absorb and accept changes in local institutes in the direction of more respect for the individual autonomy of candidates — if these changes are made at a moderate pace, are introduced without provocations, are

well explained, and occur in the context of an overall commitment to maintaining high standards of psychoanalytic training,
practice, and scholarship.

Further Developments in Israel, 1996–2003

The January 1996 resolutions have calmed the acute crisis in the
IPS, though serious differences of opinion certainly persisted.
During the next seven years, change continued, at times by consensus and at times with disagreement, but the degree of tension
subsided. To explore these years, I switch from proceeding in
chronological order to delineating the main areas of change in
training and the issues involved.

Admission Policy

The IPI, like many other institutes, has for many years used a
thorough selection process in which a penetrating examination of
the applicant's personality is attempted, mostly on the basis of
two or three long interviews. Initially, the Training Committee
conducted this examination; beginning in the 1980s, a separate
Admissions Committee assumed the role. Although evaluations
of past teachers and supervisors were usually solicited (most of
the applicants being experienced clinical psychologists or other
mental health professionals), these evaluations were often disregarded — the rationale being that they are too colored by countertransferential identifications. In the 1980s and early 1990s,
only about one fourth to one third of applicants were admitted
to the IPI, and a large group of "Institute rejects" formed among
senior members of the professional community — a situation
that often generated hostility toward psychoanalysis and a view
of the IPI (for decades the only such institute in Israel) as elitist
and persecutory.
    This policy came under growing criticism within the IPS.
With all the enormous amount of time and energy invested in
the process, some members claimed that many of the rejected
applicants were as competent as those admitted and that the cumulative impact of numerous rejections of experienced and

highly esteemed clinicians and teachers harmed the future of psychoanalysis in Israel. The system, critics argued, favored average
applicants who seem acceptable to everybody over more original
and creative applicants who may be inherently more controversial. Moreover, the Admissions Committee rarely paid much attention to the applicant's intellectual potential and broader
interests (the application form included questions about clinical
work but none about teaching or publications) and seemed to accept inadvertently Kernberg's (1996) tongue-in-cheek advice "to
maintain a relatively uniform student body in terms of . . . professional aspirations" (p. 1037).

Other critics raised the negative effect the situation has on mo-
tivations to apply. They felt that it strengthens narcissistic elements, in that candidates want to join the "chosen few" rather
than want the training for its own sake. Another painful issue was
the experience of accepted candidates, who often, as suggested in
chapter 3, suffered "survivor guilt" toward friends and colleagues (and spouses in some instances) who had been turned
down.

Another issue that came up was that an interest in intersubjectivity requires paying more attention to the dynamics of
the interview process. The wish to evaluate applicants objectively often implied, as discussed in chapter 3, downplaying
personal sources of countertransference reactions in interviewers. The applicant's behavior during the interview was attributed to intrapsychic processes — which disregarded the impact
of the interviewer and the evolving dyadic pattern. For some
reason, long-term supervisors had been assumed to be subjective and therefore unreliable, whereas one-time interviewers
had been seen as objective and dependable. At times, the same
analyst whose opinion as an interviewer was crucial after a
one-hour interview was disregarded when expressing an opinion about a supervisee of several years. The implied disbelief in
the possibility that undergoing an analysis could help an applicant overcome personal difficulties was also raised.

After numerous debates, changes began occurring in the admission policy. No formal resolutions were passed, but, over the
past few years, a considerably larger proportion of applicants has
been admitted, including many that had previously been turned
down repeatedly. A willingness to give applicants the benefit of

the doubt has increased. The feeling now seems to be that there must be strong reasons to turn down a competent professional who is willing to make the enormous investment implied in analytic training. In addition, the old system of admitting a class every two years was abolished, and new candidates were allowed to start their training at the beginning of every trimester, in line with the new curriculum (to be discussed shortly). More recently, after many newly admitted candidates flooded the insufficient number of existing seminars, a change was made to allow them to start at the beginning of the academic year after their admission — which would thus allow for better planning.

Personal Analysis

Although the term *training analysis* has become less popular in view of the realization that an effective analysis of candidates should be as therapeutic as any other analysis and should not be didactic in atmosphere, a personal analysis has always been considered central to training in Israel. Applicants are required to be in analysis at least three times a week for at least a year before applying to the IPI, so that their application is based on firsthand experience and not only on intellectual knowledge. The latter regulation was introduced a few years ago and was supported by all even though, unlike many other changes, it made the IPI more demanding. Candidates are expected to undergo, during training, at least 500 hours of analysis with a training analyst (four times a week), though most analyses are much longer, and to be in analysis when they begin their supervised cases (formerly in the third year of training but now usually in the second year).

Intrusions into candidates' analyses are now rare. The practice of reporting had been abolished in Israel decades ago, and the demand to switch analysts if admitted while in treatment with a nontraining analyst has also, as I described, been modified. The difficulty the IPS had in absorbing this change, however, is interesting. A year or two after the change had been made, it was mentioned in a business meeting, and the member who wrote the protocol inadvertently quoted the old policy (mandatory switch) as being in effect — having repressed the change (option of not switching). The protocol was amended after protests. Another year passed, and the Training Committee distributed supposedly up-to-date training regulations in which the change was again omitted, and again a new version had to be printed.

By then, though, the option of asking for continuation of an ongoing analysis, versus switching to a training analyst, had "sunk in." However, instances of asking for continuation decreased, because becoming a training analyst was easier. Of the candidates who apply for ad hoc approval of their analysts, the majority is answered positively, but these applications still arouse tension and uncertainty. The major criterion used by the Training Committee seems to be experience, and requests involving recent graduates tend to be turned down.

Choice of Training Analysts
(and Admission to Full Membership)

As I mentioned, training analyst appointments are now based on actual experience and do not require a vote. As a result, the number of appointments has increased considerably (to almost half the members), which allows for real free choice of personal analyst and supervisors, who can also be switched by the candidate "with no questions asked." (Free choice has been the official policy for decades, but it was practically meaningless when the number of training analysts in each city was very small.)

This reform also signifies changes in the definition of training analyst—from being evaluative to being factual, from being an analyst of better quality to being an active, experienced older analyst. Merit issues regarding training analysts were therefore withdrawn from collective IPS or committee judgment and were handed over in practice to the serious personal consultations candidates usually initiate with senior analysts they trust. "Did we leave the control in the hands of our candidates? Yes! They, the consumers of our teaching and supervision, will choose according to free-market rules," suggested Bar-Lev Elieli (2001, p. 33). But I would add that candidates make their choices on the basis of their great motivation to have the best analysis possible and that they do not wish to just "go through the motions" and waste time, money, and emotional investment on an analysis that is not experienced as helpful.

Similar to what I wrote regarding admission interviews, this change in training analyst appointments goes hand in hand with an intersubjective emphasis that casts doubt on absolute "objective judgment" of quality. As I suggested, even the most senior analysts may be admired by some and disliked by others, and variations in theory and in style have a role in this heterogeneity: What one values as consistency another suspects to be rigidity, what one welcomes as flexibility another derides as impulsivity, and so on. Unlike committee or group vote, personal choice by candidate gives full weight to the candidate's subjective preferences and intuitions. My own subjective impression is that the quality of training analysts appointed in Israel has been equally variable at all three stages (secret decision by Training Committee, open debate and election by all members, appointment based on factual criteria). If we use the only empirical criterion of success available – the personal analysts and supervisors chosen by candidates (undoubtedly a flawed criterion in some ways) – the conclusion is the same.

What became an issue in recent years was the emergence of a group of experienced and highly esteemed members who could not become training analysts because they remained associate members for many years after graduation (becoming a training analyst depends on full IPS membership). These members, many of whom were successful teachers and clinical supervisors, had not presented a theoretical paper, which used to be a requirement for full membership. After long debates in 2001–2002, a large majority voted that a change in the bylaws be enacted to create three parallel pathways for becoming a full member – theoretical paper (as before); two-year peer seminar covering issues of theory, practice, and supervision; and cumulative activity as a committee member or as an instructor at the IPI and in its psychotherapy programs (for beginning mental health professionals and for advanced therapists). All three pathways can lead to full membership after a vote (secret ballot, two-thirds majority required for acceptance). Analysts are heterogenous in their talents and capacities, supporters of the change argued; requiring a theoretical paper of all full members was based on an idealized vision in which all experienced analysts are expected to be theoreticians as a step toward fulfilling the idealized image of the training analyst as a superior author-teacher-clinician-supervisor-leader. In reality, theoretical, clinical, didactic, supervisory, and administrative skills may be distributed unevenly among analysts — being only partially related to one another — and different profiles should be acknowledged as legitimate and worthwhile within the psychoanalytic community.

Choice of Candidates' Analytic Cases

For many years, each of the three analytic patients a candidate was expected to treat — four sessions a week, at least two years each, though most analyses were longer — was screened by the IPI. In each city, one or two consultants were appointed to conduct screening interviews and determine if a patient was analyzable and suitable for a candidate. These cases were usually new, as converting from psychotherapy to psychoanalysis was considered an inferior move. Nevertheless, if a patient from a candidate's private practice was to be considered a potential analysand, an interview with the appointed consultant was deemed necessary.

Unlike some other changes discussed here, this practice was never formally abolished — it evaporated sometime in the 1990s. Candidates, usually seasoned psychotherapists in their late 30s and 40s, now tend to find their own analysands, either from their therapeutic practice or from new referrals. Gradually, they stopped referring prospective analysands for screening ("There is often no other means of correcting such inexpedient laws than by boldly violating them"; Freud, 1926, p. 235) and instead began discussing the potential analysand with the supervisor who would be supervising the analysis. No one seemed to miss the old system, which had often led to complications and split transference patterns (the interviewer as the real parental figure and the younger candidate/analyst as a substitute, etc.) that had visibly infantilized the candidates.

After describing this change, Bar-Lev Elieli (2001) asked, "Does this mean that we trust our trainees more than before? Does it mean that we are afraid of losing any opportunity for an analysis? Does it mean that nowadays we feel more skilled in handling difficult cases in psychoanalysis, or that we have more trust in psychoanalysis? Are we more flexible, less rigid? . . . Or are we operating as part of a wider cultural transition where youngsters can have a louder voice?" (p. 31).

This shift can also be understood in the context of growing doubts about analyzability as an objective attribute of the analysand alone—doubts that were raised in chapter 3. Balint's (1969) argument "that any kind of technique and the criteria for selection are interdependent" (p. 101) has become more influential. Paying serious attention to countertransference and to intersubjectivity makes it clear that a patient unanalyzable by one analyst may prove to be analyzable by another analyst using a different model or having a different personality or (especially relevant in training!) a different supervisor. In other words, in our present theoretical climate, the goal is no longer objective assessment by an impartial expert (who must meet the analysand directly in order to bypass the candidate's possible distortions) but rather in-depth examination of the pros and cons of a potential analysis by the analyst and the supervisor, the two individuals who will be involved in the analysis for years and whose actual subjective experiences may have a crucial role in its success or failure.

Personally, when approached by a candidate with such a question, I strive not to make an objective diagnosis and prediction (I believe, in any case, that individuals with severe pathology can benefit from analysis) but instead to make sure that the candidate is aware of potential risks and complications and of countertransferential stumbling blocks and does not begin the difficult journey with naive expectations, unsublimated rescue fantasies, or major denied emotions. In most cases, I expect the candidate to make his or her own decision after we have reached more clarity about the initial dynamics in the dyad and their relevance to a potential analytic process.

The change in this area is also related to the growing interest in conversion of psychotherapy into psychoanalysis (Skolnikoff, 1990; Stolorow, 1990; Rothstein, 1995). The greater acceptance of this possibility is related both to pragmatic reasons (fewer patients who decidedly seek analysis) and to theoretical reasons— the lesser emphasis on "uncontaminated" anonymity in contemporary psychoanalysis; greater trust in working through analytically the patient's experience of the analyst's exposure and subjectivity.

In terms of the candidates, the different way of accepting analysands has increased their autonomy and their trust in developing their own unique analytic identity (which may include preferences as to whom to analyze) versus adopting some standard, "correct" way of analyzing ("analytic false self"). In addition, this change abolished one source of "long periods of waiting in uncertainty" (Kernberg, 1996, p. 1032). In general, these changes weaken the control of the Training Committee over candidates while empowering the individual supervisor as the actual representative of the institute and empowering the supervisor–candidate dyad.

Curriculum

The curriculum of seminars has evolved. Gradually, their content became varied, nondogmatic, and flexible; recent graduates could become instructors; instructors were free to develop their interests and viewpoints. In the past, coursework continued until graduation, which depended on a case presentation (to be discussed later). A few years ago, a limitation of six years was applied to courses.

Although content was flexible, structure was rigid. Each admitted class (one every two years) went through its own sequence of theoretical and clinical seminars, which were all mandatory. Candidates often complained of the change from their earlier studies (e.g., psychotherapy programs), in which they could take elective courses, to their more advanced IPI studies, in which there were no elective courses and personal interests could not be pursued. Moreover, in settings with an elective structure, seminars considered ineffective usually disappeared from the curriculum because of low demand, whereas lack of choice in IPI studies allowed weaker seminars to be continued year after year. (An attempt was made to collect evaluation forms from candidates at the end of each seminar, but, in the intimate or incestuous atmosphere of the institute, completion and processing of such forms proved difficult.)

Lack of elective courses is also relevant to the issue of training analysts teaching their own analysands. Although I agree with Kernberg (1996) that a strict rule forbidding such teaching may be part of a strained anonymity encouraging unanalyzable idealization (p. 1034), attention should also be given to the complications of such teaching. One complication is inhibition of critical discussion when participants are aware that the instructor is the personal analyst of one participant. My preference is not to teach my analysands, but I feel this issue should be left to each analytic dyad to resolve. In a structure that consists of only mandatory courses, however, a faculty member who preferred not to teach an analysand had to give up teaching an entire class, and a training analyst with several such analysands in various classes had to give up teaching altogether.

Two additional drawbacks of this structure were the impossibility of having joint seminars of candidates and graduate analysts (Kernberg, 1996, p. 1033) and the great impact of the group dynamics of a particular class. Experience showed that such dynamics differed. In some classes, the climate was of solidarity and mutual encouragement; in others, it was of competitive tension and constant mutual criticism. In the former, studying together for six years or more was a pleasure and a firm foundation for a sense of belonging to the analytic community; in the latter, studying was a burden, as the persecutory aspect of the institute shifted from faculty to peer groups.

In the late 1990s, the IPI offered two elective seminars in which both candidates and graduate members (including faculty) could and did participate. The success of these seminars may have encouraged the Training Committee (chaired by Rivka Eifermann) to initiate a new curriculum. Starting in 2000, a completely different structure was instituted — one based on the academic model of accumulating credits in elective seminars, which can be chosen freely according to a list of categories, at times with some prerequisites. The goal was to tailor curricula to different candidates with divergent needs and wishes.

Paradoxically, although most faculty and members (including recent graduates unhappy with the curriculum they completed) saw this change as a welcome move toward liberalized training, many candidates became worried and resistant. The yearly candidates' weekend meeting,[2] which took place around

---

[2]These regular yearly meetings, reintroduced in the late 1990s after a long absence, clearly signify the greater autonomy of present candidates, who plan and conduct the meetings with no outside help.

the time of transition, was stormy. Participants expressed concern that the new structure would break up existing classes and make candidates more isolated and weaker vis-à-vis the institute. Rather than enjoying the greater freedom and individual flexibility promised, they foresaw and experienced loneliness and confusion.

Nevertheless, the change was implemented. Now, the atmosphere is more balanced, and candidates usually see both pros and cons in the new structure, which has coincided with higher admission rates. From being elitist and relatively cohesive (solidarity of the chosen few), the IPI seems to have become more open and more anonymous.

Gradually, the main difficulty with the new structure became apparent in clinical seminars. As these seminars were the setting for group supervision and their composition changed every trimester, candidates became insecure and inhibited. In response, a reform was introduced: Theoretical seminars would remain electives, chosen anew each trimester to keep the composition unique, but candidates would be encouraged to form self-selected groups (usually with colleagues admitted around the same year) that would ideally stay together for their clinical seminars. The hope was to balance the need for freedom and variation (expressed in the theoretical seminars) with the need for stability and continuity (expressed in the clinical seminars).

Evaluation of Candidates

For many years, a central characteristic of the IPI was thorough evaluation of candidates by the Training Committee. Supervisors submitted reports frequently, and long meetings were dedicated to discussing the personal characteristics and dynamics of each candidate. Some candidates were expelled. Later, in the early 1980s, attempts to expel certain candidates aroused strong reactions. When the Training Committee considered terminating a candidate's training because of one supervisor's negative reports, other supervisors disputed the negative evaluation and protested, and their opposing views made a decision impossible.[3]

---

[3]Some colleagues who were almost expelled then are now successful training analysts.

This new development was influenced by a greater heterogeneity of faculty, signified reduced confidence in impartial objective authority, and became part of a more skeptical stance regarding the impact of strict institutional evaluation.

In recent years, the Training Committee of the IPI became much less preoccupied with evaluating candidates and more invested in improving training. Evaluation and feedback were delegated to each candidate's three supervisors, who have practically become the main representatives of the institute vis-à-vis the candidate. Supervisors and teachers do little formal reporting, in spite of some attempts to resume it. The subcommittee for evaluation changed its name and now defines itself as a subcommittee accompanying candidates through their training.

Recently, some faculty members have expressed concern that evaluation is now insufficient. They have begun looking for ways to reintroduce more systematic evaluation and have warned that otherwise "every new applicant we admit is assured of becoming a training analyst in due time" (criticism of the new procedure for becoming a training analyst is clearly implied). Other faculty members (including me) believe that supervisors should be encouraged to give more critical feedback to their supervisees and that committee evaluation discussions can be reserved specifically for problematic candidates but are not needed as a matter of routine.

I have not observed any lowering of standards since evaluation was minimized. Most candidates seem invested in their training (which is burdensome in terms of time, money, and emotional energy) and eager to improve their knowledge and skills. Their private superego functions seem quite effective usually, even without formal external reinforcement. In addition, the attentiveness and thoughtfulness of candidates (e.g., in group supervision) seem to supplement faculty input in encouraging serious scrutiny of one's functioning as a beginning analyst.

Graduation

Considerable changes were gradually introduced to graduation requirements, but the centerpiece of these requirements — a written report about one analysis conducted during training, plus a brief theoretical discussion — has remained the same. Some faculty members who oppose the case report say that it is influenced too much by the views of the supervisor, but the majority of faculty members favors maintaining this tradition.

On the other hand, in the 1990s the institute abolished the practice of voting on whether to admit an IPI graduate into the society after the candidate's case presentation. "His teachers and supervisors have implicitly already voted for him," suggested Bar-Lev Elieli (2001, p. 32), who became IPS president in 2002. The candidate now makes his case presentation to an ad hoc reading committee that then meets with him to discuss it (this practice replaces secret discussion by the entire Training Committee—discussion that used to take place without the candidate present); after approval, or after making required corrections, the candidate presents the case publicly, as a graduation event. Becoming an associate member of the IPS is now automatic on IPI graduation.

Writing a case report is a source of considerable anxiety, even without the voting. The case report is experienced as one's resume, and candidates are often afraid that they will be seen as insufficiently competent. I suspect this fear is an unavoidable aspect of training. Anxiety often inhibits writing, and some candidates end up presenting their case a few years after being allowed to submit it (which is when they completed their coursework, and all three of their supervised analyses had been ongoing for at least two years).

In most cases, the meeting with the reading committee is benign—and friendlier than what the candidate imagined. Some reading committees have been more critical, at times asking for sections of a report to be revised or for some theoretical aspects to be explored more fully. A few other reading committees have refused to approve a report that was too disappointing. Although the candidate in each of these cases eventually graduated—after more revisions, appointment of a second reading committee, and so forth—rumors about these situations certainly increased candidates' fears and inhibitions and aroused the experience of being dependent on a capricious and unpredictable authority, possibly torn by its own internal conflicts. Paradoxically, some candidates have suggested that a (resumed) formal evaluation may safeguard them against unpleasant surprises at the final stage.

Indeed, in at least one case of disapproval by the reading committee, differences in opinion about quality (the supervisor thought the case satisfactory; the committee, weak) coincided with theoretical disagreements as to what constitutes a serious psychoanalytic treatment. The present heterogeneity of the IPI may in this respect become a threat to the candidates—a topic I address in chapter 7. What one supervisor, for example, sees as a welcome expression of analytic holding and provision another faculty member frowns on as a confusing boundary violation— and the candidate may be caught in the cross fire.

What occurs after the report has been approved by the reading committee—the public case presentation—has also undergone changes. With there being a much larger membership and a larger candidate group, general attendance is no longer expected, and often the audience consists of the candidate's supervisors, friends, and classmates and only a few "outsiders." Moreover, some candidates ask for a case presentation "by invitation only" for reasons of confidentiality, especially when the analysis discussed is of a mental health professional (this consideration may coincide with the candidate's fear of exposure). In the past, the candidate read the entire report, and then it was discussed. Later, to avoid boredom, the candidate was asked to make only a few brief introductory comments, but this task gradually evolved into writing a second report (updating the clinical material, adding another theoretical aspect, etc.), which multiplied the candidate's chores. Recently, an attempt was made to abolish the second report and to devote most of the meeting to debate involving an invited discussant (who attempts to explore alternative ways of understanding the analysis presented) and the audience.

Tel Aviv Institute for Contemporary Psychoanalysis

Another development relevant to our topic is the establishment, around 2000, of the Tel Aviv Institute for Contemporary Psychoanalysis (TAICP), an independent group unaffiliated with the IPA.

Although most new institutes in psychoanalytic history are created through splits in existing groups (Roudinesco, 1990;

Kirsner, 2000), such a split did not occur in Israel. A split was considered a potential outcome of the Controversial Discussions of the 1990s, but the compromise averted it. In spite of radical disagreements (many of which persist), IPS members seem reluctant to split the society. This reluctance may come partially out of emotional needs (e.g., fear of disrupting friendships and professional collaboration) and partially out of concern for the well-being of candidates, who could be faced with traumatic conflicts of loyalty, a need to choose between their analyst and a favorite supervisor, and so forth.

For a while, this reluctance seemed to mean that there would always be only one psychoanalytic center in Israel (there are Jungian and Lacanian groups, but these are separate). To the surprise of many, however, the TAICP was established by a group of senior psychoanalytically oriented therapists, many of them faculty members of various psychotherapy programs and experienced supervisors in mental health centers. Ten of the TAICP founders, encouraged by the model of independent psychoanalytic centers begun mostly by psychologists in the United States, decided to pursue self-regulated psychoanalytic training while intending to train new candidates later.

This development aroused profound disagreements within the IPS. Initially, some IPS members were involved in the plans to establish the TAICP, but at present there is almost no overlap between the two groups. However, several central members of the IPS—including some of the protagonists of the Controversial Discussions, such as Yecheskiel Cohen, Raanan Kulka, and me—accepted the invitation of the TAICP to help it by offering supervision and seminars as guest faculty. Our feeling was that TAICP members are serious and that coexistence of two training centers in Israel will be beneficial to psychoanalysis there and to the IPS, which has often been resented because of its monopolistic status.

At the other extreme, other central members (notably Shmuel Erlich, IPS president, 1999–2002) saw the new initiative as illegitimate, portrayed the TAICP founders as charlatans (how can they start an institute before being trained as analysts?), refused to collaborate with them (or with the new *Israel Psychoanalytic Journal*, initiated by them), and condemned IPS members who helped them. These opponents warned that the TAICP would lower the standards of psychoanalysis in Israel, and they challenged us who teach there. How can we accept coexistence of differing requirements at the two institutes — three analyses at four times a week in the IPI and only two supervised analyses (one at four times a week, the other at three or four times a week) in the TAICP? Although acknowledging that the entire situation is problematic, those of us willing to help the TAICP (more than a dozen IPS training analysts) feel that these anomalies are unavoidable transitional complications in a development that in the long run will be beneficial.

This new controversy peaked in 2001, when a new chairperson was to be elected to the IPS Admissions Committee, and the committee's candidate, Meir Winokur, was a training analyst who also supervises at the TAICP. Some members expressed the opinion that Winokur should be disqualified because of his divided loyalty. Nevertheless, he was elected by a considerable majority, and later Yecheskiel Cohen was elected to the IPS Ethics Committee, so it became clear that the IPS membership does not support any blacklisting. In view of the divergent opinions, however, no one in the IPS has proposed any formal resolution about its attitude toward the TAICP; it is not likely that any clear-cut position (be it support or condemnation) could win a substantial majority.

The question often arises as to whether recent changes at the IPI (notably, increased admission rates and the new elective curriculum) were made in response to the appearance of the TAICP on the scene. Basically, the answer is no. These changes are the outgrowth of gradual processes within the IPS, and many of these processes matured before the TAICP was founded. Paradoxically, one might say that the TAICP was created too late, as it was more badly needed in the 1970s or 1980s, when admissions were very limited (some of the TAICP founders were among those rejected then[4]) and training was more rigid. Still, I believe that the

---

[4]At times, some IPS members use this fact as an argument against the TAICP founders. My view is that starting an independent psychoanalytic program is a constructive response to rejection by an established program and that it should be contrasted with the fiercely antipsychoanalytic responses of some professionals who were also rejected by the IPI.

role of the TAICP is constructive and that some of the opposition
to changes within the IPS may become less vocal because of the
competition. For example, a return to lower admission rates at the
IPI will clearly result in applicants' turning to the TAICP, and
awareness of this situation will weaken the elitist IPS position of
looking for the "few who really deserve training," which in the
past was reinforced by the monopoly enjoyed by this society.

The future, I believe, will lead to collaboration and friendly
competition between the IPI and the TAICP.

The Process in Perspective

There seems to be a widespread feeling among members, faculty,
and candidates that the changes in the IPS and in the IPI are
mostly for the better — that they have resulted in reduced infantilization and authoritarianism, improved morale, greater identification with the institute and with psychoanalysis, and more
effective learning.

This experience, I believe, shows that a shift within traditional
psychoanalytic organizations to a more open, pragmatic, egalitarian training climate, freer of mystifying idealizations and of
persecutory elements, is possible and that it could be effective in
reducing the toxic influences of analytic training.

The present status quo at the IPS guarantees the continued
centrality of training analysts in its analytic education and maintains a situation in which structure and generational stratification
are important. Stratification, however, is now much less determined by internal political influences. Being a training analyst no
longer involves the pretense of guaranteeing an analyst of better
quality — an issue that many came to feel cannot be collectively
determined but instead should be left to informal personal judgment and consultation.

In addition, the intellectual and educational message to candidates has gradually become more flexible and complex. On one
hand, the IPI has not adopted a laissez-faire policy, and it continues to view clear rules as vital. On the other hand, unique individual needs and autonomy are legitimized and better respected.
Indeed, as I suggest in chapter 3, such needs are seen more often
now as a crucial element that must be taken into account by the

educational structure than as something that must be judged a rebellion against that structure. The changes also imply growing recognition by the IPS of the potentially infantilizing and persecutory qualities in analytic training as well as a serious commitment on its part to combat their possible impact.

The IPS debates regarding the optimal balance between structure and flexibility, between institutional authority and individual autonomy, continue. The common wish seems to be to maintain an agreed-on framework and a more moderate climate capable of containing ideologic and personal controversies. This tactic works at times and collapses at other times. There is always the risk, of course, that latent persecutory elements may merely "change address." Less severe evaluation of candidates during training may, for example, lead to a wish for harsher admission procedures or to a more formalistic demand for completing forms and submitting them according to exact procedures; more liberal admissions are raised by some members as an argument in favor of stricter evaluation. Abolishing discussions of the personal merit of potential training analysts may move the voting on full member acceptance into the new arena of political manipulation and vengeful reactions.

Moreover, new issues and new tensions unavoidably come up. Candidates are now much more exposed to the heterogeneity of psychoanalysis and to the inner conflicts of the IPS. This exposure prevents mystification and an awe-inspired idealization of psychoanalysis as some ultimate truth but can become stressful and confusing in itself and arouse the experience of growing up with parents who are at war with each other. I return to these issues in chapter 7.

Arousing much anxiety among candidates were recent discussions by the Ethics Committee and the Training Committee of an ethical complaint submitted by a former analysand against a candidate. Among candidates, questions were raised as to the thin line between innovative technique and unethical boundary violations; as to how much backing the candidate will receive from the former supervisor of the case; as to whether the candidate's theoretical orientation may become a factor in the discussions; and as to whether the candidate could be used as a scapegoat in the theoretical controversies within the IPS. These tensions reintroduced persecutory experiences and created a degree of renewed toxification. When considering a less conventional intervention with a difficult patient, some candidates anxiously asked their supervisors, "Will it get me in trouble with the Ethics Committee?" In a daylong ethics conference initiated by the IPS, some members and candidates protested that the specific case was not openly discussed, and others pointed out that open discussion may be impossible for reasons of confidentiality.

"The end of history" is surely a naive illusion, both in the international scene and in the psychoanalytic world.

5

The Trainee's Personal Analysis and Its Dilemmas

And lastly, we must not underestimate the advantage to be derived from the lasting mental contact that is as a rule established between the student [analysand]¹ and his guide.

—Sigmund Freud
"Recommendations to Physicians
Practising Psycho-Analysis"

Trainees in psychoanalysis and in psychotherapy usually undergo personal analytic treatment during their training. The complex dynamics of this analysis or therapy is the topic of this chapter.

A central characteristic of the trainee's own analytic treatment is the complex dialectic it creates between (a) analysis as a process focused on the inner reality of the analysand and (b) analysis (or analytic therapy) as representing a professional requirement or expectation originating in the outside world and continually influenced by it. Elements of this dialectic are present in the treatment of all mental health professionals (viz., in a considerable part of all treatments conducted), but the literature does not fully acknowledge its massive influence on the treatment process. This difficulty, to which I return later, must be considered in the context of a broader issue — the controversy about the place of "external" reality in the psychoanalytic conceptualization of mental life and of the dynamics of treatment (Bromberg et al, 1991), which is explored in chapter 2 as a central heritage of the Freud–Ferenczi and Klein–Winnicott debates.

---

¹Strachey translated "student," though the original German text refers to the analytic patient. This is actually a unique early reference to the therapeutic value of the analytic relationship itself, apart from serving as a setting for interpretation and insight.

In this chapter, I outline major aspects of the object relations of trainees and other therapists in analytic treatment; discuss the unique significance such analysis may acquire in their emotional life, including the potential role of the analysand as the analyst's fantasied therapist or supervisor; and review incestuous elements in these analyses, some of their interactions with the training process, and dilemmas regarding boundaries. The fruitful exploration of many of these issues, I believe, is facilitated by an open-minded intersubjective emphasis in conducting the analysis.

Trainees in Analysis: Object Relations

A central factor in the analysis of trainees and other therapists is the appearance of the same emotional motives at the core of the analysand's vocational choice and in the analytic situation (Berman, 1995a). The same aspects of object relations appear, and a world of mirrorings, identifications, and comparisons is established. The dilemma of being a helper or needing help, of being therapist or patient, is omnipresent. Treating and being in treatment, giving and receiving, may be unconsciously equated.

In some cases, neediness and the wish to be helped can be experienced only when projected out, onto a weak and needy other, while the therapist clings to a sense of strength and mastery. This situation may be seen most clearly when a therapist enters a first analysis, or a first serious therapy, after several years of treating others. Such an analysis may prove to be very painful, because its success depends on the "return of the projected," on reowning denied dependency needs, on shaking an overconfident self-image.

A transparent example: My analysand comes late to his session and explains that he is late because he extended the session of his own patient, who "needs it much more badly." In extreme cases, the narcissistic blow of acknowledging the need for help may lead to a negative therapeutic reaction.

Another pattern is seen in an analysand's choosing to be trained as an analyst or a psychotherapist in response to a successful analysis. In principle, such a path could be more promising, but several questions should be asked: Was the identification with the analyst worked through? Are idealization fantasies still active? Can the future therapist develop an autonomous identity divorced from the wish to "become one's analyst," which (as discussed in chapter 3) may evolve into a "false analytic self"?

Gabbard (1995) described therapist-analysands who crave the attention of both their patients (e.g., use transference interpretations excessively) and their analysts and hope to be adored and idealized as a compensation for childhood lacks. At the other extreme, he suggested, therapists who survived adverse childhood situations by attempting to satisfy the narcissistic needs of others may repeat this solution both with their patients and their analysts.

Isaacs-Elmhirst (1982–1983) gave several examples of similar repeated patterns. In one, her analysand reported a dream in which Elmhirst's figure was merged with the figure of one of his patients. The combined figure represented the sick baby; the dreamer appeared as the reliable adult.

The reappearance of the same object relations in the analysand's transference to us and in his or her countertransference to patients is not limited, however, to direct equations between one's analyst and patient. More complex connections may be understood with the help of Ogden's (1983) conceptualization: The entire bipolar object relationship is internalized, and the subject can alternate in taking on one pole ("self" of childhood) or the other ("object" of childhood) while activating the second complementary role in the other person by projective identification. This alternation may explain seeming inner contradictions in a person's character.

The interchangeable quality of one's needs as a therapist and as a patient is prominent in this example from my work:

A patient had been in treatment twice before but had experienced varying degrees of disappointment and had felt that her needs were not being sufficiently met. In spite of her intense conscious yearnings, many of our sessions were dominated by her lengthy monologues, which I interpreted as an unconscious blocking of any chance to receive—related to intense fears of rejection. She described great dedication to her patients and endless efforts to meet their needs. She shared with them many details of her personal life and was disappointed that I was not prone to such sharing. I felt that she envied her patients for the warmth they received from her — and that she kept seeking that warmth from her therapists but never felt gratified.

This pattern reminds me of some aspects of the Freud-Ferenczi relationship and of Ferenczi's attempts (especially through the "relaxation technique" and mutual analysis) to offer his patients the warmth and openness he felt lacking in Freud. On the other hand, as described in chapter 1, Ferenczi (1933) came to criticize his own "active technique" (emphasizing forceful authority and abstinence) as relying on identification with the aggressor (Frankel, 2002), possibly also on his own identification with Freud as an aggressor. Such trends also appear in analysand- therapists, at times in the form of turning oneself into a "'false copy' of the mockingly idealized analyst" (Orgel, 2002, p. 440). The analysand may, for example, apply analytic anonymity and nondirectiveness in professional tasks in which they are ineffective (e.g., in supervising students or in dealing with a crisis on a psychiatric ward). Isaacs-Elmhirst (1982–1983) gave another example: She had been late to an analytic session, and then her analysand was late to a session with his patient.

In analysis, some analysands avoid talking about their patients out of anxiety regarding competition or judgment. Others may unconsciously express their own conflicts in the course of describing their patients. Unlike Gabbard (1995), I conceptualize this not as resistance but as a valuable though cautious communication. The conscious rationale may be an appeal for supervision. An analyst who responds mostly as a supervisor (focusing on the specifics of the treatment described) may do so at the expense of pursuing the fuller analytic goal, which requires relating such contents to the analysand's own inner life and transference. Yet, the analysand-therapist's use of the analyst's approach may in any case have intrinsic supervisory value, just as one may "borrow" supervisory experiences for inner goals that are substantially therapeutic (further discussed in chapter 6). Kantrowitz (2002) described a candidate who experienced similarity between his own conflicts and those of some of his analysands: "This had enabled him to apply his own analyst's view of himself to them" (p. 957).

The connection may at times be conscious, as in this example: My analysand reported a dream in which a patient he had interviewed but had not accepted for treatment (because of her unbearable rage and bitterness) reappeared in his clinic. I commented that the patient did come back, in the dream. My analysand interrupted me, "Don't you encourage these feelings to come back here!"

Analysands' conscious comparisons of the analytic process they experience and the treatment processes of their patients may have an influence that is both inhibiting and facilitating: "When I heard you got married, I felt hurt you didn't tell me. Then I realized I didn't tell my patients when I got married, so how can I complain?" Here, identification with me as a colleague blocked dependency needs and transferential fantasies approaching consciousness.

In another example, a comparison gradually led toward greater insight and flexibility: "I am frustrated when you say nothing. My supervisor told me I must say something to my patient in every session. On the other hand, I realize how ambivalent this is. I recall my borderline patient, who always demands to know what exactly I think of her, but I actually know she only wants to hear good things."

At other moments, an analysand turns to his or her self-image as a therapist as a rescue from the vulnerability of being a patient: I commented on my analysand's tendency to put down my interpretations. He said that this is related to his need for mastery. His next associations were to his need for mastery as a therapist and to his work with a supervisee on the supervisee's need for control. I realized that the fast movement of identities — analysand, therapist, supervisor — indeed allowed him to regain mastery.

The fluidity of identities moved in the opposite direction in a situation described by another analysand: "In the middle of a therapy session, my patient told me her best friend is in therapy with you. I got all confused. In a split second, I turned from therapist to patient."

Discovery of a New World — Or,
A Rite of Initiation into a Chosen World?

For analysands who are not mental health professionals, analysis may be a unique, unprecedented experience, completely different from their familiar world. They learn a new language, adopt a new outlook on life. This may be both difficult and exciting. The analyst may be the only representative (besides remote figures like Freud or literary and cinematic analysts) of this new world.

In contrast, trainees and other analysand-colleagues may experience analysis as a fateful rite of initiation into a world they chose — a world now experienced as an intrinsic part of their personality. Studies, work, analysis, at times marital and social life, are all part of the same integral whole. The same discourse dominates different segments of this universe. The analyst may be a model for internalization (or imitation?) in one's professional-personal identity (in our field, nothing can be purely professional). Still, the analyst is only one of many well-known representatives of the same world.

This situation invites comparisons and splits (Heimann, 1954). Transference may be split between the analyst and a significant supervisor: "When I feel depressed, I'd rather meet my supervisor; it's easier for me to lean emotionally on a woman." There may be fantasies of being in analysis with a teacher or a supervisor, who may be the analyst of the analysand's friend. Yearnings unfulfilled with an analyst may be achieved in displaced side transferences: An analysand made great efforts to mobilize me into a "male alliance" against his mother and wife. While attempting to interpret this wish, I realized that it had already been gratified with a (male) supervisor to whom my analysand presented a highly resistant female patient who annoyed them both.

Although our initial (possessive?) response may be to treat such splits as resistance, we may eventually use them to understand transference more fully — including its split-off extra-analytic branches. An attempt to base all our analytic work on the analysand's direct responses to us may be too narrow and misleading (Berman, 2001a).

The attitude toward analysis and work as a fateful "package deal" becomes evident in moments of crisis. Analysis experienced as stuck leads to doubts about vocational choice: "If I can't be helped, how can I help others?" The colleague-analysand does not have the option, available to other analysands, to retreat from the "new world" to the safer and more familiar "old world." Blaming the analyst is also more difficult, because putting down one's analyst necessitates putting down many colleagues who think highly of him or her. Being in this position may arouse a fantasy of being the child in "The King's New Robes" — a lonely, frightening place.

Another solution is masochistic self-devaluation: "If I don't progress in my analysis, it proves my choice to become an analyst [or a psychotherapist] was wrong. If my patients say I help them, and my colleagues respect me, this means I manage to fool them all. I am really an impostor."

Such expressions may be seen as a request for confirmation from the analyst, but they may convey a deeper and more painful experience. Professional knowledge may be mobilized for harsh self-diagnosis: "If you say I have difficulty in trusting anybody, this means I am paranoid." Gabbard (1995) spoke of therapists' fear of having a psychotic core; here the fear is angrily projected onto me. Another case does not involve projection: "I identify in myself all the signs Kernberg lists for borderlines." The connotation is that analysis cannot help with such severe pathology.

In this case, a perfectionistic ego ideal was evident. Its contents were new (integration, insight, contact with affects, avoidance of splitting), but the perfection demanded, and the constant self-devaluation about failing to reach it resembled the parents' attitudes toward other ideals in the analysand's childhood (responsibility, honesty, conscientiousness, morality). In the inner world of this analysand, there were two cores of superego demands, "professional superego" and "familial superego," with contrasts that made being a servant of two masters a hopeless task. Expressing certain associations disappointed family values of avoiding gossip and slander; withholding them meant failing professional ideals of openness and nondefensiveness.

Just as an experience of failure in analysis may lead to thoughts of abandoning the profession, so can professional failures arouse an impulse to quit analysis. Failing a certification examination, being dismissed from a job, not receiving referrals, being rejected by an institute, and receiving harsh criticism from a supervisor may all arouse a fantasy of "slamming the door." The analyst may be unconsciously seen as responsible for one's training and career. There may be several versions — anger at the analyst who does not help enough; concern that the analyst justifies what happened ("accusations that I share the outsider's opinions"; Orgel, 2002, p. 425) or maybe even influenced it ("I know the institute is nonreporting, but maybe your disappointment with me leaked to some members of the Admissions or Training Committee?"); fear that the analyst is now disappointed, ashamed of the analysand, or concerned about being seen as responsible by colleagues; apprehension that the analyst will now invest more in "successful children" who will glorify his or her name with their achievements.

Switching now to the countertransference side, I must say such fears may not be unfounded. The analysis of trainees and colleagues is conducted "in a fishbowl" (Gitelson, 1954). Indirect countertransference, related to the imagined look of others (Racker, 1968), may be particularly powerful. At times, the analysand stimulates our anxieties directly, by giving hostile reports about our work to esteemed colleagues. But even without provocation, we may be disturbed by thoughts such as, "How does he talk about me with X or Y?" When one of our analysands is not admitted to our institute, or when the analysand's graduation paper is criticized or rejected, we may wonder if this conveys a negative evaluation of our own work. The tendency to blame therapists for their patients' problems was beautifully portrayed by Ekstein, Wallerstein, and Mandelbaum (1959). Meyer (2003) had good reasons to suggest that the dependence existing between the candidate and the training analyst is reciprocal.

When an analysand who is a trainee or a colleague terminates analysis unilaterally, the unavoidable pain of any such rejection may be accompanied by the concern, "How will my colleagues see it?" We may be tempted to violate confidentiality by spreading our own version of what happened.

Treating trainees and other colleagues unavoidably triggers our judgmental, evaluative look. Our professional concern is activated, and at some moments we cannot avoid the thought, "God, and this person is going to treat others!" Gabbard (1995) spoke of a fantasy of "policing the profession through analytic surveillance" (p. 721). Moreover, we may again become concerned that the analysand's failures will be interpreted by the professional community as the analysand's "report on *me* and on his or her analysis" (Orgel, 2002, p. 432). Anxious reactions may appear between the lines of our interpretations and may confirm the analysand's worst fears. Channeling such important counter-transference reactions into effective, empathic work requires of us a thorough working through.

Such judgments in the minds of analyst and analysand may reduce the capacity for regression in these analyses (Balint, 1954). Certain forms of transference—psychotic, dependent, impulsive, perverse, seductive, and so forth—may be artificially inhibited ("If *this* comes out, it will be clear I can't be an analyst!") and covered up with "more acceptable" neurotic-oedipal dynamics. But these experiences are influenced not just by the analyst but also by the milieu in which analysis takes place. We must face the incestuous climate of this milieu.

The Incestuous Dimension: Burden and Benefit

Several of the examples I have provided point to the incestuous element in analyzing professional colleagues, particularly trainees. In these analyses, the incestuous element is, as a rule, more intensive and widespread. This phenomenon was operating within Freud's circle. The complex relationships between numerous analytic dyads—Freud and Ferenczi, Ferenczi and Jones, Freud and Elma, Freud and Loe Kann (Jones's spouse at the time), Jones and Joan Riviere, Freud and Joan Riviere—were all part of a loaded interconnected network. And the phenomenon is still prominent within contemporary professional circles, both in intimate smaller communities, where it is unavoidable, and in the largest cities, where it is reinforced by requiring trainees to undergo treatment with the faculty of their own institute, even if numerous outside options are available. Such requirements demonstrate, I suspect, that economic, power-related, and ideologic motives ("Only our own faculty provides the right kind of analysis") have the upper hand—casting aside analytic awareness of the emotional burden posed by an incestuous milieu.

Under these circumstances, analyst and analysand cannot create a closed-off, intimate world that functions freely as a

transitional space. Their relationship is part of a complex, three-
or four-generation network that resembles an extended family or
a tribe. In fact, this network can be graphically described as an an-
thropological genealogy, a family tree. In drawing it, we may
need many colors and many styles of lines if we want to acknowledge the multiplicity of relationships within the network. These
relationships include both the professional (analysis, therapy, supervision, teaching, joint work) and the personal (marriage, divorce, love affairs, friendships). And they are subject to change —
and along with them their accompanying emotions, such as affection, resentment, admiration, rivalry, scorn, and so forth. Included persons, in addition to belonging to the same institute and
society, are frequently interconnected through additional current
and historical professional affiliations, as psychiatrists, psychologists, university faculty, and so forth, and the dramas of each
context add colors to the emerging picture. The network is multifaceted and in constant flux, never static. Even its composition
changes; for example, it expands whenever a new class of candidates enters an institute.

In this family tree, a particular middle-aged analyst may be, at
a certain point in time, part of the second generation. The training
analysts who analyzed and supervised him or her are first generation. The analysand-trainee is third generation, and this analysand's patients, often younger students or younger colleagues,
are fourth generation.

Each participant is tied to every other member of this network
through a variety of direct, indirect, and crisscrossing lines. Some
are central, others peripheral, but with time each acquires meaning and affective coloring. One learns more and more through direct contacts, through others' accounts of their contacts, and
through gossip (Olinick, 1980) and rumors. Impressions, generalizations, and emotional reactions from numerous sources con-
verge, clash, confuse, or crystallize. The same person is known, at
different moments, as one friend's admirable supervisor, as another colleague's frustrating analyst, as a third person's intrusive
boss at the hospital, as one's own intriguing seminar teacher, and
so forth (Berman, 1995a).

The candidate's own analyst is no exception. The fantasied
ideal conditions of analytic anonymity and "pure culture" transference, espoused in older textbooks (and never fully attainable

in the first place), are plainly impossible in the training analysis. Direct meetings at the institute are unavoidable, and so is the exposure to information and opinions regarding the analyst. His (or her) behaviors with other analysands, his functioning as a supervisor to other candidates, his political situation at the institute, and, of course, his personal life — all become known to a lesser or greater degree. Although the candidate's needs may have a role in the amount of exposure, exposure is ever present, because our analysand knows other patients we see, our supervisees, our colleagues, and our past and present analysts and teachers or becomes a student or supervisee of colleagues who have other important roles in our emotional life.

Another result is that many figures in the analysand's interpersonal world are directly familiar to us. This familiarity makes it more difficult to respond to these figures on the level of internal object relations, to translate actual interactions into unconscious meanings. The actual acquaintance arouses concrete visual images and existing affective responses (Jacobs, 1983). We may find ourselves thinking, while listening during the session, "how accurately she describes him" or "how he could miss what is so evident about her." We may be more sensitive to the pathology leading our analysand to fall in love with someone we despise, and we may be more empathic if the object of the analysand's love is someone we care for. (In a parallel way, it is easier for us to translate the contents of an analysand's professional argument into its deeper underlying significance if the analysand is, say, a physicist — versus a psychologist debating issues that are close to our heart.)

The incestuous situation influences the analysand constantly. When describing an argument with a friend, for example, the candidate may be aware that this friend is a patient, student, or colleague of the analyst. Will my analyst also hear another version of my story, and which will she believe? Even if not, does she evaluate my view critically, given her acquaintance with the other person? Such doubts and anxieties are aroused frequently.

When analysands know that we are acquainted with persons in their life, they often apply caution when speaking of them, both out of concern that we may identify with these persons more than with the analysand's experience of them and out of guilt about possibly damaging these persons' images. The situation may also threaten these persons, who may become concerned about the way they are presented in the analysis: "X must be bad-mouthing me on your couch," I have been told more than once. The analysand may sense a cautious attitude from some people since they found out who the analysand's analyst is. The result could be a loss of spontaneity in significant relationships — a heavy price to pay for the analysis.

Our analysand's friends may also choose to ask the analysand to keep certain things secret from us. Such requests create a conflict of loyalties and burden associative freedom. They may be understood at times as attempts to sabotage analysis. Analysands differ in the degree to which they allow such requests or honor them. Making such alliances may become a way to avoid full exposure. Similarly, an analysand's protectively concealing the names of persons mentioned during analysis may convey doubt regarding the trustworthiness of the analyst, the solidity of boundaries, the ability of the analyst to respond therapeutically while avoiding the temptation to abuse the analysis for the gratification of personal curiosity. Accepting the mystifying style of "someone said" may indicate the analyst's not confronting a deep-rooted layer of mistrust.

Realistically, we do face the risk of allowing our curiosity to become excessive intrusiveness. Maintaining boundaries is not always easy. When we are hurt by some comments about us, quoted on the couch, we may later meet the quoted person and be unable to clarify things openly. Treating trainees and colleagues may leave us lonelier and more vulnerable.

As mentioned, another result of the incestuous situation is that the analysand is flooded with information and impressions about the analyst's personality, life, and functioning in various professional contexts. The degree of flooding depends on the extent of overlap in the professional circles of analyst and analysand but also on the analysand's needs. These needs are on a continuum. Curiosity and inquisitiveness, at one pole, may reflect a need for control, a fear of being caught by surprise, a struggle against the humiliation of unilateral exposure, or, at times, infatuation, intrusiveness, or addictive preoccupation. The opposite, defensive, pole is dominated by "turning a deaf ear" and a request not to be told things; this pole may represent anxiety that the intimate relationship will be destroyed by outside input, at times against the background of a family history in which cherished dyadic ties were sabotaged by excluded or envious family members.

In most cases, the available information is vast. The impact of extensive exposure is very different from the impact of the occasional exposure occurring in any analysis. Extensive exposure may foster consistent inhibitions and blocks in associative flow, caused by guilt over knowing forbidden secrets and over elaborating them in fantasy. These secrets rarely come to the foreground without the analyst's clear encouragement. Let us remember Klauber's (1981) rhetorical question: "Is it really sound to act as though the patient had no knowledge of one's private life and family, or even of the severe blows that fate may deal one?" (p. 212). Absorbed stories confirm fears and hopes, inflame envy and anxiety, arouse scorn and admiration, and constantly amplify both conscious and unconscious transferential fantasies.

Let me give an extreme example of what may happen when an analyst is unable to help the analysand work through his actual knowledge. In a study I conducted (Berman, 2002b), a respondent described an analysis he had in his youth with an older senior analyst. He had found out by chance that the analyst's wife was having an affair with another man, and he brought this burdensome knowledge into the analysis. The analyst, apparently unable to deal with the analysand's experience, maintained a blank screen and turned "loudly silent" for some time. "Luckily, in later therapies . . . I was able or enabled to break out of these death-like hours on the couch," the analysand wrote (Berman, 2002b).

On hearing stories about the analyst, the analysand crystallizes a picture of the analyst's general (transferential) attitude to the professional community, to colleagues, and to students. The picture becomes meaningful for the analysand—no less meaningful than the analyst's direct behavior in their interaction. Following Racker's (1968) view that transference is always reactive to the analyst's countertransference, we may add a hypothesis: This general attitude of the analyst, even though it is not experienced firsthand in the sessions, also arouses transference feelings that incorporate, of course, elements from the analysand's unique inner world.

For example, out of all she had heard about me, one analysand responded in particular to my image as someone independent and defiant of authority. She identified with this trait—it encouraged her expression of her own rebelliousness—but it also aroused her anxiety that I, her analyst, might be in danger and that she might be endangering herself by following in my footsteps.

Another analysand responded much more to my active involvement in many professional settings, to my papers and public talks. This involvement contrasted sharply with the analysand's passivity, with his fear of humiliating exposure. Early in analysis, the contrast left him feeling hopeless—that I would never be able to understand him. Later, his ambition was aroused, and his wish to "come out of the shadows" and assert his presence, as I had done, became prominent.

A third analysand was particularly sensitive to my tendency to become a mentor to promising beginners. She wished I could play such a role for her, but she feared that doing so was hopeless, both because of the boundaries of analysis (she felt she got the short end of the stick—my inhibited and formal side) and because I came to see how disturbed she was.

In all these cases, the picture mirrored by the analysands was realistic and could by no means be defined as a distortion. Yet, the pictures differed, and each was visibly influenced by the analysand's family background, life experiences, and dynamics.

Crastnopol (1997), who found much value in exploring analysands' experience of the analyst's private life, also warned that "knowing too much about the analyst's extratherapeutic life can put an excessive burden on the patient to conform in some way to whatever role he or she imagines the analyst might want the patients to play, a role which can be inferred from the analyst's life circumstances" (p. 262). Professional life circumstances can offer the same knowledge—and increase the risk.

Only when verbalization of such impressions and fantasies is seriously encouraged (Aron, 1996a), only when we work on them nondefensively and overcome the fear of our analysands' penetrating intelligent look, can we reach fully the intrapsychic needs and conflicts involved. Along the way, we may learn important new things about ourselves.

Let me provide a clinical example to illustrate the impact of the incestuous context on the trainee's analysis. This example consists of elements derived from several real situations; the complexity of the described constellation fully matches the complexity of these actual situations.

A male candidate undergoing a training analysis became sexually involved with his female supervisee. The supervisee, a former student of the candidate's analyst, told the candidate that she experienced his analyst as seductive—which aroused intense excitement and anxiety in the candidate.

On one hand, as the candidate constantly struggled with compulsive seductive impulses, he identified with his analyst. He imagined the two of them involved in a secret male comradeship, and he felt that he had finally reached the analyst on a personal level, from which he had previously felt deprived. Homosexual fantasies emerged at the far end of this feeling.

On the other hand, the candidate feared that his analyst would punish him for "stealing" a woman from him, and he felt guilt over this oedipal victory. He tried to speak as little as he could about the affair—which became a source of resistance. Later, when he began experiencing the woman as destructive and hostile, he fantasized that both he and his analyst were castrated by the same woman, and he was disappointed that his analyst was as vulnerable as he himself was to her dangerous charm.

Additional bits and pieces of information strengthened these fantasies. The candidate, hearing that students of the analyst had described him with excitement, saw this as supporting his view of the analyst as seductive. Hearing that the analyst had been angrily arguing with a colleague at a meeting of the psychoanalytic society enhanced the candidate's fear of the analyst's potential aggression toward him. When he met a former male supervisee of the analyst, the supervisee told him that the analyst had criticized him unjustly—which further contributed to the candidate's castration anxiety. Later, the candidate heard someone describe the analyst's wife as unattractive—which fed into his sense that the analyst was castrated and therefore afraid of feminine women.

What I have described so far is, of course, only the tip of the iceberg—something that cannot be understood entirely without a fuller account of the candidate's life history and dynamics, the analyst's countertransference, and the dyad's evolving relationship—but it suffices for illustrating the double-edged impact of the incestuous situation.

On one hand, the reality inputs were powerful triggers that brought to the surface many issues deserving analytic exploration. In a less incestuous setting, the same issues probably would have emerged, but the process would have been slower and less dramatic. As it turned out, incest had been part of this candidate's life history, and the anxieties aroused by the current "psychoanalytic incest" were gradually connected to their developmental sources.

On the other hand, the candidate/analysand found it difficult to separate reality and fantasy, perceptions and projections. He brought up actual events and quotations and at times suspected that exploration of their unconscious meanings might be a defensive reaction of the analyst, a response to the threat of genuine exposure. The situation was also complicated for the analyst, who may have realized that he had unnecessarily lost his temper at the meeting of the psychoanalytic society, for example, and now he was confronted with an admixture of his analysand's transferential castration anxiety and a realistic reflection of his own aggressive impulses. Interpreting the former without dishonestly denying the latter may not be so easy.

Or, consider the female supervisee. The analyst, knowing her, predicted from the start the negative turn events would take; he even felt an overprotective countertransferential urge to warn the analysand of the danger of his being hurt. But the analyst inhibited his impulse, because he felt that such an intervention would be inappropriate and that his own jealousy may have been driving him to intervene. He continually struggled with separating his reactions to the supervisee from his analysand's reactions, because he wanted to make sure that he was interpreting the analysand's feelings without projective identification. This complication may have inhibited the analyst in his working with the situation.

The analysand also felt inhibited. He feared that his reports on the matter would lead the analyst to act vindictively toward him and toward the female supervisee. His also feared for his own career; transferential fantasies of punishment again got mixed up with realistic possibilities. Although the institute in question had a "no reporting" policy, the candidate was aware that information may leak out in informal ways. He felt that his questionable professional ethics (a love affair with a trainee in supervision with him) might become known and might lead to his expulsion from the institute.

The impact of the incestuous setting may burden the delicate process of analytic training with additional difficulties. Such a situation invites analytic exploration of relevant issues — oedipal dynamics, primal scene experiences, incestuous elements in one's family, and sibling rivalry — but, paradoxically, it may also inhibit such exploration and reduce the intensity of related expressed emotions (Balint, 1954). An analysand may find crying more difficult, for example, when he or she knows that at the end of the session someone familiar may be coming up the stairs. (A colleague once told me that he cries in his analysis only on certain days, when he is the last patient seen.) My sense is that this situation may be one of the reasons that earlier, more primitive experiences may be less fully explored in training analyses and may be clouded by later issues or by a facade of pseudo-normality (Gitelson, 1948). A "fishbowl" is not the ideal setting for regression, for the exploration of our deepest and most disturbed fantasies, for the development and testing of basic trust. Moreover, life within an intensive network of curious and psychologically minded individuals may put the candidate on guard in many situations. The pressure to function well, to prove one's adaptation and competence successfully, is intense.

These realities, however, are to a great extent unavoidable. If handled openly and courageously, with a genuine willingness by the analyst to be a partner in intersubjective exploration, they may be worked through and can become a source of growth.

Obstacles to Studying the Analysis of Trainees

As suggested at the beginning of this chapter, studying the analytic treatment of trainees may be hampered if sharing a profession and a training setting is viewed as a superficial factor, marginal in its impact — as part of a theoretical view of psychoanalysis as a purely intrapsychic search. In this context, a traditional one-person psychology approach may have defensive functions for the analyst. The actual importance of these supposedly "external" factors, however, has been gradually gaining recognition in the literature

on training analyses in psychoanalytic institutes, to which I return shortly. Many important issues are not limited to narrowly
defined training analyses alone but arise in the treatment of students in clinical psychology and social work, of psychiatric resi-
dents, of trainees in various psychotherapy programs, and of
practitioners in all these areas.

Incomplete exploration of some of the issues involved in analyzing trainees and therapists may also be influenced by the
problem of confidentiality, another derivative of the incestuous
dimension (Aron, 2000). Analysands who are colleagues and
students, as well as their friends and acquaintances, attend conferences at which we present papers, and they read journals in
which we publish. The risk of exposure is greater.

It is possible that analysand/colleague cases are underrepre-
sented in our literature. Also, these cases may be presented under
thick disguise, involving alterations in professional identity.
Such disguise naturally blocks any discussion of the place of this
identity in the analytic process.

Radical disguise, we have come gradually to realize, may confuse and mislead the reader (Klumpner and Frank, 1991). Little
(1951), for example, described an analysand's anxiety after a radio talk and shortly after the death of the analysand's mother.
Lacan (1988, pp. 30–33), in discussing the case, interpreted the radio audience as an anonymous audience, which could include the
living and the dead, such as the analysand's mother. But this interpretation lost ground when we learned (Little, 1990, p. 36) that
the audience was anything but anonymous — the "radio" was Little's disguise, in an actual autobiographical episode, for a lecture
she had delivered to the British Psychoanalytic Society.

Confidentiality was an issue in my preparation of this chapter. Because of my concern about the confidentiality of my analysands, and because of my reservations about "thick" disguises, I
have limited many of my clinical examples to brief vignettes.

Another difficulty in our exploration is related to the fact that,
in most of the literature, analysts describe their work with their
patients but rarely describe their own experiences as analysands.
We hear, then, about only one side of the coin and are less able to
decipher the full intersubjective picture. Experiences of analysands, in particular of professionals in training, are more often
the topic of oral informal discussions — common among

therapists and trainees—about their own experiences as patients, for better or worse. This form of discussion, which can be called the "reverse case conference" (a professional version of the witches' sabbath?), is rarely made public and seldom put in print for the benefit of the professional community (for notable exceptions, see Guntrip, 1975; Little, 1990; Simon, 1993; Lichtenberg, 1998).

This bias may be one source of the proclivity to write about therapeutic successes more than about failures. The vital discussion of therapeutic failures, so it seems, is banished from the central ("high") professional discourse and is relegated to marginal channels (Berman, 2002b). Another channel through which failures can be explored — besides the reverse case conference — is analysts' discussion of the failures of other analysts and therapists, notably former analysts of their own patients. Professionals in training are indeed prone to have been in more than one treatment, and this is in itself an additional component of the incestuous dimension in our field. The emotional triangle a person forms with two analysts, especially when the second analyst is expected to fulfill what the first one missed—is potentially quite loaded.

Discourse about what happened in an earlier treatment runs the visible risk of scapegoating. Just as in our professional rescue fantasies we are prone to imagine ourselves as better parents than the patients' actual parents, our competitiveness and determination to do better are naturally activated when we accept a patient who is unhappy with a former treatment.

Still, from my extensive experience of being patients' second (or third) analyst, I can say that my transferential feelings toward their former analysts and therapists vary tremendously, irrespective of my knowing or not knowing them directly. With some, I experience an imaginary alliance, gratitude for helping my patient in the past, or identification vis-à-vis repeated difficulties. With others, I experience a distance, as their focus seems to have been so different from mine. And with others still—envy (as my analysand describes them with longing, making me feel like a stepparent) or anger (because I feel they were destructive, and I have to deal with the posttraumatic impact of their work).

Naturally, the question sometimes crosses my mind: How would the next analysts of some of my own patients experience me and my work?

With all its limitations, the understanding we reach of past analyses is a valuable source of insight into the present analysis and can contribute to a better understanding of the unique issues of analyzing trainees.

Analysand as Analyst's Therapist and Supervisor

Searles (1979) suggested that a therapeutic impulse of the patient toward the therapist is universal, an outgrowth of the child's need to cure the parents of their shortcomings and limitations. Searles emphasized that this tendency is not unique to patients who are therapists. I suspect, however, that the deeper roots of the choice to become an analyst or a therapist guarantee the intensity of this motive in the analysis of professionals. In addition, the fuller knowledge the analysand-colleague may have about the analyst and the diagnostic sensitivity cultivated by training allow this analysand to identify even more astutely the analyst's Achilles heel. Indeed, D. Shapiro (1976), conducting a follow-up study of analysts, reported that most of them who were unhappy with the outcome of their own analysis attributed the difficulty to their analysts' personal qualities or conflicts.

An analysand I treated when I was single told me, "Because you have no children, you turn your students into your children. You must prefer brain children to flesh children."

My immediate experience was of insult and hurt. This was followed by an impulse to interpret the analysand's comment as resistance, as an avoidance of her own conflicts, but I soon realized that my impulse was vindictive and defensive. I also noticed that the analysand's tone was pained, not hostile. And, above all, I knew she was onto something, though the calm word *prefer* in her statement was far from the actual loaded conflictual emotions the topic carried for me.

Eventually, I interpreted mostly her fear that my own difficulties would prevent me from helping her to resolve her own conflicts around potential parenthood. Without confirming or denying her interpretation, I let her feel that her wish to help me was legitimate and that I could perceive its empathic element, combined with her hope to make me a better analyst for her own sake (Berman, 1995a).

Searles (1979) commented that a parent's difficulty in viewing a child's wish to "cure" the parent as legitimate and benign stems from hearing the child's voice as a scolding parental voice. That the patient is also a therapist increases this danger for the analyst. In the vignette I have given, my initial response to my analysand was as though to a parental figure. Her comment was close to the comments that my own analyst made around the same period. My aggression, which resulted from feeling in the cross fire of two critical parents, dissipated when I recognized that the emotional source of my patient's comment was not hostile.

Isaacs-Elmhirst (1982–1983) offered a Kleinian view of the same fantasy reversal. If in many analyses the analysands are experienced countertransferentially as the analyst's damaged inner objects, the analysand-colleague may be seen more specifically as a parent who was damaged and became a helpless child. However, Isaacs-Elmhirst's paper, which brilliantly interprets fantasies activated by the analysis of colleagues, is striking in that it does not explore the possibility that such analysands may actually recognize the analyst's inner damage.

My experience is that analysands often know and sense a lot about us (not only fantasies) and that, when analysands are our trainees or colleagues, this deep knowledge is multiplied. In this respect, my thinking resonates with Crastnopol's (1997) view, "that the patient's subjective experience of the therapist's private life has an important impact . . . [and] the analyst as a *person* plays a critical — and generally unacknowledged — role in the patient's subjective experience of the endeavor" (p. 261). As Crastnopol wrote, "the patient constructs multiple overlapping images of the analyst and of the analytic relationship. One of these internal images is a function of the patient's subjective experience of the analyst's multifaceted identity" (p. 262). This experience can be the springboard for a deep-rooted curative effort.

On a parallel issue, we may agree with Langs (1979) and others that every analysand is our supervisor — teaching us more than anyone else about the impact of our interventions. Most analysands do so implicitly. Analysand-trainees may adopt a supervisory role much more explicitly. Whether they verbalize it or not (of course, things are easier when responses are verbalized), they can evaluate the analyst's interventions in comparison to standards internalized during training and out of identification with teachers, supervisors, and books.

This advantage involves a paradoxical risk. By assuming a supervisory stance, the analysand may become a less effective "supervisor." The competitive, judgmental side of this position, potential undertones of contempt and devaluation (Gabbard, 1995), reduces its emotional authenticity and pushes the analyst into a defensive corner.

For example, when an analysand tells me spontaneously, "For the past few minutes, I feel very remote," I tend to reexamine my preceding intervention. If I see that it was an intellectual interpretation, I may offer my analysand the hypothesis that my interpretation may have distanced him, and I explore with him his emotional reaction to it.

On the other hand, if an analysand-trainee tells me, "Your last interpretation was too intellectual, and it distanced me," I am more likely to feel uneasy because of his blaming tone. He may be correct, and he actually "saved me work," but his professional formulation conveys that he is isolated now from the feelings of disappointment and loneliness possibly aroused by my heavy-handed intervention. He may have reacted to my distance with a defensive move into the role of a supervisor-critic who needs nothing. The professional identity is here mobilized defensively, and this process itself now requires interpretation. Still, in the long run, these analysands' criticisms may become a valuable source of stimulation in improving our analytic skills.

A related issue, which I just mention here, is analyzing therapists with a theoretical orientation different from our own and dealing with their evaluative comments, which may be based on goals that we do not fully share. I also just mention the important implications of treating therapists whose vocational background differs from our own. In such situations, tensions between the disciplines unavoidably enter the consulting room. As a psychologist, I may notice a psychiatrist's flooding me from the couch with medical terms I do not understand, or a social worker's triumphantly reminding me of Casement's similar background. This level, too, is interweaved, naturally, with personal dynamics.

The Institute and the Candidate's Analysis

Starting with the classical discussions of the 1950s and 1960s (e.g., Balint, 1954; Heimann, 1954; Bernfeld, 1962; Kairys, 1964; McLaughlin, 1967), we realized how much the actual psychoanalytic institute — its regulations, atmosphere, evaluation methods, and reporting policies — is present in the consulting room during the candidate's analysis (see Wallerstein, 1993). Extreme examples, reported by Lampl-de Groot (1954) and Anna Freud (1983, p. 259), are the cases (particularly in "reporting" institutes) in which anxiety immobilizes the training analysis, or makes it dishonest, so that only after graduation a second analysis becomes open and fruitful.

The complications and repercussions of "official" training analyses led Anna Freud to a radical conclusion: "My colleagues who first advocated the introduction of training analysis at the Marienbad Congress [1936] — if they had known of all the dangers, of the positive and negative transferences, and splits, and hates, etc. — would probably never have advocated it! They would have said, 'Let them be as they are!'" (A. Freud, 1983, p. 259).

The tendency toward "pseudo-normality" among analytic candidates has been described by Sachs (1947), Gitelson (1948, 1954), and Greenacre (1966). Balint (1954) spoke of instances of "covert, insincere, even hypocritical collusion" (p. 161). D. Shapiro (1976) added, "Training analyses tend to be pallid in comparison to the emotionally heated transference reactions that often arise in analysis under non-training conditions" (p. 34).

Review of the literature on training analyses shows that many of these issues are common to training analyses and to other analyses of mental health professionals. The more dramatic difference may be in comparing analyses of both these groups with treatment of individuals from outside the therapy field. Calef (1982), in a follow-up study of his former analysands, concluded that similarities between psychiatrists who were in analytic training while in analysis and psychiatrists who were not[2] (some of whom applied later) "are more striking than the differences" (p. 112).

---

[2]Calef was discussing a period when many psychiatrists sought analytic training, which is not the case these days.

The major difference, of course, is the impact of institute dynamics, some of which were explored in chapters 3 and 4. There may be partial analogies to such dynamics outside analytic training as well — when the analyst, for example, is teaching in professional programs attended by the analysand — but most such programs do not arouse the awesome transference elicited by the psychoanalytic institute, and their impact on the analysis usually does not become that intense.

Where do institute dynamics penetrate the analytic process in the analysis of trainees? A major example is in the practice of "reporting," in which the candidate's analyst is expected to have a role in decisions about the candidate's progress — decisions about admission into training, starting supervised analyses, and graduating. Growing criticism of the intrusiveness of this practice (e.g., Kairys, 1964; Kernberg, 1986, p. 817) led to its gradual abandonment by most psychoanalytic institutes. (The London institute remains a notable exception, in spite of internal debates about this policy.) Still, as mentioned earlier, the reality of nonreporting cannot stop candidates from having anxious fantasies that what they say in analysis may leak out and influence their evaluation and status informally.

The other side of the coin is the degree to which institute dynamics "leak in" and penetrate the analyst's own work. Orgel (2002) mentioned, for example, the analyst's temptation to encourage the analysand's achievements in training through unexamined countertransference enactments (p. 421) or to mobilize "followers and caregivers from among our analysands" (p. 436). Orgel reviewed earlier debates between Fleming (1973), who encouraged training analysts to "collaborate" with analysands on certain educational issues, and Greenacre (1966) and Kairys (1964), who proposed a training analysis conducted like any other analysis. Fleming's model, Orgel feared, may encourage unexamined suggestion and manipulation.

Although the dominant tendency in recent years has been "to remove the analysis of our candidates, as far as possible, from any institutional connection" (McLaughlin, 1967, p. 230), some institutes are still active in assigning personal analysts to their trainees. This practice is especially problematic in view of the consistent finding that the analyst–analysand match is crucial in influencing the success of the analysis (D. Shapiro, 1976, p. 36; Kantrowitz, Katz, and Paolitto, 1990). Administrators may believe that they can achieve a better match than the trainee can, but to me this sounds paternalistic, grandiose, and unrealistic.

The few empirical follow-up studies of training analyses raise issues that are universal to the analytic process in general but that also highlight some unique characteristics. D. Shapiro (1976), in his follow-up of 122 graduates of the Columbia Psychoanalytic Institute, spoke of the significance for the analysand of "finally joining his analyst as colleague, co-worker, or rival" (p. 5); of "halo responses from aspects of the educational and administrative milieu" (p. 13); and of the impact of sibling rivalries and competitive pressures (p. 28) and the hierarchical structure (p. 30). Shapiro emphasized the way in which the setting, providing extensive feedback in supervision and in seminars, may also facilitate the development of insight (p. 35).

Schachter (1990), exploring analysts' reserved attitudes toward posttermination contact in comparison to its actual potential benefit,[3] noted the advantage of having analysand-trainees able to continue contact with their former analysts without having to ask explicitly for additional help (p. 478).

Craige (2002), who studied the questionnaires of 121 respondents (all American analytic candidates) and interviewed 20 of them, emphasized that they did not seem to be a "different breed from 'ordinary' patients," and "all reported having struggled with significant emotional pain." Craige's focus on the mourning implicit in terminating analysis, and on different patterns of handling it, indeed leads mostly to universal analytic issues emphasizing the crucial role of the analyst's availability and flexibility in responding to posttermination crises.

---

[3]Martinez and Hoppe (1991), studying the experience of 214 American analysts, found that posttermination therapy or analysis with one's analyst significantly correlated with perceived benefit. Follow-up contact of a collegial or friendship nature was related to the experience of the ongoing intrapsychic presence of one's analyst, and such an experience was in turn correlated with perceived benefit. Lack of posttermination contact, on the other hand, was correlated with a lower experience of benefit.

So, should we attempt to bring the analysis of analytic candidates as close as possible to a therapeutic analysis conducted in a nontraining setting, or should we strive to maintain its different nature? In a conservative critique of proposed changes in analytic training, Erlich (1996) expressed concern that "downright opposition to Reporting may also contain a basic lack of understanding of the function and place of the training analysis" (p. 31). Erlich believed that changes of the kind introduced in Israel (discussed in chapter 4) convey a disregard for the organizational significance of psychoanalytic training, including the personal analysis of the trainee, in which a triangular aspect (maintaining the organization as a third partner) is crucial. Organizational and social aspects are undoubtedly important, but, as I repeatedly attempt to demonstrate, our own organizational needs (e.g., for regulation, power, control) may at times sabotage the growth of effective future analysts.

Using individual dynamics as a metaphor for social phenomena is risky. Still, if we were to accept Erlich's (1996, pp. 31–32) suggestion to relate reporting and similar training issues to the dyadic–triangular aspect of individual development, we may, I believe, reach a conclusion opposite to the one he drew. A successful oedipal stage can be reached only spontaneously, against the background of a secure mother–infant relationship (Ferenczi, 1929). Future analysts also need the safety of an undisturbed dyadic relationship with their personal analyst to undergo a growth process with its own individual pace, in which triangular experiences come up when they are ripe. Direct intrusions of the institute into the analytic space of the dyad — the most dramatic being reporting and interruption of an analysis because of the analyst's formal status — may be experienced as destructive impingements in this delicate process (Berman, 1997c). If they hinder the personal therapeutic value of the analysis, they necessarily reduce its value as a part of training.

Analysands as Colleagues:
The Issue of Boundaries

Many times, our trainee analysand — and the analysand who has already completed training — turns to us as a colleague and presents professional questions, ideas, requests, or comments. The dilemma of how much to acknowledge our professional affinity and allow its expression is not easy. Will answering or responding concretely enhance or undermine analytic work? Each solution is problematic, each is loaded on a countertransferential level.

If we seem to be refusing to accept our equality as adult professionals, this may be experienced as infantilizing and humiliating. It may also serve defensive needs:

> Many of us have particular difficulty with analysands' observations and judgments about our functioning as analysts and as members of the analytic community. The temptation to enjoy the narcissistic rewards inherent in our positions as analysts and educators ... merges with the feelings of a parent who, with diminishing powers and shrinking time, is yielding up his or her future in every action of analyzing the patients' transference wishes. Is there any analysis in which the analyst is not at least partially a Lear awaiting the fate of being killed by the children? [Orgel, 1990, pp. 9–10].

On the other hand, a willingness to accept the analysand as a mature colleague may complicate the effort to explore the immature parts of this analysand's inner world. Personally, I do not see this risk as severe in some of the minor daily examples, such as an analysand's question, sometimes at the door, about the dates of a professional conference or about the reference for a paper. In these situations, we may apply Klauber's (1981) comment about analysts who do not reply to Christmas cards: "Is it really sound to imagine that more is to be gained by rebuffing the patient in this way than by reciprocating as a member of society with a common culture and still analysing the motives when they come up?" (p. 212). Similarly, Etchegoyen (1991) explained his choice to let his analysand know (without being asked) that a lecture he planned to attend was canceled (p. 320).

However, we must remember that the issue of boundaries may come up in more massive proportions and may have a much more profound impact on the nature of the analytic relationship. A clear example is the situation in which analysis and an actual comprehensive professional tie coexist. Should this be seen as an omnipotent attempt that endangers the effective working through of both transference and countertransference? Several historical examples of such "simultaneous" endeavors ended with ambivalent feelings on both sides: Freud and Ferenczi (discussed in chapter 1), Klein and Paula Heimann (Grosskurth, 1986), Winnicott and Khan (Hopkins, 1998), and Fairbairn and Guntrip[4] (Hughes, 1989).

I can imagine an attempt to rationalize such combinations as being based on a unique version of the "working alliance" as mobilizing a conflict-free ego sphere. However, Greenson's (1967) belief that such an alliance need not be interpreted was successfully challenged by M. M. Gill (1982). We now realize how a seemingly rational and unconflictual alliance may camouflage irrational needs ("the envy, competitiveness, and contempt that so often lie buried below"; Gabbard, 1995, pp. 720–721), which actually require intensive interpretive work. When the analyst "strengthens the alliance" by turning the analysand into a student, disciple, coworker, or political partner (Balint, 1948) or by becoming a "seductive recruiter" (Orgel, 2002, p. 428), this may unwittingly sabotage such interpretive work—and with it the full fruition of the analysis.

Moreover, a combined analytic-political alliance may lead to an exaggerated identification with the analyst-mentor as a single parental figure—not allowing the painful but fruitful conflict of competing identifications in molding one's unique and autonomous professional self. (In chapter 6, I return to this issue in addressing the phenomenon of a combined analyst-supervisor.) And if at some point the analysand enters a separation-individuation process, expressing theoretical or organizational disagreements with the analyst-mentor, there may be a considerable risk that the analyst, threatened by the distancing of a loyal supporter, interprets these moves as aggressive or even parricidal/matricidal, unwittingly abusing the analytic authority position as means for maintaining control.

---

[4]Guntrip's personal notes (Hughes, 1989) convey more disappointment than his published account does (Guntrip, 1975).

Another issue in turning analysands into disciples and students (e.g., by inviting them to become supervisees or coworkers after analysis is over) is whether we are undermining the separation process and avoiding the need for mourning. Novick (1997) raised this risk as a major issue in analyses of colleagues and related difficulties with termination to the unhappy outcome of some of them, including numerous historical cases. This issue was raised by Milner (1950): "Perhaps we, as analysts, are handicapped in knowing all about what ending feels like, for by the mere fact of becoming analysts we have succeeded in bypassing an experience which our patients have to go through" (p. 191). On the other hand, continued collaboration could enhance — as posttermination contact seems to enhance in general — the possibility of working out posttermination crises (Craige, 2002), of maintaining an experience of interest and concern without requiring that help must be explicitly requested (Schachter, 1990), and of strengthening the analyst's enduring intrapsychic presence as a helpful lively introject.

We must take very seriously the risks in both directions. We should beware of being seduced by a soothing closeness or a flattering discipleship into neglecting or undermining our analytic goals, which require striving to maintain an open-ended, exploratory relationship free of extrinsic goals and interests. As I have described, succumbing to such seduction may risk in the long run both the analysis and the personal or professional closeness. Still, we must always keep in mind a central reality. In every analysis, "analyst and patient are also two real people, of equal adult status, in a real personal relationship to each other" (A. Freud, 1954, p. 373). In the cases discussed here, we are also two real professionals, of potentially equal competence, in a real partnership with each other.

6

Psychoanalytic Supervision: The Intersubjective Turn

Teaching in itself, teaching as such, takes place precisely only through a crisis; if teaching does not hit upon some sort of crisis, if it does not encounter either the vulnerability or the explosiveness of an (explicit or implicit) critical and unpredictable dimension, it has perhaps not really taught.

—Shoshana Felman
"Education and Crisis, Or
The Vicissitudes of Teaching"

The notion of intersubjectivity has enormous implications for the analytic relationship and, I believe, for psychoanalytic supervision as well. If taken seriously, intersubjectivity points the way to potential radical changes both in the content and in the style of supervision (Berman, 2000d). This is the focus of this chapter.

Let me first briefly summarize a few central points of intersubjective and relational thinking that have direct implications for supervision. Psychoanalysis is both a "one-person psychology" (studying intrapsychic processes) and a "two-person psychology" (studying interactions). The concept of intersubjectivity attempts to integrate these aspects. The psychic realities of both analyst and analysand, it implies, are involved in their encounter and are transformed by that encounter. Transference is both an outgrowth of the patient's life history and a reaction to the personality and actions of the analyst, who can never fully become a "blank screen" or an "empty container" (Aron, 1996a). There is a continual mutual influence between analyst and analysand, though this mutuality evolves in the context of a clear asymmetry, that must be acknowledged (Aron, 1996a).

Transference, in its broader definition, unavoidably combines displaced and projected elements with realistic perceptions, and the analyst is never sufficiently "objective" to separate these definitively. We can raise questions and offer ideas about the sources of different elements, but to attempt a definitive judgment as to what is true and what is distorted in the way we are viewed implies absolute knowledge of ourselves — that is, denying that there are unconscious aspects in our own psyche (M. M. Gill, 1982).

Likewise, countertransference unavoidably combines issues stemming from the basic psychic reality of the analyst and aspects responsive to the specific analysand. Some authors (e.g., Springmann, 1986) have attempted to separate these into different categories, but I suspect this attempt is futile. In my own experience, in self-analysis, and in the supervision and analysis of candidates, every reaction that first appears as pure projective counteridentification (Grinberg, 1979) or mere role responsiveness (J. Sandler, 1976) turns out on further scrutiny to have aspects related to the analyst's unique personality (in other words, there are reasons why a projective identification can "catch on"). Conversely, the analyst may be certain he or she reacts out of a purely personal vulnerability, but fuller exploration reveals that a particular analysand powerfully activates that vulnerability, whereas others do not.

Transference and countertransference constantly activate and mold each other. Actually, they are parts of one total cyclic process that has no starting point. Studying each separately makes as much sense as studying a game of chess by analyzing the moves of only the white pieces. In this respect, the *counter* in the word *countertransference* may be misleading, as transference is also countercountertransference (Racker, 1968). The total transference–countertransference cycle generates a joint new reality, a transitional space with its own unique emotional climate in which analytic work takes place.

Countertransference Cannot Be Relegated to the Candidate's Analysis

Such an intersubjective view of the analytic relationship has, first of all, clear implications for the content of psychoanalytic supervision. It makes the option of purely didactic supervision, which avoids countertransference or delegates all of it to the candidate's own analysis, untenable. Discussing the dynamics of only the analysand, or demonstrating "correct" technique, is of limited value. If we assume that important elements in the transference are reactive to the analyst's actual personality and behavior, it follows that we cannot fully understand the analysand's experience if relevant aspects of the analyst's own personality and emotional reactions are not discussed in supervision (Berman, 2000d).

I do not believe that the supervisor has the capacity to pass a final verdict as to the accuracy of the analysand's attributions, but the supervisor can become an invaluable partner in thinking about the possible validity of such attributions. It is potentially very helpful—though not easy—when a supervisor says, "You know, I also heard that interpretation as seductive." Or, the opposite direction may be relevant, as in this example:

A supervisee raises his difficulty with the analysand's idealization of him. When listening to the material, the supervisor wonders about the supervisee's use of the term *idealization*. The supervisor actually experiences the analysand as expressing realistic gratitude to this competent and empathic analyst. Raising this issue leads to talking about the analyst's low self-esteem, which left him blind to the progress this gratitude may signify for the analysand, a person who is harshly critical of his parents and almost everyone else, and quite lonely.

If we assume that countertransference is both a clue to understanding the psychic reality of the analysand and an influence on its further development in the course of analysis, it follows that countertransference cannot be avoided in psychoanalytic supervision, including the more personal sources of countertransference, which cannot be separated out in advance. We need to know, to give a simple example, that the analysand reminds the analyst of her brother if we are to help her in attempting to clarify for herself how this association effects her countertransference and if we are to help to uncover the ways in which this countertransference unavoidably colors the analyst's actions and verbalizations and, therefore, unknowingly influences her analysand as well—changing in turn his transference to her and the entire atmosphere in the consulting room.

Bollas (1997) expressed a different view: Rather than speaking about countertransference, we should let the countertransference speak. Direct discussion of countertransference in supervision, he believed, may be too limited to the conscious level, whereas noticing its expression in the verbatim transcript of the sessions allows contact with unconscious components. At times, I suspect, this is so, but I am wary of such a generalized conclusion. In my experience, clinging to verbatim transcripts may also acquire a defensive quality, and countertransference manifestations in the analyst's verbalizations may then be clouded or rationalized away. On the other hand, a direct question posed by the supervisor, "How do you feel toward this analysand?", though initially answered on a conscious level, may become a thread leading to growing awareness of preconscious and unconscious levels as well. Therefore, though I usually encourage taking notes of the sessions and reading them in supervision, I attempt not to be enslaved by such a routine. At times, major insights about analytic work emerged in a session in which a supervisee put aside or forgot to bring the notebook.

In the framework I outline, the idea of a standard technique becomes obsolete. The alternative challenge is to follow carefully, with close attention to minute details, the analytic interaction, and to pause and consider the intersubjective implications of each verbal or nonverbal exchange. In this context, the analyst's interpretations, silences, and slips of the tongue can be examined in supervision in terms of their affective antecedents and consequences rather than on the basis of conscious intentions. In this respect, they are explored much as the analysand's associations, requests, and jokes are.

The analytic impact of interventions can be evaluated only in retrospect. What was formulated as an empathic interpretation may be experienced as an insult, what first appears as the analyst's blunder may eventually lead to an important insight, and so forth. Beyond basic ideas about the setting and its boundaries, which are important in that they make this scrutiny possible, what needs to be learned is not any list of steadfast rules but an introspective and empathic sensitivity to the actual sources and actual impact of our actions and inactions. This is a most personal learning process, which requires considerable personal exposure, and is strongly influenced by the supervisory climate.

If we accept that analysis may at times benefit from direct expression of countertransference (Bollas, 1987; Tansey and Burke,

1989; Aron, 1996a; Renik, 1999; Berman, 2001a), exploration of such an option becomes another supervisory challenge. Many beginning analysts are afraid to make any such interventions, and their avoidance may be costly at times, especially when they attempt to sidetrack an involuntary expression of countertransference already noticed by the analysand, in which case they are perceived as defensive and anxious. After thoughtful joint consideration of all risks and benefits, the potential encouragement of a supervisor to express things more directly in some instances may be an important step toward breaking a stalemate in analysis. Naturally, countertransference disclosure cannot be considered if countertransference in general is not patiently explored first. Let me give an example:

A supervisee reported that his analysand constantly blamed him for identifying with his wife rather than with him. All the analyst's attempts to interpret this as a fearful projection were ineffective. Fuller discussion in supervision made it clear that the analysand had a point: In the countertransference, the analyst experiences his analysand as a bully and the analysand's wife as a victim. This reaction turned out to have some sources in the analyst's life but was also molded by the analysand's projective identification. This analysand consciously depreciated his wife but unconsciously invited empathy toward her much more than toward himself. It became clear that the analyst's past interpretations, which implied denial of the analysand's complaints, made the analysand confused and even more suspicious. On the other hand, judicious acknowledgment of the analysand's perceptions could become a springboard to the new understanding of his marriage, not as the external battlefield he consciously portrayed but as the stage of an inner drama in which many of his own dissociated experiences as a battered child were projectively expressed through his wife.

Supervision as the Crossroads of a
Matrix of Object Relations

An intersubjective focus cannot be limited, however, to the analyst and analysand alone. Analysand, analyst, and supervisor can be "viewed as co-creators of two mutually influential dyads" (Frawley-O'Dea, 2003). Both dyads must be understood, so we need to pay full attention to the intersubjective reality created between supervisor and supervisee. Psychoanalytic supervision therefore becomes a task in which a psychoanalytic orientation is expressed not only in content but also in the nature of the process. Psychoanalytic scrutiny can be effectively directed toward our own work as supervisors, and the meta-communication achieved may allow us a critical self-analysis. We could then become, as supervisors, less preoccupied with formulating what we should do and more receptive to an exploration of what we actually do and undergo, which may not be always dictated by our theoretical rationales and goals, as we once believed. Our programmatic and ideologic discourse could be modified and enriched by accurate observation of actual processes, in the participant–observer style developed by social anthropology.

A psychoanalytic supervision that allows this meta-communication may contribute more to the deep personal growth process toward which psychoanalytic training aims. On the other hand, lack of meta-communication runs the risk of inhibiting this process at times. In such a purely "content-oriented" (or patient-focused) supervision, psychoanalysis may be underused.

Discussions of supervision that focus on the didactic exploration of the patient–therapist dyad treat the supervisory process as if it were "transparent," merely a means to know what happens in the supervised analysis. (In a parallel way, authors naive about transferential and countertransferential currents might discuss psychotherapy as a "transparent" process teaching us directly about the patient's reported childhood and verbalized experiences.) The result may be supervision texts that are about analysis or therapy but not about supervision per se. In the past, such avoidance was rationalized by the need to maintain the difference between analysis and supervision (Windholz, 1970), but I believe such compartmentalization unavoidably impoverishes supervision.

We might think of supervision as the crossroads of a matrix of object relations of at least three persons, each bringing her or his psychic reality into the bargain and thus creating a joint intersubjective milieu (Berman, 1997e) or as a triadic intersubjective matrix (Brown and Miller, 2002). This crossroads involves visible interpersonal expressions — related to issues of authority, power, gender roles, economic stratification, and so forth — as well as less visible unconscious expressions. In spite of the risks involved in introducing clinically derived terms into the study of supervision (Ekstein and Wallerstein, 1972), it may be helpful to speak also of the juxtaposition and interaction of several simultaneous transference–countertransference trends[1] in each analytic-supervisory combination.

I am aware of the hopelessness of fully deciphering all these nuances within the limited time-span of one supervisory process, and I am aware of the natural differences among supervisors (and supervisees) regarding aspects on which they prefer to focus. I am arguing, however, that all these levels should be at least acknowledged and allowed as potential legitimate contents in the supervisory discourse. If this is not achieved, some components (most typically the supervisor's subjective contribution, as well as issues of authority and power) may be defensively denied or rationalized away, and consequently supervision may become stilted or even oppressive, not allowing the potential transitional space to evolve within it. A powerful example of such a process was supplied by Shevrin in his account of his experiences as a supervisee who was a passive subject in a research project on supervision conducted by his "elders" (in Wallerstein, 1981).

The supervisor–supervisee relationship, I suggest, is always a rich and complex transference–countertransference combination, even if supervision is utterly impersonal; teachers are always a major focus of transference feelings. Naturally, the more personal approach I advocate may add complexity and intensity to the process, may undermine some of the more defensive modes of avoiding anxiety in the situation, and may increase the fear of intrusion and humiliation. On the other hand, as a partial

---

[1]The idea of using yet another term, *supertransference* (Teitelbaum, 1990), in describing the supervisor's experiences is problematic. Although Teitelbaum (1990) emphasized the negative impact of this phenomenon — loyal to the tradition of viewing countertransference as a hindrance — his suggested term paradoxically may acquire the connotation of viewing the supervisor as "superhuman," above ordinary transference.

remedy, it may allow greater awareness and better resolution of supervisory conflicts and crises by encouraging the joint exploration of the supervisory relationship itself (Berman, 1988b). The supervisor's fuller awareness of moments in which he or she was experienced as intrusive or insensitive, for example, may make reparation possible and may serve as a springboard for more tactful work, taking better into account the supervisee's sensitivities, once these were more openly verbalized.

Although the wishes of both supervisee and supervisor to make their work together instructive and fruitful are usually quite sincere, many factors make their relationship potentially conflictual. Epstein (1986) thoroughly discussed the possible negative impact of supervision on supervisees.

The analytic encounter is a very intimate dyadic situation, and a third partner in it may be a burdensome intrusion, a chaperon on a honeymoon. This may become noticeable when the analyst's spontaneity is inhibited by a preoccupation with remembering the session, sometimes to the point of taking notes during the session (contrary to Freud's, 1912b, warnings, which many generations have confirmed) so "nothing gets lost" when reported in supervision. I know of some instances in which this practice was kept secret from the supervisor — out of fear of disapproval — which naturally blocked the supervisor's capacity to notice the impact of note taking on the analysand and the process.

Analysts often have rescue fantasies involving their patients (chapter 3), projecting their own vulnerability onto them, whereas the involvement of a supervisor unavoidably reintroduces the analyst's own vulnerability and neediness into the picture. The supervisor may be experienced as a potentially superior rescuer. "I am sure you would have done it much better" is a common candidate's fantasy. It may sometimes be untrue: With difficult cases, a beginner's enthusiasm and optimism may be potentially more helpful than a seasoned professional's sober apprehension. But would the supervisor help in dismantling the fantasy?

Idealization has a broad range of outcomes in psychoanalytic supervision. It may become a fruitful spur for learning, when related to an experience of being deeply understood, influenced, and inspired. At the other end of the spectrum, in a collusively maintained overidealization, oedipal and narcissistic dynamics may at times combine in producing in the younger analyst a painful sense of inferiority (S. Gill, 2001). An image of supervisor and supervisee as fundamentally differing in their therapeutic potential may become part of the "myth of the supervisory situation" (Berman, 1988b), equivalent to the "myth of the analytic situation" as involving an interaction between a sick person and a healthy one (Racker's formulation, quoted in chapter 2). Do supervisors contribute to such mythology? Langs (1979) seemed to have a point when he observed that "even a therapist prepared to surrender an overidealized image of himself in his work with patients clings to the overidealized image of himself as supervisor" (p. 43).

In some instances, a "negative supervisory reaction" may develop, which (in ways parallel to the negative therapeutic reaction) leads to a regression in the therapeutic work of the trainee after a seemingly positive development or even a breakthrough in supervision. It is an important example of a situation in which open exploration of the supervisory experience itself becomes invaluable.

Such exploration, bordering at times on a therapeutic process, may eventually lead to the individual sources of the supervisee's reaction. Here are two examples:

After some important sessions of supervision, in which the supervisor was able to suggest new ways of dealing with a patient's resistant aloofness, the patient became much more involved in treatment. The therapist, however, started forgetting supervisory appointments, brought very short notes, and sounded alienated from her work. It turned out that the supervisor's interventions made the therapist realize how poor her past training had been and how ineffective were the methods she had developed (proudly) during several years of unsupervised work. She now felt ashamed of herself and embarrassed to present her work. The supervisor began to recognize that he may have been too active and enthusiastic and insufficiently attentive to the supervisee's anxieties.

During supervision of a first-year graduate student, several weeks went by in which the student reported a stalemate in the treatment of a difficult patient. Finally, a completely new interpretation crossed the supervisor's mind, and she suggested it to the supervisee, who greeted it as very convincing. In her next supervisory meeting, the supervisee reported that she had used the interpretation and encountered an immediate confirmatory reaction from the patient, who finally felt understood. The therapist reported this in a gloomy tone, however, and soon mentioned thoughts she had of abandoning her training. Further exploration revealed that she could not forgive herself for not thinking of the effective interpretation herself. An omnipotent fantasy was now demolished, activating deep-seated envy and resentment of needing to be supervised, seen both as a manifestation of incompetence and as a dangerous source of dependence.

In both cases, open discussion of the source of regression resolved the immediate crisis. Deeper resolution of the emotional issues involved, crucial for the trainees' professional future, remained a long-term goal, one probably requiring working through in analysis as well.

Many of the dynamic patterns that have been offered in the literature as explaining negative therapeutic reactions may also be contemplated as potential sources of negative supervisory reactions. These patterns include unconscious guilt and a need for punishment (Freud); competition with the analyst, hurt self-esteem, fear of being envied because of success, and experiencing an interpretation as an accusation or proof of dislike (Horney); envy, leading to a need to destroy the envied analyst's competence (Klein); and negativism (Olinick; these explanations are reviewed by J. Sandler, Dare, and Holder, 1979). But of particular relevance are viewpoints that do not conceptualize the negative therapeutic reaction as necessarily stemming from the patient alone. Langs (1976) raised the possibility of an "interactional negative therapeutic reaction" strongly influenced by the analyst's contribution. Stolorow, Brandchaft, and Atwood (1983) discussed the negative therapeutic reaction as resulting from "prolonged, unrecognized transference–countertransference disjunctions and the chronic misunderstandings that result from them" (p. 120). The possible application or such models to supervision requires paying attention to the supervisor's role.

Whereas in my past work I tended to emphasize sources of conflict unique to supervisors and other sources of conflict unique to supervisees, I gradually came to see their commonalities. Within supervision, too, we may speak of basic mutuality and joint vulnerability (Slavin, 1998), though they are experienced in the context of unavoidable asymmetry and inequality, which should not be denied.

A major source of difficulty for supervisees, for example, is that the learning of new skills requires acknowledgment of their lack, and such an acknowledgment arouses shame. But in good supervision, the supervisor needs to learn and change, too, and at times to become aware of one's blind spots or to admit not having satisfactory answers to the challenge posed by a troublesome analysand. And, though we often discuss the evaluation of candidates by supervisors, mutual evaluation is actually occurring, even if the evaluation of the supervisor by the candidate is often silent or muted within supervision and verbalized only outside, informally, by word of mouth. This reality turns partners into threatening judges of each other, with both being a potential source of embarrassing exposure and rejection (Berman, 2000d).

Narcissistic needs of supervisors, a possible competitiveness with younger colleagues, and fear of being displaced by them all add to supervisors' vulnerability and to their anxiety about the way supervisees describe them to their peers, to their analyst, or to other supervisors. Gediman and Wolkenfeld (1980) related the supervisor's authoritarianism to "seeing the supervisee as a potential extension of himself" (p. 246). They discussed the supervisor's "competitive feelings toward his supervisee and anxieties about the inevitability of the supervisee's eventually becoming his peer" (p. 247) and the supervisor's tendency to be "preoccupied with his teaching reputation as it is displayed to the student body . . . [and] concerned with the image of himself that his student may convey to his analyst" (p. 248). Just as in analysis the direct countertransference to one's analysand may be supplemented by indirect countertransferences (Racker, 1968) involving the reactions of third parties (e.g., a supervisor), in supervision the direct countertransference to the supervisee may be supplemented by indirect countertransferences as well (e.g., concerns about the opinion of the candidate's analyst). Disregarding this aspect of the supervisory reality implies denying the paradoxical and mutual aspects of the supervisory dyad, just as

Etchegoyen (1991) oversimplified the complexity of the analytic encounter by interpreting indirect countertransference involving the supervisor as merely a displacement of direct countertransference to the patient (as discussed in chapter 2). Such indirect countertransference reactions may be too burdensome to share with a supervisee, but the supervisor's awareness of them may be crucial so they could be worked through.

In extreme cases, the supervisor's experience may become most painful. A powerful example of a supervisor's negative countertransference toward a supervisee, supplied by Teitelbaum (1990), involved:

> (a) Dreading sessions — a wish to cancel them — a wish to get rid of the therapist ... (b) Persistent feelings of irritation, annoyance, impatience, and disdain. (c) A desire to protect his patients from him, and empathy for the patients who were not being understood ... (d) I felt deprived of seeing that my work with a therapist was having an impact ... I did not want this therapist to be my product ... (e) I often felt alone, angry, helpless and shut out ... (f) ... sadistic feelings ... (g) Feelings of frustration because the therapist ... appeared to simply screen out my reactions [p. 252].

The Conflict-Generating Triadic Structure of the Analytic-Supervisory Situation

The triadic structure of the analytic-supervisory situation leads to a possible conflict of loyalties within each participant. For the candidate analyst, such a conflict may be aroused if the analyst experiences a discrepancy between what appears to be the emotional needs of the analysand and the supervisor's views as to the preferred analytic technique. From the supervisor's end, an inherent conflict of identifications, with the supervisee and with the analysand, may also be a source of difficulty. Being a "servant of two masters," the supervisor experiences two ethical commitments: "I was well aware of feeling in a quandary as to which desperate young woman to help, the patient or the supervisee" (Stimmel, 1995, p. 613).

The dilemma surfaces when the supervisor is unhappy with the supervisee's work and becomes torn between loyalty to the candidate's needs (to develop gradually at the suitable individual pace, without feeling too criticized and threatened) and a sense of responsibility for the analysand's well-being. The supervisor may feel quite helpless in dangerous situations (e.g., risk of suicide or psychosis); this situation "often evokes a sense of helplessness and even anxiety when the student's mistakes seem to threaten the patient's safety" (Fleming and Benedek, 1966, p. 58). At such moments, the supervisee may take on the projected role of the aggressor — relieving the supervisor of his or her own guilt over the process that led to the danger. Such projection can in extreme cases lead to direct accusation by the supervisor and in more moderate situations to difficulty in maintaining full empathy with the supervisee's difficulty. At times, the supervisor may be tempted to move from impotence to omnipotence, to assume a more directive position (to put words in the supervisee's mouth, turning into a Cyrano de Bergerac), even to meet the patient directly. This may constitute an authoritarian disruption of the younger analyst's growth.

This vignette is representative:

The therapist possessed much experience and self-confidence but in the eyes of his supervisor was not particularly wise. When discussing the treatment of a depressed borderline patient, he quoted some interventions in which he had smugly challenged the patient regarding the seriousness of his suicidal ideation. The supervisor experienced growing anxiety during the session and toward its end forcefully confronted the supervisee with the dangerous impact of such challenges. The therapist now responded with anxiety himself and subsequently made efforts to avoid such risks. This supervisory intervention, which seemed unavoidable to the supervisor, had a price, however: The supervisee became more guarded in future presentations. The identification of the supervisor with the patient "over the therapist's head" (complementary identification), and his need to save the endangered patient from the therapist, led to an experience of abandonment in the supervisee, which was not easy to correct.

A similar but even more complex situation may occur during the supervision of supervision,[2] in which the senior supervisor is one more step removed from the clinical situation (Ekstein, in Wallerstein 1981), is in a way even more powerless, and may be in conflict among three competing identifications.

A supervisor in supervisory training presented in his own supervision his work with a beginning therapist treating a vulnerable young homosexual man. Both supervisors found the therapist's work rather weak and possibly marred by unresolved feelings regarding homosexuality. Both were very concerned when the therapist impulsively accepted the patient's stated wish for a (clearly premature) termination. The senior supervisor found himself so critical that he raised the question of dropping the therapist from training; he clearly identified with the patient and experienced a rescue fantasy in which the therapist (whom he had never met) played the role of the dragon. The direct supervisor, on the other hand, experienced identification both with the patient and with the therapist and responded to his teacher's suggestion by attempting to rescue the therapist (declared not guilty by reason of inexperience) from the threatening dragon (senior supervisor).

In this case, the direct supervisor's personal contact with the therapist guaranteed a sense of commitment that the senior supervisor had no way of developing. The latter acknowledged that decisions must be reached by those directly working with the trainee and not dictated "from above." I do not further discuss the issues of supervising supervision here, except to say that exploration of the relationship is equally indicated in that setting.

Equivalent issues of conflicted identifications actually appear within analysis itself: The analyst may be conflicted between "concordant identifications" with the analysand and "complementary identifications" with the analysand's inner objects, as

---

[2]In Israel, every clinical psychologist wishing to become a certified supervisor must go through supervision of supervision. In psychoanalytic training, this is less common; there seems to be an implicit assumption, not necessarily accurate, that analytic training and experience prepare one for effective supervisory work as well.

personalized through other individuals in the analysand's life (Racker, 1968, p. 134). However, once we realize that these other individuals (e.g., spouse, children) also represent unacknowledged aspects of the analysand, an integration of the conflicting identifications becomes conceivable, and both kinds of identifications become the basis of potential empathy toward the analysand. Tansey and Burke (1989) made this point, and it is an important advance over Racker's original view that only concordant identifications can be sublimated into empathy.

Similar understanding may be relevant at times in supervision as well (e.g., a resistant patient may represent a side of the supervisee, just as a rebellious adolescent may represent a side of the parent), but not as consistently. After all, the analyst has not raised the patient from infancy and often has not chosen the patient (as we choose friends, lovers, or spouses on the basis of unconscious identifications). Therefore, the conflict of identifications of the supervisor is more difficult to resolve.

The role of supervisors in supervisory dynamics and difficulties receives scant attention in most of our professional literature. The literature is written mostly by supervisors, just as analysis is usually reported by analysts, and written reports by analysands are rare. The other side of the coin, as already mentioned, is often thoroughly explored in candidates' informal discussions of their analysts and supervisors (Fraser, 1996; Jaffe, 2000), but these are never recorded or published — a fact that deprives us of a major source of insight about success and failure in analysis and in its supervision. A notable exception is Pergeron's (1996) account of the way his expression and exploration of feelings toward his supervisor opened up important aspects of both the supervised analysis and of his own self-analysis.

Seminars attended by supervisors alone are, against this background, limited in their potential. An ideal forum for exploring intersubjective aspects in supervision would therefore jointly involve both supervisor and supervisee. Such a forum was successfully created at the 1997 IPA Conference of Training Analysts in Barcelona (Szecsödy, 1999), where dyads of supervisor and supervisee brought up their respective experiences in supervision for discussion in small groups of analysts. At times, their two-sided accounts allowed for much better understanding of the supervisory process and dilemmas. This format was established in spite of the objections of numerous analysts, particularly from France and Britain, who were concerned about boundaries being eroded, complained that candidates expected to present become overexcited, and expressed fear that the joint presentation might destroy the psychic process of supervision (Brenman-Pick, 1997).

The Supervisor–Patient Relationship

To fully understand the triadic dynamics of analysis and supervision, we should also recognize the evolving relationship between the supervisor and the analysand discussed in supervision. This relationship may develop in fantasy and ultimately may gain a powerful real impact, both of the two related parties on each other (even though in a mediated manner) as well as on the "mediator," the analyst.

Many analysands are aware of possible supervision, especially those who are themselves mental health professionals. Some analysands may find out who the supervisor is or may develop (wishful or anxious) hypotheses about the supervisor. Many more develop a mental image of the supervisor and a transference reaction to this imagined person (Berman, 1997e).

In this context, too, we discover splits and conflicts. I briefly mention a few divergent themes as examples: "You are too young and inexperienced to understand me, but your supervisor will help you out." "I feel that our relationship is very close, but it's hard for me to be open because you talk about me to a stranger." "You and your supervisor must have a field day, laughing about my stupidity." "Bring this dream to supervision. I feel we are stuck with it." "Were you in supervision today? This interpretation did not sound as your own."[3] "You probably raise my fee because you were told in supervision you allow yourself to be

---

[3]I share Casement's (1997) experience that, when supervision is used too directly, "patients will sense that there is a different hand at the helm in sessions immediately following a student's supervision" and may guess the day of weekly supervision (p. 264).

exploited." "As a man, you cannot understand menstruation, but hopefully you have a female supervisor." B. MacCarthy (personal communication) described an applicant for an analysis who refused to go to a fully qualified analyst and preferred to wait for a candidate — saying he felt safer that someone outside the analysis will be in control. In another instance known to me, an analysand asked his analyst to arrange for him a meeting with her supervisor, who could, he hoped, mediate in a crisis between them.

Mayer (1972) related the tendency to idealize the supervisor while denigrating the therapist to life histories involving traumatic disruptions of the tie to the parents as well as the presence of alternative caretakers within the family. Windholz (1970) described a case in which a patient attempted to exclude her analyst (experienced as a competitive brother) from her relationship with the "maternal" supervisor.

Luber (1991) offered another intriguing example. After five years of analysis under the auspices of an institute, a patient who correctly sensed Luber's being close to graduation developed intense anxiety about the possible switch to private patient status. Analytic exploration revealed that the patient was fearful about losing the background presence of Luber's supervisor (never alluded to before) and remaining alone with her analyst. Transferentially, the analyst came to represent her brother, with whom she experienced incestuous feelings, and the supervisor represented a protective father.

Luber (1991) suggested that such split transferences to analyst and supervisor may belong to two main categories — attempts to split off one side of an ambivalent transference from the analyst to the supervisor and cases in which the transference is primarily triadic, based on the patient's past involvement with two related figures. In my view, these categories are not mutually exclusive. The initial split in the patient's history may have also been related to splitting off, as in Fairbairn's (1954) analysis of the Oedipus complex, as an externalization of the initial ambivalence regarding the mother.

Naturally, the analysand's transference to the supervisor may influence both the analyst's countertransference (e.g., feeling put down or, to the contrary, seduced into an exclusive alliance) and the supervisor's countertransference to the analyst (e.g., seeing

the analyst as weak because the patient yearns for reinforcement) or to the analysand (feeling a guardian angel or, at the
other extreme, an unwelcome intruder). Consequently, it may
influence the supervisory relationship, and its impact is another
potential focus of an intersubjective exploration in supervision.
Barron (2003) presented and thoughtfully analyzed two fascinating cases of convergence between patients' fantasies about
supervisors and the analyst's experience of these supervisors.

In addition, each supervisor may develop an autonomous and
unique countertransference to any analysand being discussed —
affection, curiosity, annoyance, and so forth. This affective response also becomes interconnected with the supervisory relationship, and various (counter)transferential triadic patterns evolve
(Winokur, 1982).

Let me mention three potential basic patterns, each of which
creates a different supervisory climate, the latter two being particularly destructive for growth in supervision:

1. Supervisor and analyst form a close alliance as the concerned and mutually supportive parents of a problematic child.

2. Analyst and analysand form a close and secretive involvement; analyst withholds in supervision part of what goes
on (self-disclosures, affective expressions, active interventions;
see Yerushalmi, 1992; Mayer, 1996; Jaffe, 2000) and reports sessions in a guarded form — the result being that the excluded supervisor becomes bored and uninvested in both supervisee
and analysand.

3. Supervisor is deeply interested in the appealing analysand,
is critical of the analyst's unempathic work, and develops a fantasy of rescuing the analysand from the analyst, as in the example
presented earlier. The result may be a harsh critical attitude leading to a crisis in supervision and a report to the training committee that the candidate is unsuitable.

Greenson (1967, pp. 220–221) discussed a supervisee who
failed to express interest in the health of an analysand's sick child.
Greenson was very attentive to the analysand's hurt but was not
empathic to any potential vulnerability at the bottom of the
supervisee's guarded inhibition or to the supervisee's possible
hurt when scolded and sent for more analysis (Teitelbaum, 1990).

In my reading, an opportunity for change within supervision itself may have been missed, against the background of a triadic transferential entanglement.

Difficulties in Supervision as a Topic of
Supervisory Discourse

An intersubjective focus should turn difficulties in the supervisory relationship into a legitimate topic within the supervisory discourse. Avoiding these difficulties may set the supervisor up as a bad role model and undermine the supervisor's encouragement of constant attention to the affective nuances in the analytic relationship and their verbalization. Empathy toward the analysand, in the absence of empathy toward the supervisee, creates a confusing, mixed message (Sloane, 1986; Ricci, 1995). On the other hand, "the more fully and freely supervisor and supervisee represent the intricacies of their own relationship ... the more completely and effectively the supervisee can engage with the patient in identifying and speaking about the relational paradigms operating within the treatment" (Frawley-O'Dea, 2003).

Acknowledgment of the supervisor's possible role in difficulties (Sarnat, 1992) is not only crucial in creating a nonthreatening atmosphere but is also vital for a rich, truthful understanding of the dyadic process. Both supervisor and supervisee should hope to learn a lot from understanding the repeated gaps between their conscious wishes and the actual outcomes of their encounter.[4]

---

[4]The same rationales apply to exploration of group process in group supervision. In group supervision, we may enjoy the added benefit of amplifying insight through the consistent response of numerous group members; in other instances, respective group members, in their differential responses, dramatize various aspects of the presenter's countertransference, respond to conflicting aspects of the patient's personality, or reenact different roles that were or are present in the patient's family. In addition, an effective supervisory group, one in which all participants become active members of a supervisory team, invites and encourages development of a supervisory capacity in each therapist. The result may be to demystify the supervisory process and provide greater insight into conflictual aspects of both the supervisee's role and the supervisor's role. Open discussion of group processes helps in crystallizing such insight.

The interrelatedness of the two levels of discourse can be seen in an example — a supervision in which dealing with the seductive behavior of a male analysand emerged as a major source of difficulty for his female analyst. Our open and fruitful work on this issue was enhanced by prior discussion, during our first supervisory session, which took place before the analysis started. As is usual, I encouraged the supervisee to tell me of any past interactions we had had that might influence her feeling in supervision. She brought up an interaction from years back, when we had been acquainted professionally in another setting, in which she had experienced a compliment I gave her as seductive. Our straightforward conversation about that episode turned out to be a valuable springboard for our subsequent work on erotized transference issues, because the possible resonances between sexual currents in analysis and supervision (e.g., the erotic atmosphere that might evolve in supervision when the analysand's sexual fantasies about the analyst are discussed) became less threatening to both of us as a result of the effective working through of such themes in our own relationship.

Exploration of the supervisory relationship was historically introduced and legitimized through the idea of a parallel process (Searles, 1955, 1962; Arlow, 1963; Doehrman, 1976) in which there are direct influences of the patient–therapist relationship on the supervisory dyad. This was a valuable starting point, but today we can better recognize the risks involved in that conceptual framework. Ekstein and Wallerstein (1972) mentioned that "parallelism can work in reverse as well" (p. 196), and this point, which is often disregarded, was elaborated by Langs (1979) and by Gediman and Wolkenfeld (1980). Even more critically, Lesser (1984) listed parallel process as one of three illusions surrounding supervision (the other two being "the supervisor knows best" and "the supervisor is objective") that help the supervisor to avoid supervisory anxieties. Stimmel (1995) suggested, "Parallel process . . . may be used also as a resistance to awareness of transference phenomena within the supervisor in relation to the supervisee" (p. 609).

The difficulty is that the notion of parallel process simultaneously calls attention to the supervisory relationship and yet allows for displacement and rationalization of its difficulties, away from the supervisory dyad itself. When used unidirectionally and defensively, it may amount to a covert message from the supervisor to the supervisee: "The trouble you and I seem to experience is not really our own; it comes from your patient, and, if you solve it there, we'll be okay, too." Such attribution of issues to a third party, and the attempt to structure a dyadic relationship in a roundabout way through that third party, is what family therapists call *triangulation* (Winokur, 1982).

Parallel processes should be understood as one potential aspect of the complex network of cross-identifications within the supervisor–analyst–analysand triad (Gediman and Wolkenfeld, 1980; Wolkenfeld, 1990; Baudry, 1993). A dogmatic expectation to find exact parallels may become arbitrary and forced. Some supervisory stalemates may develop irrespective of who is the supervised analysand, and these stalemates require full attention despite being "unparalleled." What may be more productive is thorough thinking about the overall dynamics of the entire triad; these dynamics may include a potential "interdyadic transference–countertransference situation based on sequential identifications," as Frawley-O'Dea and Sarnat (2001, p. 174) redefined parallel process from a relational viewpoint.

Harris and Gold (2001), exploring a treatment case discussed in their joint supervisory work, spoke of a "highly complex, mutually constructed system of effects carried in the multiple dialogues of analytic work. In particular, we consider the bidirectional highway from supervisor–analyst dyad to treatment" (p. 366). The debate that subsequently developed between Brenneis (2002) and Harris (2002) about that case focused on, among other issues, the dominant direction in that bidirectional highway: Was it the impact of the patient's dissociative tendencies on the "fog" that supervisor and supervisee experienced during supervisory sessions, as Harris and Gold (2001) concluded, or the impact of the supervisor's thinking about dissociation on the therapist–patient dyad, as Brenneis (2002) suggested? Harris (2002) pinpointed an additional aspect, relevant to our conception of supervision: If "identity formation is seen as an experience emerging in the center of a dyadic interaction," is it seen as a "rather violent act of colonization" or in more benign intersubjective terms? (p. 1014).

When the supervisor–supervisee relationship is well understood, Kantrowitz (2002) demonstrated, noticing how the analyst's

encounter with the analysand influences the relationship may
also be possible. For example, if the direction proposed by a supervisor is ineffective with a particular analysand, the result
may be mutual disappointment and tension between supervisor
and supervisee (p. 961). Kantrowitz's detailed study of four
analysand–candidate–supervisor triads, based on interviews
with both candidate and supervisor, offers a valuable example
of the rich benefits of such intersubjective exploration. Kantrowitz chose to study only triads having beneficial effects, but,
as one of these cases underwent a change in supervisors, the experience of mismatch also arose.

The valuable contribution of joint exploration of the supervisory relationship was demonstrated by Sarnat (1992), who sum-
marized her main example:

> A supervisee's character problems became a focus of su-
> pervisory attention. The supervisor's conflicts (i.e., her im-
> patience to see her supervisee change, and her need to
> assert her own competence by too-active intervention)
> played into the student's problem (i.e., submissiveness),
> contributing to the development of a supervisory crisis. . . .
> The supervisor's acknowledgment of her contribution to
> the crisis seemed to shift the interpersonal context to one in
> which the supervisee could safely and vividly experience
> and process her own conflict. . . . Had the supervisor tried
> to "help" her with this problem, while pretending to be the
> uninvolved expert, the supervisee would very likely have
> felt humiliated and endangered [p. 399].

We must also keep in mind the risks involved in joint exploration of the process. I soon return to the issues of blurring the
boundaries between supervision and analysis and of possibly
pathologizing the supervisee. Another major risk has some com-
monality with a risk inherent in a "here-and-now" emphasis in
analysis itself: In both cases, a focus on the dyad may augment an
intense narcissistic absorption of the two partners in their exclusive relationship. In analysis, this can lead to a neglect of serious
issues in the analysand's life situation (Berman, 2001a). In supervision, a strong emphasis on the supervisory relationship can
lead to forgetting the patient. Similarly, a supervisory group may

actually turn into a group process workshop and abandon its supervisory goals.

There may certainly be stages (e.g., around crisis points) when such transformations are productive, and flexibility is beneficial. One criterion for successful resolution of a supervisory crisis, however, is a gradual return to the natural balance, in which understanding of the analysis or therapy is primary and understanding of the supervision itself is important but secondary.

Let me give now a fuller example of a supervisory process that ran into difficulty:

A supervisory session began with my supervisee telling me that she had met outside my building another candidate whose supervisory session preceded hers. She had told him that she would blame him for her arriving late, and he had laughed at her for taking things too seriously.

She then described two sessions she had had with her analysand after a vacation. In the first session, the analysand had smiled at her warmly when entering; later, he told her he had wanted to give her a good feeling. He had missed her during her vacation, but he had not felt shaken up, as he had during a previous break. He had almost gotten into his customary acting-out but thought of her and avoided it. Unlike before, he had been less prone to assume that she had gone skiing abroad — a change that for him implied seeing the two of them as less distant (for him, skiing signified her being an upper-class "lady"). He had apologized that he was still not in the mood for work, and he said that serious analysis would begin in the next session. He had expressed a wish to sit up, and mentioned that he had almost done so when he came in.

The analyst had then made an interpretation that today the analysand had come to the "absent her," but the analysand had not been able to understand what she meant. I admitted to my supervisee that I was not sure I understood either. (In retrospect, I see that "I don't understand" may have been a euphemism for "I disagree.") She apologized and said that she was in a holiday mood herself and was happy that work would resume only gradually. I suggested that both she and her analysand had too easily agreed that "no work was going on," whereas this session was very valuable. The analysand had described an important transition in the transference — a feeling of intimacy rather than of awe, a greater capacity to use his analyst as a protective internalized object, a deeper capacity to experience gratitude, and much less of his customary depreciatory self-blaming.

The supervisee then attributed her own reaction in the session to her need to give "deep" interpretations, and she related this reaction to a difficulty that had arisen between us recently — around her disappointment that I do not help her to develop such deeper interpretations. Her comment coincided with my feeling, which I shared with her, that she experiences me (as she sees the candidate who came before her?) as too "light," as belittling the severity of her analysand's condition. She disagreed with my use of the word *belittling* but felt that "making light of" indeed described her experience. She and her analysand, she commented, both have "heavy" superegos. I told her that I felt a bit clearer as to the source of the difficulty between us.

In the second session, she now reported, the analysand had arrived late and felt very guilty. She had tried to reflect his harshness in judging himself — he worked very hard and had to schedule his sessions at peak-traffic morning times so as not to neglect his work — and his attempt to turn her into a scolding boss. He had responded by expressing disbelief that she really was not shocked by his coming late. I asked her whether she had pursued his disbelief further. When she said no, I wondered about it. (I think that I may have been influenced by the way our session had begun with her own fear of being late, but this did not come up directly in our discussion.) I also shared with her a thought — that she repeatedly tries to confront her analysand's rigidity but that something in the atmosphere of the sessions does not supply an alternative pole, an option of "playing" and not only "working." She responded that her patients rarely laughed during sessions, although there were individual differences.

These related issues, in the analytic dyad and in our own relationship, were further explored in the next sessions. A few months later, my supervisee told me that she wanted to switch supervisors. For several weeks, we discussed her wish, explored her expectations for supervision and the way they diverged from our actual work, and discussed our mutual experiences of each other. I supported the legitimacy of her wanting to switch supervisors and saw this option as an expression of the freer atmosphere in our institute. At the same time, I told her that I was sad that we were apparently not able to fully resolve our difficulties, in spite of repeated efforts.

I also found myself concerned whether her leaving might deter other candidates from seeking supervision with me, but I felt that such concerns should not be shared with her at this time. (Naturally, supervisor self-disclosure is an option to be contemplated with full attention to both possible benefits and potential risks, such as unduly burdening the supervisee.)

In retrospect, I feel that her decision indicated that I may not have been sufficiently empathic and patient in my attempts to encourage this talented trainee to allow herself to become a "lighter," more playful analyst. Possibly, I failed to understand fully what she found appealing about being "heavy" — her apparent equating of depth, seriousness, and severity. Was I a "bull in a china shop"?

When discussing this issue with the supervisee some years later, after she had read a draft of this chapter, she suggested that we did not give sufficient attention to the impact of the theoretical differences between her mostly British sources of inspiration (particularly Klein, Bion, and Meltzer) and the relational American emphases in my own work. Our theoretical differences, she felt, may explain the difficulties we had better than the more personal differences I had emphasized.

I believe that, though our discussions did not stop her from switching supervisors, and though we never reached full agreement about the nature of our differences, our frank and open exploration of these differences helped lead to a nontraumatic outcome for our supervisory crisis and to our maintaining a good relationship.

The Triad in the Context of
Institutional Dynamics

The analytic-supervisory triad does not exist in a vacuum. An intersubjective understanding, for me, also requires paying attention to the influences of broader organizational, cultural, and historical currents on the subjective experiences of all individuals involved — which may be described as moving from a two-person psychology toward a multiple-person psychology. The supervisory relationship is often colored by its institutional context and its atmosphere (Shane and Shane, 1995; Fraser, 1996; Jaffe, 2000) and by the transferential feelings both supervisor and supervisee develop toward their organization.

Except for supervisions arranged privately, most supervisory dyads operate in the broader institutional context of an analytic/clinical training program or of a treatment agency. The institution typically has its own agenda — ideologic commitment to a particular therapeutic or analytic approach, economic considerations (which may dictate preference to longer or to shorter treatments), recommending hospitalization (if budgets depend on "filling beds") or avoiding it, safeguarding its reputation, and so forth. Besides having such specific goals, most institutions are invested in maintaining control over staff and trainees (maintaining control involves collecting a considerable amount of information about these people). All these goals, though not relevant to the quality of learning in supervision, may yet be the source of considerable pressure on both supervisor and supervisee — and are at times rationalized by the organization in order that it might continue to appear to be motivated by more intrinsic values.

The influence of the institutional context can also be conceptualized as an additional set of transferences. If the patient is seen within an institutional setting, the patient is likely to develop a unique transferential attitude to the setting (clinic, hospital, etc.) that is often distinct from the transference to the therapist: "You understand me, but they don't" or "I am mad at you for leaving, but I trust them to assign me another therapist, hopefully one more experienced." Reider (1953) described traumatized patients who were unable to sustain an intimate relationship and who found it easier to fantasize being cared for by a motherly institution, the hospital. Meyerson and Epstein (1976) talked of analysands who split off their unreliable candidate/ analysts from the psychoanalytic institute, which they experienced as reliable and nurturant. I would argue that these are extreme forms of a widespread phenomenon that may often go unrecognized in its subtler forms, possibly because it threatens the therapist's self-image.

The therapist, as an employee or trainee, naturally has transferential feelings toward the setting (as a prestigious place to which one is proud to belong, as a disappointing substitute, as generous or exploitative, etc.); so does the supervisor, as an employee or faculty member (gratified or frustrated, secure or struggling for recognition, etc.). Besides having a transference to the setting as a whole, therapist and supervisor each may have transference–countertransference patterns with specific authority figures within it (e.g., being the director's favorite or rival).

My point is that all these transferential currents (I am using the term in its broader sense, which does not exclude realistic perceptions) may influence the supervisory process. The different agendas and feelings may coincide or clash. Let me give a few examples:

1. Patient, therapist, and supervisor create an alliance to prove to the clinic director that continuing treatment for another year is crucial—though contrary to clinic rules or economic interests.

2. Analysand and candidate/analyst both feel that, at the present stage of the analysis, conducting it face-to-face will be better, and they view the institute's insistence on using the couch as dogmatic and coercive. The supervisor, identified more with institute ideology, may see their decision as acting out—or may fear for his or her status if their new way of conducting analysis is legitimized.

3. Supervisor is secretly, maybe unconsciously, gratified that treatment is failing, because assignment of the case (or admission of the trainee into the program) was decided by another faculty member whom the supervisor despises and would be delighted to expose as incompetent.

In a similar direction, Ehrlich (2003) analyzed the way the unique meaning of training for the candidate influences the analytic process with this candidate's patients. This unique meaning, Ehrlich demonstrated, is more influential than the general universal impact of training, which receives more attention in the literature.

Many clinical and analytic training programs view the sharing of information about supervisees as highly desirable. Indeed, one can think of instances in which the impressions of a supervisor clarify for a colleague the nature of a confusing impasse with the same trainee. On the other hand, sharing supervisors' views before a new supervision begins may reduce the chance that a new pattern would unfold in the new dyad (Langs, 1979, p. 90; Shevrin, in Wallerstein, 1981). In some situations, moreover, group discussion may lead to an impasse in an ongoing process, as in this example:

In a faculty meeting, a supervisor was surprised to discover that his (moderately positive) evaluation of a supervisee stood in marked contrast to the harsh judgments made by several colleagues. Although he defended his supervisee during the meeting, the supervisor was left burdened with concerns that he had been manipulated by his supervisee, that he had been too lenient, and so forth. Over the next few weeks, he found himself responding to the supervisee's reports with much more criticism. The trainee, an anxious young man who had previously experienced this supervisor as his only ally in the program, became even more anxious and isolated, and his clinical performance deteriorated.

Shevrin (in Wallerstein, 1981, p. 315) raised the hazard that interpretations of individual transference in supervision may be abused to deny the reality of influences of an institutional context — in his case, the power structure of a psychoanalytic institute (cf. Berman and Segel, 1982). The possibility of such abuse must be recognized, as serious exploration of the supervisory encounter should be based on a full understanding of its realistic setting (including transferences to the institution by both supervisor and supervisee) rather than on denial of reality factors.

Open joint exploration of the intersubjective dimension of supervision itself, including the supervisor's personal contribution, becomes even more crucial if we want to counteract these risks and learn "how to supervise without doing harm" (Wolf, 1995).

The institution has a major influence on evaluation. Around evaluation, power becomes most visible. Harris and Gold (2001) reminded us, "If power is not yet adequately theorized in the analytic dyad, it is surely even less elaborated in supervisory dyads" (p. 367). Joint exploration of the impact of the supervisor's evaluative role may become vital, as this role may potentially sabotage supervision as a meaningful mutual learning process—tilting the crucial balance between comfort and challenge (Kantrowitz, 2002, p. 959).

Inherent in any serious supervision are critical-evaluative elements—enthusiasm or concern, pinpointing of blind spots, suggested changes. Within the functioning supervisory dyad, vulnerability to criticism can be contained and worked through, and possible insults can be discussed and resolved. This work is easier when the supervisor avoids assuming an omniscient position and is willing to examine her or his role in difficulties—putting evaluation too in an intersubjective context. Such openness, and basic trust in the candidate's capacity for future growth, creates a background of safety that makes it possible for the supervisor to express criticism honestly. Exploration of personal aspects of countertransference, some of which may be experienced as arousing guilt or shame, is also naturally easier in a more egalitarian and friendlier atmosphere: "Transmission . . . occurs most effectively when a particular content, strongly and sincerely believed, is communicated from one person to the next in the context of a loving relationship" (Druck, 2000, p. 897).

In contrast to straightforward face-to-face criticism within an intimate dyad, reports to institutional committees take evaluation out of its intersubjective context, give it the pretense of selfless objective judgment, and cut it off from the setting in which criticism can promote change. Committees may spend long hours discussing trainees' personalities—in what borders on a clinical case conference or degenerates into gossip—but they can do little to help in the development of a troubled younger colleague. Moreover, existence of an elaborate evaluation system may allow the supervisor to "pass the buck" and avoid developing an honest critical discourse within supervision. As mentioned in chapter 3, anonymous institutional feedback often leads to a defensive, anxious confrontation while reducing the chance for more serious in-depth learning within the supervisory dyad. Effective learning, I suggest, is most enhanced by a supervisor who is openly critical but also self-critical and who is willing to explore openly the way this criticism is experienced—reducing as much as possible any reporting to external authorities, and discussing any such reporting openly within supervision (Caruth, 1990; Sarnat, 1992). "When candidates feel more confident, they are less prone to fear criticism or experience shame, and are more receptive to learning something new" (Kantrowitz, 2002, p. 960).

Of course, extreme cases (ethical misconduct, dangerous incompetence) raise the question as to whether a younger colleague's training or work should be discontinued, and then deliberations by a committee may be necessary. Luckily, such cases are rare. When they occur, a special initiative may have to be taken — one that would not burden all other trainees with ongoing stressful discussions and endless evaluation forms. Even if the institution needs a formal evaluation of trainees toward the conclusion of training, in my experience such procedures can be easily minimized if learning itself, rather than control, is the purpose.

In supervision taking place outside any institutional context — in which the supervisee is an independent professional who has completed training — issues of power and of intrinsic (informal) evaluation may still appear on a deeper transferential emotional basis, and these issues still need to be addressed. One way to transform their impact may be through peer supervision or mutual supervision (Harris and Ragen, 1993), in which exploration of countertransference and of the analytic process is conducted in the spirit of joint self-analysis.

Boundaries Between Supervision and Analysis

My focus on exploring personal experiences in supervision — countertransference to patient, kernels of truth found in patient's view of analyst's personality, transference to supervisor and to institution — naturally raises the old issue of the boundaries between analysis and supervision. In a way, my approach could bring me closer to the view of the Budapest school (Balint, 1948) — that the ideal supervisor is the trainee's analyst.

Nevertheless, I disapprove of this suggestion and on this rare occasion agree with Eitingon's opposite view. A trainee's having his or her analyst as supervisor (simultaneously or even if supervision is planned to start after analysis), in spite of its learning potential, may undermine the depth of the analysis, discourage the expression of negative transference, dilute work on termination, and introduce an unanalyzable collusion. The situation may lead to a total uncritical identification with an analyst-supervisor-mentor as an exclusive transferential figure — undermining the conflict and complementarity of competing identifications, which in the long run are conducive in the search for one's unique and autonomous analytic self. Moreover, as discussed in chapter 5, analysis of future analysts benefits from being a very private affair, not directly mobilized for training goals and therefore unregulated and uninterfered with by training settings. The basic positions of a supervisor (loyal, as I described earlier, to both supervisee and patient, and to institutional goals as well) and of an analyst (loyal, in my conception, to the analysand alone) are substantially different.

My image of good analytic training thus maintains the coexistence of, and at times the troublesome split between, a personal analyst (preferably more than one along the way) and several supervisors; a degree of overlap between the contents of analysis and supervision (Lester and Robertson, 1995); and continual exploration of their complex interaction within analysis and at times within supervision as well. Each candidate–personal analyst–supervisor triangle may arouse new meaningful issues, and the significance given to the different figures may not match their declared functions. The total milieu of the institute creates a complex transferential network in which various transferential roles are played by different figures (a phenomenon often observed in group analysis). In this context, the planned division of labor between analysis and supervision may become partial and secondary for the candidate. Supervisors may be experienced as auxiliary analysts — and the analyst as an auxiliary supervisor. Actually, "candidates often speak informally of their selection of a supervisor to compensate for perceived deficiencies in their training analyst" (Kantrowitz, 2002, p. 960). Moreover, when the candidate's problems are similar to those of the analysand, the supervisor's understanding of these problems "may in displacement be therapeutically beneficial," even though it may at times generate too much anxiety and interfere with learning (p. 964).

The next example, coming from an analysis, clarifies the way in which supervision may become, in the candidate's inner reality, an extension of analysis:

The analysand described a dilemma he had experienced with a case not in supervision — a young female patient in psychotherapy. The patient had been enraged with her mother, with whom she lived, for not pampering her enough, for not buying her the cinnamon rolls she loved eating in the morning. The therapist was torn between two different inner voices suggesting how to react to the patient's rage. One voice advocated challenging the patient to explore how she could pamper herself more and encouraging her to grow out of her prolonged dependency. (He identified this voice with me. In the past, he had told me that he noticed that at times I do not encourage regression in his analysis, which was both a relief and a disappointment to him.) The other voice advocated fully empathizing with the patient's regressive yearnings. (This voice he identified with one of his analytic supervisors — a female analyst who saw regression as a major curative element.)

In principle, the therapist knew that the dialogue between these two voices — and maybe also with the voices of his former analyst and of other supervisors — could be enriching and productive in gradually fostering his own individual integration. But emotionally he was torn. He was reminded of a period, during his army service, when he had had two commanding officers. He recalled how one had often shouted, "Faster, faster!" and the other had said, "Calm down, slow down." The combination of the contrasting voices made him anxious.

He was also reminded of a period of crisis he had experienced with another patient and of his feeling a gap between what had emerged from his work with me and with that supervisor. In that crisis, he had found an effective interpretive direction that had drawn on both voices — taking what suited him from both his supervisor and me. He said that he realized that doing so was easier then because of his awareness that the supervisor and I were good friends.

The therapist's parents had divorced during his childhood, and the breakup had been total. They had lived utterly different lifestyles, in two different cities. His home, he once joked, had been on the bus in between. He had identified entirely with one parent and maintained an emotional distance from the other, in spite of regular visits. The new spouse of one parent had often criticized the other parent. To avoid conflict, the boy had avoided talking about each parent with the other. There had been no hope of integration.

He now realized how new the present situation was for him. He spoke with his supervisor about his analysis, and he spoke with me about his supervision. Our different views, to which we both seemed very committed, did not stop his supervisor and me from being friends, and he did not feel that either of us demanded total loyalty of him. Still, handling our differences was not easy for him.

This analysand "borrowed" the analytic experience with me as an indirect supervision (making me a potential role model) and "borrowed" the supervisory work with my colleague as a partial analytic experience. In that supervision, he received legitimization for regressive needs, which he found were less gratified with me. Did he want to encourage me, I wonder, to allow more space for his own yearning for his version of a cinnamon roll?

Although the analytic setting offers ideal conditions for full exploration of such a process, I also experienced fruitful discussions of similar dynamics with some supervisees, and this exploration aided in improving supervisory work.

Telling trainees to "bring it up in your analysis" is of no use in my experience, for many reasons. It is intrusive and unrealistic (a genuine analytic process cannot follow assignments); it deprives supervision of the understanding of crucial issues, without which we cannot figure out what goes on in the treatment discussed and in the supervisory relationship itself; and it may be experienced as conveying a rule- or role-dominated avoidance rather than involvement and openness to full analytic learning.

When I am totally unaware of a supervisee's private life and major personal concerns, I may be grappling in the dark in an attempt to understand many issues in his or her work with analysands. Communicating with the supervisee's analyst (DeBell, 1963) would be a violation of confidentiality on both sides. Such paternalistic informal conversations often turn out to be detrimental to both analysis and supervision (Langs, 1979) — interfering in the formation of a unique relationship in each setting and supplying both analyst and supervisor with "forbidden knowledge" that is not usable because of its external source. The ethical option is to create in supervision a tolerant and attentive atmosphere that will make it easier for trainees (only if they wish, of course) to share personal associations and feelings whenever they appear to be potentially relevant to the task at hand or whenever their relevance is intuitively sensed.

A personal example of facilitating such exploration comes to mind. I sensed that a supervisee had responded intolerantly to her analysand's cancellation of some sessions, which had come as a consequence of progress in the analysand's vocational and personal life. I shared with my supervisee a spontaneous association to my own feelings of frustration and jealousy when my daughter had less time to spend with me as a result of her expanding involvement with her peers. The supervisee then recalled similar themes with her own children and related them to her countertransference toward her analysand.

Without direct communication about personal matters, we may remain at times in the dark as to the significance of what we observe in supervision, as in this example:

A supervisee's behavior in sessions was marked by a strict routine, pedantic reading of process notes, and intellectualization. I tended to see these as character traits, until I brought up my observations. It turned out that the supervisee was in many situations intensely emotional, spontaneous, and impulsive and was very concerned that her behavior might harm her work as a therapist and her chances of learning. In her fantasy, supervision became a testing ground for a yearned-for capacity for mastery and control. Our discussion led to her greater flexibility.

In principle, no personal topic is, for me, out of place in supervision. A supervisee's impending divorce may be a major influence on countertransference to analysands; a childhood event may be the source of identification with a particular patient; a dream may offer the key to the stalemate in a certain case.
Another example:

A young trainee assigned an older female patient immediately expressed concern that the patient seemed to resemble his mother. After the first session, he reported with relief that he saw no similarity. A month later, however, he described annoyance with the patient, hope that she would miss her sessions, and difficulty in remembering their interactions. On exploration, he indicated that these are his typical reactions vis-à-vis his clinging, dependent mother. Further discussions of both mother and patient eventually enabled him to differentiate the two better in his mind and to empathize more with the patient.

When the connection between a supervisee's personal history and the case presented does not come up — out of a feeling on either side that "this does not belong here" — the countertransference may remain utterly clouded. When such a major emotional reality remains unverbalized, supervision may acquire an "as if" quality. Supervisor and supervisee go through the motions of discussing the patient or even some "safe" aspects of countertransference (e.g., annoyance about resistance, aspects of role responsiveness that can be attributed to the patient and that are not personally revealing), whereas emotions that for the supervisee are most powerful during the sessions (those related to personal associations) remain hidden, with no chance that their influence will be discussed.

Naturally, even when personal issues come up openly, the extent, direction, and style of exploration in analysis and in supervision differ significantly. I do not advocate turning supervision into a "mini-analysis." The personal analyst, attempting to reach the deepest and broadest understanding, proceeds openmindedly with no immediate goals; the supervisor, much more selective and goal oriented, focuses on these aspects of the personal theme that can be directly related to visible consequences and dilemmas in the trainee's work with patients and within supervision itself.

Likewise, the supervisor wants to identify the supervisee's transference toward her or him but without searching for its deeper historical roots — at times simply relying on the trainee's account as a summary of analytic work already done. The more crucial focus within supervision is instead on possible reality influences (e.g., impact of the supervisor's personality) and on effective resolution of troublesome consequences of transference-countertransference entanglements in supervision (e.g., anxiety, inhibition, antagonism, estrangement).

Whereas in analysis negative transference, or erotic transference, must often be allowed to develop fully, and premature attempts to dissolve it are usually counterproductive, the supervisor is more likely to try to quickly establish (or reestablish) a calmer, friendlier atmosphere that is more conducive to fulfilling the shared goals of this team.

We must bear in mind that a more personal focus of supervision, of the kind I advocate here, increases the risk (which exists in any supervision) that supervisory work will become intrusive and threatening for the supervisee. Exploration of the supervisee's transference to the supervisor or countertransference to the patient may unwittingly evolve into infantilizing or "pathologizing" the supervisee. This is particularly true when the discussion is imposed by the supervisor without much attention given to the supervisee's wishes, when it is conducted from a position of omniscience and pseudo-objectivity, and when the supervisor avoids exploring his or her own countertransference. Consider this example:

A supervisee reported to his supervisor that he had consulted another faculty member regarding his case. The supervisor noticed a smile on the student's face and interpreted it as an expression of sadistic victory over her. She further discussed sadistic elements in the student's personality. The student knew there was a point to the supervisor's comment. However, he felt unable to acknowledge it or to discuss it openly, as he felt too threatened by his condemning supervisor, who would not acknowledge her own sadistic side, evident in the harsh formulation of the interpretation. The tension was never fully resolved.

A supervisor willing to discuss some of his own countertransference as well (Langs, 1979, p. 193) stands a better chance of bringing about a freer discussion of pathologic aspects of the supervisee's reactions without becoming intrusive and humiliating. A mutual search into both partners' contributions to a difficulty is more likely to lead to greater trust and to a relief of tension originating from transferential fears and distortions. Coburn (1997) discussed an interesting case of self-disclosure by a supervisor, but Brown and Miller (2002) pointed out its boundaries: "The supervisor's impatience and sense of constriction towards her supervisee [were] highlighted, but with no reference to what [these] meant to her personally" (p. 815). These authors' work on mutual self-disclosure, including dreams the supervisor and supervisee shared with each other, expressed a move beyond resolving supervisory difficulties and toward fuller exploration of the triadic intersubjective supervisory field — uncovering the "confluence of the interlocking unconscious processes of the patient, analyst and supervisor" (Brown and Miller, 2002, p. 814).

Transitional Space Evolving in Supervision

In supervision, a warm and open personal atmosphere and an "ambience of self-disclosure" (Coburn, 1997) may facilitate much fuller creative use of the supervisory situation—which in turn, aided by giving attention to immediate affective nuances and to reverie, may approximate what Ogden (1995, part iii especially) described in speaking of the "analytic third." One might also say that what develops is a "supervisory fourth" (Brown and Miller, 2002, p. 820) with its own new life.

The inner freedom achieved may allow supervision with an intersubjective focus to evolve into a transitional space, within which the dyad generates new meanings not accessible by the intrapsychic work of each partner in isolation. Supervisor and supervisee become a true generative dyad.

Consider this session with a supervisee:

The supervisee began our session by telling me of his difficulty in writing down the sessions he was having with the female analysand whose analysis I was supervising. The sessions themselves, however, he experienced as being quite good. At times, his analysand arrived five minutes early, and he enjoyed meeting her need and starting early, which he had rarely done with other patients. During the sessions of the preceding week, he had found himself feeling drowsy. The analysand praised him for his soft, gentle side, which "enables her things."

I voiced my thoughts about two possible meanings of his difficulty in writing: Was he deeply relating to an early, primary, preverbal side of his analysand, which was difficult to put into words, or was his avoidance motivated by anxiety?

He recalled that his analysand had said about some topic that he should discuss it with his female supervisor. (In Hebrew, one cannot say "supervisor" without specifying gender.) The supervisee's other analysand, a man with whom he felt much more on his guard, referred to a male supervisor, whereas that case was actually supervised by a woman.

Drawing on our past conversations, I commented how issues of masculinity and femininity come up here in a complex manner. He conveyed to me that, in the analysis with the critical male analysand, he was constantly feeling threatened and attacked, whereas with his female analysand and me, whom he seemed to experience as feminine-motherly, he felt relaxed, drowsy, more in a "being" state that inhibited "doing" (writing).

I reminded him of recent episodes in which his female analysand had criticized him for not being strong (manly?) enough. In one instance, when she had felt that he had not done enough to stop some noise that was irritating her, she went at the end of the session to protest to the noisy person herself, as if she were telling her analyst, "If you have no balls, I'll take command." This phallic side of her, I recalled, had aroused anxiety and embarrassment in him.

He then began describing the sessions. The analysand had spoken of the anxiety she experienced when she heard an alarm in the house of a bereaved neighbor, a woman who had lost her child in a terrorist attack. The analysand had had a fantasy that her neighbor might have committed suicide. Then, suddenly, she had commented, "From the place you sit you see bodies." They had both been perplexed by this comment, and I told him I was too. The Hebrew word she had used, *gufa,* implies a dead body but is close to the word for a live body, *guf.* He said that her comment had made him more attentive to her *gufa.* When I asked if that was a slip of the tongue, he told me of a slang expression (which I had not known) in which a woman's body is referred to this way. I spoke of the defensive significance of this slang usage and related it to common jokes based on the multiple significance of another Hebrew word, *shahav* ("lay down"), which has both a strong sexual meaning (roughly equivalent to "slept with") and a connotation of death (the biblical "lay down with his forefathers").

The analysand had then spoken of her tendency to buy ornamental items for her house, and my supervisee said that he had felt reserved then because he experienced her as being too "or-nate." She had specifically talked of an unidentified item that she called "tomba" and described as seeming to be like a coffin. She had commented that she was building a little temple in her house.

This material brought to my mind a recent visit to Egypt. I told my supervisee of a comment a guide there had made about the small investment ancient Egyptians made in their lifetime houses compared with the enormous investment they made in their "death houses," their tombs. My supervisee related this to the Jewish traditional view that life is but a corridor to the parlor of afterlife.

Then I recalled that this analysand had sought treatment im-mediately after her neighbor's child had been killed, and I sug-gested that only now were the emotional reverberations of that event surfacing for her. Her saying "From the place you sit you see bodies" attributes to the analyst an awesome perspective of an eternal observer who sees generations come and go, babies grow up, become children and then adults, grow old and die. Her "little temple" represented her preoccupation with death, which she had difficulty integrating with other sides of herself as a practical and goal-directed woman.

The analyst then recalled that, during the next sessions, the analysand had found lying down on the couch difficult. Our time was up.

The analyst's difficulty in writing down sessions—not being defined as necessarily a resistance or an obstacle to our work—proved to be a springboard for further understanding. During the session, our focus shifted from issues of gender identity and affec-tive states to issues of life and death, sexuality and annihilation anxiety.

For me, this supervisory session is a rich example of the way in which transitional space can evolve in the supervisory dyad and allow it to generate meaning in a way equivalent to, resonant with, and supplementary to the analytic dyad. Although we did not discuss any purely personal contents (my supervisee's or mine), the atmosphere of the session was personal and close, which I believe helped make it more creative.

The combined analytic-supervisory team may allow intersub-jective trends in the triad to develop and come into awareness—

promoting their verbalization and elaboration in a way that is at times more difficult to achieve in the isolation of the unsupervised analytic dyad alone. It is to be hoped that this generativity in the supervisory space will in turn extend into the analytic space as well.

A Broad Range of Options

I do not strive to crystallize a new general technique of supervision. Not believing in a standard analytic technique, I certainly do not advocate a standardization of supervision. I highlight certain dynamic processes and try to legitimize their open exploration, but undoubtedly the specific focus and style of each supervisory dyad will always depend on the unique personalities of both partners and will be also influenced by the analysand, by the candidate's analyst, by the institute or an equivalent setting, and by contemporary values and national culture (Berman, 2000d).

Supervision benefits from evolving through a flexible mutual adaptation in which the needs of both partners have a role, as each is recognized as a subject by the other (Slavin, 1998). Supervisors are different as individuals and as analysts. Some may use their awareness of nuances in the supervisory relationship as a basis for improving supervision without ever discussing the relationship directly, whereas others may be more prone to bring it up as a topic. Supervision requires making constant choices, as what comes up in each session can be understood on numerous different levels. These choices may be wiser when based on attentive analytic understanding of the intrapsychic and intersubjective dynamics involved; routine solutions of any kind may endanger the freshness and depth of the needed scrutiny.

If we stick rigidly to a preformed agenda, if we allow supervision to become routinized, we may unwittingly transmit an inflexible mode of interaction that will show up in the trainees' clinical work as well. If difficulties in the supervisory process remain unexpressed, supervision runs the risk of developing into a narrow, formal interaction in which the most powerful emotions present in the room are taboo. Such a stifling situation may breed an "as if" supervision.

In my own supervisory work, I find myself being quite different with various supervisees. The degree to which personal issues come up and the nature of boundaries in general vary considerably, and this variance seems to be influenced both by the conscious wishes of supervisees and by more subtle transference–countertransference patterns in each relationship. In some supervisory dyads, the process itself is explored in joint curiosity; in others, it remains quiet in the background. Imposing one's values and preferences (e.g., insisting that the supervisee share his or her life story or deeper transferential reactions toward the supervisor) is counterproductive. Enforced egalitarianism (possibly based on a fantasy of "rescuing the victim," e.g., the underprivileged candidate; see chapter 3) could be as aggressive as authoritarian paternalism and even more confusing. Moreover, in the course of one supervisory process, there may be different stages and unique moments that require new creative approaches.

In my earlier work on supervision (Berman, 1988b), the issue of resistance to supervision, and of the supervisor's counter-resistance, had a central role. Over the years, the notion of resistance has become less meaningful to me, both in analysis and in supervision. Today, I focus more on inherent conflicts between dyad members' differing wishes and goals, which may include conservative goals such as avoiding pain or embarrassment. Although I still believe that in some instances supervisees resist supervision per se — because of fear of threatening change, because of envy, and because of other individual dynamics that block any new learning or any learning that is not autodidactic — my guess is that the more common source of difficulty is a specific and often unverbalized conflict between supervisor and supervisee, who do not manage to work out together a supervisory agenda that suits both of them. In extreme cases, this process may create stagnation, impasses, and negative supervisory reactions that are unconsciously coconstructed by supervisor and supervisee.

In conclusion, my hope is not to offer any universal methods but to outline a broad range of options that supervisors and trainees alike can take advantage of in facilitating, molding, and enriching their personal ways of learning.

7

Training for the Future

What we need . . . is a new orientation of our training system which must aim less at establishing a new and firm superego but more at enabling the candidate to free himself and to build up a strong ego which shall be both critical and liberal at the same time.

—Michael Balint
"On the Psychoanalytic Training System"

The greatest mistake we could make is to consider our present training system as a final, or even settled, solution of our many problems.

—Michael Balint
"Analytic Training and Training Analysis"

Expectations of the future are crucial in shaping the present. In this chapter, I take into account the role of social and cultural processes as I explore some of the implications of a future perspective for present-day training.

I have confidence in the future of psychoanalytic treatment, but I assume it may undergo radical changes in the years to come. My confidence is related to a broad definition of psychoanalytic treatment as a synonym for a "talking cure" rather than as any specific technique related to any particular theoretical model. Freud's genius, I believe, lay first and foremost in discovering the rich potential for understanding and transformation inherent in the continual patient and attentive dialogue of two individuals—in which the dynamics of the dialogue itself are of interest and through which the emotional currents of each individual become illuminated.

Core and Periphery

Use of a couch, specific frequencies and durations, additional "rules of the game," theoretical concepts regarding mental life—

227

all these can further facilitate this process of transformation, but they also run the risk of ossifying and inhibiting it. In the coming decades, the specifics may change in many ways, including ways we cannot foresee, but the core of listening to affective nuances, observing subjective and intersubjective subtleties, looking for words for them, struggling with the conflictuality of the process — this backbone, I believe, will survive.

My conclusion is that the core of psychoanalytic training is not the teaching of any specific technique or any specific theoretical model but the development of a unique state of mind and of particular sensitivities that facilitate better empathic and introspective perceptiveness. Another crucial component is in-depth work on the unavoidable defensive processes that inhibit and sidetrack such perceptiveness in the analyst (Berman, 2003b).

The intellectual counterpart of this work is developing a critical understanding of the history of psychoanalysis, which may enable the future analyst to take advantage of the many fascinating theoretical models offered in this field over the past 120 years, while placing each of them in a social and biographical context. Such learning immunizes against dogmatism and ancestor worship and encourages a continual process of creative personal theorizing — attempting to generalize from one's own life experiences and clinical experiences, as our theorists did, rather than seeing their ideas as a binding absolute truth.

This combination has the best potential to educate analysts who not only will be competent practitioners in 2010 but could also help in reshaping psychoanalysis to meet the unknown challenges of 2030 or 2040.

Let me give an example of the differentiation between core and periphery — the issue of defining psychoanalysis in comparison with psychoanalytic psychotherapy. Exploration of differences between psychoanalysis and psychotherapy is of interest, but, in a social reality in which all the talking cures have come under harsh attack, an overemphasis on such inner dividing lines may serve the narcissism of small differences while neglecting the crucial contemporary debate about the legitimacy and value of psychoanalytic treatment as a whole. Moreover, when Kernberg (1999) discussed indications for psychoanalysis versus those for psychoanalytic psychotherapy, he did not allow for the possibility that many such choices are nowadays made mostly by patients. In the experience of many analysts, the major difference between patients in analysis and patients in psychotherapy often does not reside in any diagnostic criteria but in the fact that the former have consented to come several times a week (which is desirable to most analysts), whereas the latter declined (Berman, 2001a).

How can we define analysis in the context of training? Although numerous intriguing attempts have been made to differentiate the goals of analysis from those of therapy (Wallerstein, 1989; Kernberg, 1999), the most clear difference is often in the setting, and only the setting can be legislated as part of training. At the same time, the relation of the setting to the depth of analytic process — our substantial goal — may not be linear.

I consider the couch a marvelous invention. In many analyst-analysand dyads, it facilitates for both partners the capacity for freer expression and self-observation and thus paradoxically allows better understanding of the analyst–analysand interaction (Ogden, 1996). Still, in some other dyads, or at some stages of certain analyses, it may become a hindrance that fosters schizoid tendencies or inhibits communication. Similarly, numerous sessions a week — in my personal experience, four, but I could imagine enjoying the luxury of having five or six — usually allow for greater continuity, for a freer space for all levels of discourse (past and present, reality and fantasy, dreams and momentary experiences), for a better chance to be surprised by unexpected developments. On the other hand, when the number of sessions is experienced as burdensome and as arbitrarily imposed (being nonnegotiable), these benefits may be nullified. If a patient feels captive or fears being used for the analyst's needs (to have an "acceptable" case), the therapeutic value of this treatment may be compromised.

Training requires structure, and at the outset of one's analytic training a preliminary definition of what constitutes analysis is of value. At the same time, open exploration of the analytic process (fortified by an understanding of the historical context of psychoanalysis) supplies tools for gradually deconstructing this very definition.

At the Israel Psychoanalytic Institute, for example, candidates are expected to conduct three analyses of four sessions a week, on the couch, under continual supervision. I support this structure:

I greatly benefited from it in my own (second) training, and I believe so do my present analysands and supervisees. Still, when the question of a possible change comes up in a particular analysis (e.g., a shift to a face-to-face arrangement or to three sessions a week), an open negotiation process (Mitchell, 1993) is crucial. In this negotiation, I believe, the training needs of the candidate (which are often known to the patient) are a legitimate topic and consideration but cannot be the single decisive factor. When such a negotiation takes place, the candidate–supervisor dyad also needs the freedom to contemplate what serves best the analytic process and the analysand's needs as we understand them, and the institute must be tolerant of some exceptions to its rules.

Moreover, it is very important for me as a supervisor to emphasize that the needs of the patient come first, even if they clash with institute rules to a degree that may disqualify the case in terms of the requirements. For example, if an analysand of a candidate insists on switching to only one or two sessions a week — for reality reasons or because of emotional factors, and these often intermingle — this is no reason to stop treatment. The ethical responsibility of the clinician, I believe, is not nullified even if the patient breaks his initial commitment to greater frequency of sessions. Treatment should proceed according to what is feasible — whether on the couch or not is an issue to debate in terms of clinical effectiveness alone — and the candidate may have to look for another analytic case to satisfy institute requirements.

A decision to stop treatment if the patient will not come four times a week, on the other hand, even if justifiable on formal grounds, may be quite destructive and might raise serious ethical questions. This decision may leave the patient with an experience of having served as a guinea pig, as a tool for the analyst's personal goals, and the ensuing bitterness may sabotage future treatment as well. The trainee, in other words, is first and foremost a responsible independent clinician loyal to patients' needs; being an analytic trainee supplements this primary identity, never replaces it.

If training is successful in establishing a firm empathic foundation, allowing serious exploration of the significance of different treatment settings for each analysand, future flexibility will increase, it is hoped. In my own practice, the boundaries between analysis and therapy are fluid, as I make an effort to tailor settings to the needs of individual analysands. I may see some analysands face-to-face four times a week, because this arrangement works better for them; I may see others (typically long-term analysands who reduced their frequency but still enjoy the reclining position, or past analysands who returned) once or twice a week on the couch. When confronted by colleagues who insist on a firm boundary between analysis and therapy, I do not know how to define my work with some of these patients. Is it "theralysis" or "anarapy"?

When the boundaries between analysis and therapy are defined too sharply, patients can sustain numerous types of damage. For example, there is the danger that an experienced therapist who did good work with a patient will become much less effective after the patient begins analysis as part of the therapist's analytic training. The therapist may suddenly become much more passive and inhibited, out of awe (analysis as a sacred activity requiring "purity"), anxiety, or concern about the supervisor's opinion (Slavin, 1992, 1997). On the other hand, when the trainee manages to hold onto the good relationship established in therapy and then enriches it through the much closer scrutiny that the analytic setting allows, the new stage may be most beneficial in clarifying and gradually resolving issues that were quite unclear and mystifying when sensed, for example, in the procrustean bed of once-a-week therapy.

Another situation involves an analysand who goes into a serious crisis, can no longer tolerate the lack of eye contact, and is wisely seen face-to-face but is also being told by the analyst that the analysis is now terminated, because what is needed in a crisis is psychotherapy. The analysand may feel demoted or expelled or may see himself or herself as a failure, as no longer deserving the "real thing." A more flexible approach, without entering a debate about therapy versus analysis (labels that may be of little interest to individuals outside the professional milieu), would have enabled a pragmatic adaptation with no feeling of loss as well as a freer space to consider later whether the change should be temporary or permanent.

Not surprisingly, I view quite favorably the involvement of analysts and of psychoanalytic institutes in psychotherapy training—a role that some European colleagues are apprehensive about, as they fear a blurring of boundaries. Such involvement may have various forms, depending on local conditions and beliefs. Training in psychoanalysis and in psychoanalytically oriented psychotherapy may become a continuum in one comprehensive program, as at the New York University Postdoctoral Program in Psychotherapy and Psychoanalysis. Or, at the Israel Psychoanalytic Institute, it may be divided into separate interconnected programs, with considerable overlap in faculty. Israel Psychoanalytic Institute candidates train only in psychoanalysis (as mentioned in chapter 4, they are as a rule experienced psychotherapists already). However, two additional three-year programs are offered[1] — one for beginning clinical psychologists, social workers, and psychiatrists (a program on the fundamentals of dynamic psychotherapy) and the other for experienced professionals (a program of advanced courses and group supervision by analysts and senior analytic candidates, but without the extensive requirements of analytic training proper). Some of the more ambitious graduates of these programs end up seeking training in psychoanalysis as well.

Naturally, analysts can also make a valuable contribution in the initial training in psychotherapy of psychology and social work students, in practicum and internship settings, in psychiatric residency programs, and so forth. Although this book focuses on the dynamics of psychoanalytic training per se, many of the issues I raise are relevant in all these varied settings of dynamic clinical training.

Only time will tell which settings will be characteristic a few decades from now (and whether psychoanalysis and psychoanalytic psychotherapy will be perceived as different or as synonymous), but I hope our present trainees will be able to help mold the methods suitable for the social milieu of tomorrow.

------

[1]In addition to these programs, officially sponsored by the Israel Psychoanalytic Institute, several other psychotherapy programs exist — most affiliated with the universities, one organized privately by a group of analysts — in which many analysts teach and supervise. Some faculty members of these programs initiated the Tel Aviv Institute for Contemporary Psychoanalysis, mentioned in chapter 4.

Knowing and Using Oneself

I view the analytic process as coconstructed by analyst and analysand and as unique to each such dyad. I therefore dislike the terminology of "applying a technique" and instead value giving intense attention to who each trainee is and who his or her analysands are and to the unique mutual influence they exert continually on each other (the transference–countertransference cycle in its broadest definition). I believe it is within such sensitivity to the intersubjective context that richer familiarity with unconscious fantasies and unconscious processes evolves (I avoid the reified concept "The Unconscious").

A fuller appreciation of the antecedents (conscious and unconscious) and consequences (often unexpected) of each move of the analyst—whether an interpretation, an enactment, or a subtle emotional expression—is crucial in deciphering that cycle, as I tried to describe in chapter 6. Steadfast rules as to "what is analytic" are a hindrance to such sensitivity—a superego pressure that disturbs our listening. The useful place of superego voices in clinical psychoanalysis is in helping us develop and maintain ethical standards, which for me are the only absolute rules as to what can happen in psychoanalysis. Sensitivity to the risks of exploitation and abuse of patients is vital, and I believe training should be attentive to such risks, some of which evolve inadvertently.

Interest in figuring out "who one is" and what kind of an analyst one wishes to become could be a goal in many training analyses (Berman, 2003b), though we must beware of gaining too much confidence in our experience of "who we are," which can always be challenged by our analysands. Crastnopol (2003) spoke of the need "to factor in the influence of the practitioner's characterological underpinnings . . . discover aspects of the candidate's individuality that are likely to outlive the training analysis" (p. 381). Work in this direction counterbalances the unavoidable pull to identify with one's analyst(s), supervisors, and teachers. Although I believe that identification may have benign and constructive aspects, it may also have elements of "identifying with the aggressor" (Frankel, 2002) and may lead (as described in chapter 3) to the formation of a strong "false analytic self" component in one's evolving analytic identity, at times under the impact of a utopian New Person fantasy.

Today's theoretical diversity—to which I return later—reduces the risk of a uniform image inviting conformity, but at the same time it creates conflicts between competing identifications (as in the example I give in chapter 6), which can be resolved only with the help of patient self-exploration.

Clarifying the personal significance of various components of analytic style (firmer or more flexible boundaries, being more cautious or more expressive, putting the weight on intrapsychic interpretation or on intersubjective exploration and self-disclosure, etc.) and clarifying the personal sources of attraction and reservations toward competing theoretical models may clear the way to a freer and better integrated self-definition. This result (as described earlier) also requires exploring and working through relationships with authority figures past and present, issues of submission and rebellion, tendencies to acquiesce or seek approval, and so on. These questions are apparently the kind not asked in Ferenczi's analysis with Freud, with dire consequences in the long run.

A crucial aspect is exploring the appearance of such topics within the transference ("Am I expected to represent you?") and the countertransference ("Do I need to turn my analysands into disciples?"). In my own experience, a degree of self-disclosure by the analyst is at times helpful in working through such issues. During some of the crisis points in my society and institute, the positions my analysands took vis-à-vis my well-known involvement became crucial topics in their analyses.

My emphasis on giving continual attention to "who and where one (really) is" emotionally at any given moment is related to my belief that all aspects of countertransference can be used productively by the analyst. Naturally, we all have ego ideals, and as analysts we strive to be as competent and as effective as possible—developing various theoretical notions as to what is curative in psychoanalysis—but this wish can be dialectically counterbalanced by our lively attention to what actually happens beyond our choice and control. When the balance is tilted, a determination to be a certain way decreases our inner freedom and spontaneity and as a result reduces our capacity to understand more deeply. Overconfident models of the desirable analytic role may paradoxically reduce the usefulness of psychoanalysis as an open-ended setting in which unexpected insights and new experiences can evolve creatively. Some of the ideas regarding the desirable analytic position (scientific objectivity for Freud, achieving a corrective emotional experience for Alexander, empathic immersion facilitating our use as selfobjects for Kohut, etc.) can also be defined as prescribed countertransference.

Expanding the range of affective states that the analyst can identify, accept, and use reduces the suffocating inner pressure to respond "correctly" and helps replace guilt-ridden rhetorical questions ("Why am I not more empathic, more objective, more . . .?") with real questions ("What happens to me now in this dyad, and how can I understand it better?"). Giving up the "promise of magical union" (Poland, 2000), which can possibly be an aspect of our self-romanticization within a rescue fantasy, allows for a more secular, realistic psychoanalysis (Berman, 2000b).

Bollas (1987) wrote, "An analyst who is, as far as the patient can see and know, always helpful, kindly and understanding, may seem to that patient to be a wonderful man . . . [but] he may not have the feeling of having been fully known. This analyst will not have *lived through* the patient's childhood. This analyst will not feel the frustrations of the parents or the destructive ability of the child who is furious with the parent" (p. 253).

I find this quotation valuable as a warning against a view that limits useful countertransference reactions only to those that are directly empathic, only to feelings based on one of the two components identified by Racker (1968) in countertransference — on concordant identifications, in which we find ourselves "in the analysand's shoes," while rejecting complementary identifications with the analysand's objects, through which the "analyst acquires a further key of prime importance for the understanding of the transference" (p. 175). Tansey and Burke (1989), as I mentioned in chapter 6, further pursued Racker's line of thought by emphasizing that the objects in one's life also represent aspects of one's self, and, therefore, the "potential for an empathic outcome also lies in the successful processing of complementary identifications" (p. 58). Although the complementary emotional state may be momentarily adversarial, "what the therapist is experiencing at a particular moment may very well be something that the patient himself has experienced," and, therefore, the "initial complementary identification serves as a vehicle for an eventual concordant identification" (p. 59). This idea resonates with Ogden's (1983) analysis of the "formation of two new suborganizations of the ego, one identified with the self in the external object relationship and the other thoroughly identified with the object" (p. 234). Ogden concluded that Racker's complementary identification "involves the therapist's unconsciously identifying with the aspect of the patient's ego identified with the object" (p. 234). The subjective experience of the analyst, in whom such identifications may arouse guilt because of their unempathic and "treacherous" nature, is therefore misleading, as the identifications potentially form a springboard for a much richer and more complex empathic understanding.

An attempt to base one's analytic work only on concordant identifications—out of an idealization of immediate empathic immersion, of "being at one with the analysand"—sidetracks this dialectical relationship. It is problematic for several reasons (Berman, 2001a):

1. Such an attempt is forced, and it may lead to inner censorship of parts of the analyst's multifaceted spontaneous experience with the analysand—an experience that is in its totality a major source of insight into the analysand's emotional life. If aggressive reactions, for example, are cast aside by the analytic superego, we may end up with a depleted "prescribed countertransference."

2. Such determination may bind the analyst to certain aspects of the analysand's conscious self-experience (e.g., being victimized by others) while cutting off denied and projected aspects of the analysand's inner world, which may initially be expressed only by proxy (see example on p. 189).

3. Subsequently, a full intersubjective exploration of the evolving dyadic relationship is undermined, and the relationship may remain in the dark and possibly reach an impasse.

4. This artificial selection may reach the analysand's awareness and reduce her or his trust in the analyst's actual caring ("Your empathy is just a technique. Who knows how you really feel?") or contribute to the analysand's self-image as a weak, vulnerable child with whom one cannot speak openly.

5. The analyst's always positive attitude may contribute to guilt feelings in the analysand, who is not always feeling positive

toward the analyst. Anger and criticism may be experienced as ingratitude.

6. The analysand may wonder: If my analyst cannot tolerate his or her own aggression, it must be a very frightening area. What is my chance of dealing with it?

7. The analyst's repressed or denied affects may find uncontrolled outlets in acting out (especially if the analysand becomes rebellious or wishes to leave) or may result in an inner experience of distance or alienation.

On Personalizing and Theorizing

The newly discovered centrality of the personal dimension of analytic identity — strongly influenced by the legacy of Ferenczi and of Winnicott — is also one of the sequelae of our disillusionment with the beliefs in uniform psychoanalytic theory, in standard psychoanalytic technique, and in a "generic analyst" (Mitchell, 1997).

Such notions are first found in Freud (1912b): "Let me express a hope that the increasing experience of psycho-analysts will soon lead to agreement on questions of technique and on the most effective method of treating neurotic patients" (p. 120). Even Ferenczi shared such expectations at times, in spite of his greater investment in the subjective dimension (chapter 1; Berman, 2003a). I must say, however, that the complex thinking Freud and Ferenczi developed about the uniqueness of individual personality eventually gained the upper hand, and it influences our views today more than the positivistic scientific aspirations that led them to the utopia of universal laws and of standard procedures.

As I suggested, exploration of the impact of the analyst's personality, character, style, subjectivity, and broadly defined countertransference (these are partially overlapping interrelated aspects) is a crucial component in analytic training. This exploration can take place mostly in two settings, personal analysis and supervision. Although I support the total separation of these two settings at the institutional level (delicate regulation of supervision, staying out of personal analysis), I believe the trainee can use them in a combined, mutually enhancing way. The same issue (e.g., a particular character pattern or countertransference reaction) may come up and be fruitfully examined in both settings.

As I tried to show in chapters 5 and 6, such an issue — including its childhood antecedents and its comprehensive manifestations in the trainee's object relations — is likely to be explored more broadly in analysis. Is the trainee's annoyance with a patient's neediness or demandingness, for example, similar to feelings experienced with one's spouse and children? Are all these related to past relations with mother?

An understanding of one's impact on the other can be advanced through work on the transference–countertransference cycle, especially when the analyst is interested in intersubjective processes and can contemplate judicious expression of his or her experiences with the analysand. Such understanding may also be promoted by the analyst's interest in other central relationships in the analysand's life, in which insight into the experiences of significant others can be increased with the help of the analyst's complementary identifications, which become a key to the fuller understanding of extratransferential relationships beyond their conscious representation in the analysand's narrative (Berman, 2001a).

The same experience (i.e., annoyance with a patient's neediness) may simultaneously be explored in supervision, mostly through close attention to nuances in the trainee's interaction with the patient. When does that annoyance arise? How is it expressed in the content or tone of interventions? Do we have indications that the patient perceived it consciously or unconsciously? How can it account for the patient's subsequent withdrawal, anger, or attempts to pacify the analyst? Most important, how can our growing insight into the evolving intersubjective pattern become a springboard for meaningful exploration in the treatment being supervised?

This crucial work cannot be done (as argued in chapter 6) if supervision is mostly "patient oriented," if personal issues and countertransference are relegated by the supervisor to the trainee's personal analysis alone. Cresci (2003) well described the effective exploration of a trainee's personal impact in supervision: "In that intimate experience, a good supervisor can get a sense of the candidates' inherent personality that is displayed in a variety of analytic dyads.[2] Tendencies to be empathic, confrontational, reflective and thoughtful, playful, anxious, intimidated or intimidating, responsive or distant . . . would be evident in the process material and discussions . . . These qualities can best be discussed and appreciated in a non-judgmental supervisory relationship" (pp. 433–434).

One way in which issues regarding the trainee's impact on patients come up in analysis (and in supervision, if it is open enough) are through statements such as, "If I am like this [too emotional, too cerebral, too impulsive, too anxious, etc.], I am not fit to be an analyst." Such depressive, self-depreciating reactions, often based on comparisons with idealized others (one's analyst, a favorite supervisor, a revered author), convey belief in a required model experienced as hopelessly remote. Although there may indeed be some individuals whose personality structure turns out to be an insurmountable obstacle to their becoming effective analysts (a major issue for admissions committees), I believe the situation is not so hopeless in most cases. At times, a desperate view disqualifying oneself becomes a masochistic weapon and paradoxically also exempts oneself from the arduous effort of working through certain character traits, striving for greater flexibility, and learning how to notice, understand, and use analytically the reactions of patients to one's unique character.

One more example: Both incessant talkativeness and long stubborn silences of the analyst may sabotage the development of an analytic process. But if we eliminate these extremes, patients may benefit from work with a broad range of analysts along the continuum of style between chatty and quiet/laconic. The main issue is the analyst's nondefensive willingness and capacity to explore the meaning of his or her style in this respect, as well as the impact of this dimension on the patient and on their evolving relationship. Is the talkativeness experienced as conveying liveliness, involvement, and assertivity or intrusiveness, domination,

---

[2]One implication of this thought is that the traditional expectation in psychoanalytic training—that the candidate continually brings into a particular supervision only one case, and a wish to discuss other cases may be interpreted as resistance, fear of exposure, or so forth—also has its drawbacks.

and not leaving enough space? Is the quiet presence of the analyst experienced as attentive, contemplative, and respectful or as disinterested, passive, and withdrawn? What past experiences of the patient become related to the way the analyst is perceived? How does this connection facilitate identification or disidentification? What patterns of the patient's personality are transferentially activated in response to this experience?

Group supervision (with attention to mutual perceptions within the group), group therapy, or group process workshops (unfortunately, rarely initiated in analytic training programs) may go a long way toward facilitating such insights — offering useful feedback that can later be contemplated and worked through in one's personal analysis and individual supervision. I think mostly of longer term group work, unrelated to any institutional evaluation processes, that can generate a "background of safety." In such an empathic climate, a comment such as, "Don't be surprised your patient is afraid to tell you things. I also get intimidated at times by your harsh critical reactions," can hopefully be experienced as useful input and not predominantly as a devastating insult.

A productive way to help trainees in their search for a deeper and more integrative combined personal-professional identity is to encourage them to read discussions by seasoned analysts, from various theoretical backgrounds, who openly discuss the way their personal history and central emotional themes have influenced their lives, their analytic work, and their countertransference. Such fascinating works range from Ferenczi's (1932) *Clinical Diary*, through Guntrip's (1975) classical account of his analyses, to recent moving papers by Crastnopol (1997), Mitchell (1998), and Schwaber (1998).

Let me turn to the theoretical side of training. Undoubtedly, a capacity for critical comparative evaluation of theoretical models and of their implications is most useful. As I tried to show in chapters 1 and 2, this capacity can be gained better in conjunction with learning the historical, cultural, personal, and interpersonal context in which such models evolved. At times, an interest in the life of prominent analysts is downgraded as mere "gossip" or "voyeurism." The anxiety aroused by knowing "too much" about conflictual aspects in the lives of major theoreticians is at times related to a fear of discovering that the "king is naked." This betrays a conventional expectation—that our "kings" and "queens" be attired in majestic robes—as if psychoanalysis has not taught that all of us, senior and junior alike, are naked under our robes, are basically human and imperfect. Maintaining such blind idealizations, as I have commented throughout this book, stands in the way of developing an independent, mature analytic identity—and can be compared to inhibiting curiosity in analysands, who cannot work out central issues in their own lives as long as what they sense in the analyst, or know about the analyst, remains a secret taboo or else something "irrelevant" that gets trivialized and brushed aside defensively, blocking real exploration of the evolving transference.

I view a personal interest in the lives of leading analysts as legitimate, serious, and beneficial—as a springboard for understanding the way theories developed organically in the personal and professional life of these "forefathers" and "foremothers," for studying "how the analyst's intrapersonal and interpersonal psychic life is expressed in his or her theoretical writings, and how the latter has affected his or her clinical work" (Crastnopol, 2003, p. 384). Such understanding can offer us a model for the potential development of theoretical thinking in our own lives as well—not at an abstract and remote level but as a lively extension of daily experiences.

The Perils of Diversity

In chapter 4, I described the changes at the Israel Psychoanalytic Institute that gradually reduced infantilizing and persecutory aspects in training. I assume it is no coincidence that these structural changes evolved during a period in which graduation papers (case presentations) at the institute seemed to rely less massively on theory and on diagnostic considerations and to refer less to "The Unconscious" and to the inevitable repetition in the transference while taking into account much more of the analyst's presence, personality, and subjectivity (Stein, 2000).

These changes also took place against the background of much greater theoretical diversity, which also brought about diversity in views about what is expected of an analyst. The Israel Psychoanalytic Society, originally quite classical and later dominated by ego psychology, gradually became enormously diversified, having strong competing influences of Klein, Bion, Winnicott, Kohut, and intersubjective-relational trends. I view this as a welcome development, but I must say that some candidates find the situation difficult, and I have heard a few express a yearning for the consistency of more uniform training (e.g., Kleinian training in London). The open and at times stormy debates contribute to demystifying and deidealizing psychoanalysis—clarifying its personal and subjective nature—but the same debates may also generate confusion, anxiety, and conflict.

The most painful situations I have encountered are those in which candidates have felt that the "fight is being held on their back." The difficulty may begin already in individual supervision, when there may be some confusion between the contrasting recommendations of various supervisors. Still, this is more manageable, as the candidate chooses the supervisors, and each works on a different case. Moreover, one could hope that at least some of the supervisors are closer to Aron's (1999) "supervisor Z," who asks many questions in order to figure out the unique significance of a particular analytic dilemma within the intersubjective space of a particular dyad, rather than to "supervisor X" and "supervisor Y," who have definitive answers to that dilemma, out of their firm belief in abstinence (X) or in a corrective emotional experience (Y).

Candidates have different strategies for dealing with the complex scene of divergent supervisory lines. In choosing supervisors, some candidates seek diversity, and others opt for consistency, but even the latter may discover that three supervisors who all admire Winnicott interpret him in three different ways. Kantrowitz (2002) highlighted how choosing supervisors is related to the identity of the candidate's analyst. "Choices of similarity" reflect positive feelings about one's analysis—but at times also idealized transference to the analyst, fear of conflict with the analyst, and protectiveness "of the candidate's narcissistic vulnerabilities or the narcissistic vulnerabilities that the candidate attributes to the analyst" (p. 965). "Choices of difference" express a wish for increased autonomy but may also be a way to split the transference or to express protest against disagreements with the analyst (p. 966).

The tension may be greater in seminars. A faculty member may express antagonism to opposing views of candidates, who come to represent for him or for her these candidates' analysts and supervisors, with whom the instructor is in deep disagreement. Things become most difficult when a case is presented in a clinical seminar, and the instructor in the seminar is critical of the candidate's work, which is influenced by the beliefs of that case's individual supervisor. As I mentioned, what one analyst sees today as firmness another may see as rigidity, what one sees as vital provision another may see as confusing acting-out. When the instructor finds a way to express a differing view in a tolerant and respectful tone, this may be illuminating; when the differing view acquires harsh nuances (an implication that working as the candidate does blocks unconscious communication or is countertherapeutic), this becomes devastating.

Crastnopol (2003) listed some of the dangers in a multitheoretical approach: "No one position would be presented thoroughly enough . . . candidates would be overwhelmed by the slew of less than compatible formulations . . . the candidate would become so confused that he or she would prematurely foreclose exploration . . ." (p. 386). Lester and Robertson (1995) emphasized the competition, often unconscious, for the candidate's allegiance. Diversity unavoidably brings turmoil.

Still, in today's intellectual climate a diversified curriculum is crucial, and a historical perspective may put diversity in context and make it less confusing. In my experience, studying the Freud–Ferenczi relationship (chapter 1) or the Klein–Winnicott relationship (chapter 2) goes a long way toward understanding their theoretical differences better. There is much to be gained from seminars that, rather than admiringly teach one perspective, have a critical-comparative element. Of course, it is inspiring to learn Klein from a Kleinian and Kohut from a Kohutian, but, if instructors are too strongly identified with their mentors, the divergent ideas will remain isolated and idealized. Candidates benefit also from reading and evaluating papers that are critical of various theoretical models and pinpoint their shortcomings. Still, the curriculum of each institute is influenced by the interests and views of faculty members. Some institutes may naturally be more unified and others more diversified. If there are several options in the same geographical area, candidates can make educated choices.

A capacity for a systematic comparative evaluation of various theoretical models, as I mentioned, is particularly valuable in this heterogeneous reality. But such a capacity may not be widespread, and it may be unrealistic to expect it from many psychoanalytic faculty members, even those who are successful in other forms of analytic teaching. A serious evaluative comparative study, transcending polemics (e.g., "My model is deep and innovative; the other model is shallow and dated"), requires degrees of metatheoretical abstraction and of knowledge in the history and philosophy of ideas, which are not easy to develop (Berman, 2003b).

I assume some individuals in many analytic institutes are prone to this sophisticated kind of metatheoretical thinking, and they can be encouraged to develop such seminars for the candidates. Such seminars, in turn — I can guess — will fascinate certain candidates and intimidate some others. The range between relying mostly on personal clinical intuition and using theory more fully is another area of dissimilarity among analysts. Some analysts develop a phobic-resistant attitude toward theory and view it as potentially dogmatic, as coercive, as depriving the analyst of a freedom to develop an authentic emotional involvement with one's patients. Such attitudes have their risks, too: "As valuable as we have found the stance of tolerating not-knowing, and the reflection on uncertainty, it is unquestionably dangerous to move from that stance into an ideal of not-knowing" (Benjamin, 1997, p. 797).

I share Benjamin's (1997) view: "Pluralism will make new knowledge demands on psychoanalysts. Analytic training should include the development of critical abilities that help to meet these demands within a context of education as a collaborative, democratic process" (p. 781). In this spirit, I believe that creative teaching can help analysts — even those who rely mostly on intuition — notice the implicit theoretical assumptions in their own supposedly atheoretical clinical work and become sensitized to the unavoidable impact of common concepts, widespread interpretive models, and current cultural assumptions. Paradoxically, such awareness may enhance one's freedom for more daring personal expressiveness, whereas a theoretical naivete may support a thinly disguised conventionality.

One way to strengthen the comparative-evaluative meta-theoretical component in analytic teaching is to train as analysts and as future instructors colleagues from the humanities and social sciences, who have a richer background in the history of ideas and in the philosophy of science than most psychologists, psychiatrists, and social workers do. Such an invitation opens up many practical, ethical, and legal issues and requires developing sets of prerequisites that will allow these interested colleagues to compensate for their lack of past exposure to the mental health field. Still, recruiting such colleagues can be most productive.

From my experience, on the other hand, inviting nonanalytic academics to be guest lecturers rarely has a positive long-term influence. These individuals may be most sophisticated in a relevant area, such as theory building, paradigm shifts, narration, or hermeneutics, but, because they lack a clinical analytic background (and possibly a therapeutic drive), they fail to communicate their vast knowledge in a way that becomes meaningfully internalized by clinician-students. A combined academic and psychoanalytic background promises a better chance for truly effective and generative teaching, based on the instructor's long personal odyssey of seeking to integrate the different disciplines. Such teaching may help more in promoting the evolution in each analyst of a unique analytic identity, which it is hoped could integrate critical intellectual sophistication while remaining meaningfully grounded in the analyst's individual personal characteristics and in the deep emotional needs that resulted in this particular choice of our "impossible profession."

Training and Social Reality

Although early psychoanalysis, in its struggle to gain legitimacy for an intrapsychic focus, often turned a deaf ear to the impact of social reality on the analytic dyad, we can now see that such an impact always existed. Freud (1905) analyzed Dora with exclusive attention to her unconscious fantasies and drives, but later authors showed convincingly to what extent that analysis was influenced by factors never mentioned by Freud—images of women in European culture at the time (Moi, 1981, and many others), limitations on their actual roles, the affinity between Dora and Freud as Jews in an anti-Semitic political reality (Decker, 1991), their similar socioeconomic background, and so on (Berman, 2002a). Beyond acknowledging the social reality of the training setting, emphasized throughout this book, we must notice the implications of an even broader social, economic, political, and cultural reality. Exploration and working through of such issues need to find their place in our training as well.

The issue of gender in psychoanalytic training, for example, is part of the way training is influenced by the broader social context. Early analysts were all men (who mostly treated women ...), and Freud had to veto the wish of some of his Viennese colleagues to officially limit membership in their new society to men, as was done by numerous professional organizations at the time (Gay, 1988). Gradually, women began joining, and today they may be taking over.

Is this the reason for a stronger emphasis on preoedipal issues, on maternal analytic functions? Does it strengthen the trend for "embracing the maternal ideal of holding or mirroring in contrast to the phallic image of the penetrating knower" (Benjamin, 1997, p. 793)? It is difficult to say. Paradoxically, as mentioned in chapters 1 and 2, these aspects were most forcefully introduced by analysts, Ferenczi and Winnicott, who were both childless men. In any case, my hope is that in our training we will facilitate development and recognition of many nuances of transference (paternal, maternal, fraternal—*see under Ferenczi*—and all combinations thereof). An intellectual climate that focuses exclusively on a particular pattern (be it oedipal, preoedipal, or any other) may lead to reductionism and blind spots. And, though undoubtedly the proportion of women in the profession is increasing, we all need to be in touch with both masculine and feminine identifications in ourselves so that, I hope, our theories will not be determined by our actual gender, which may become a straitjacket if taken too literally.

Gender may influence training when various gender-related social roles and conventional expectations influence faculty and trainees alike. An empirical study of supervisory dyads, for example, showed that, regardless of supervisor's gender, "supervisors did not encourage female students to break out of a pattern of deference, but did encourage male trainees to increase their use of high-power messages" (Holloway and Wolleat, 1994, p. 35). Frawley-O'Dea and Sarnat (2001) concluded, "Any male supervisor who does not actively attend to the subtle ways that women supervisees defer to him, or to the pull he may feel to relate to them as sexual objects, runs the risk of blindly perpetuating traditional gender patterns" (p. 101). Frawley-O'Dea and Sarnat also discussed the importance of men's difficulties in tolerating women who are in roles of authority — another important issue when women become the majority in many psychoanalytic faculty groups.

The growing number of women in training is related to another reality shift — the growing demedicalization of psychoanalysis and psychotherapy. This process, influenced, of course, by the strong biological-pharmacologic trend in psychiatry, arouses concern about its implications for the place of psychoanalytic psychotherapy in public mental health settings, many of which (both in the United States and in Israel) were run by psychoanalysts 20 or 30 years ago. If analysts leave these agencies, they unavoidably abandon large parts of the population and limit their practice to the affluent and the educated.

Economic factors also directly influence training. Although clinical psychologists and social workers, now our main professional reservoir, are predominantly women (also an important topic to explore), men may also be more reluctant to undergo analytic training because of economic reasons. The high overall cost of training — combining tuition, personal analysis, supervision, and the loss inherent in spending many hours a week with low-cost analysands instead of better-paying therapy patients — becomes prohibitive when one sees oneself as the family's main provider, as many men do. This economic obstacle has severe social implications and contributes to the rather narrow identity pattern of analysts in numerous countries.

In Israel, the mainstream image of psychoanalysis has slowly become a topic of discourse. Recently, a candidate presented a graduation paper describing the case of a patient, of Mideastern background, who had grown up in a remote "development town" populated mostly by new immigrants — and the candidate hinted at the patient's background in the title of the paper. Some participants remarked that the patient's background is irrelevant to the "real (intrapsychic) issues." Other participants disagreed: Are psychodynamics unrelated to issues of ethnicity and social class? Might some aspects of the patient's mental pain and symptoms be related to experiences of marginality, exclusion, and humiliation?

Israeli psychoanalysis, as one member remarked in that debate, is an exclusive membership club. There are no Arab analysts. (None ever applied, and the number of Arab clinical psychologists is small. Psychology does not seem a popular subject among Arab youth.) The number of analysts and candidates with a Mideastern background (the background of roughly half the population of Israel) is small. Very few are orthodox. There are barely any gay or lesbian analysts (not because of direct discrimination but because they rarely apply, possibly because of the rigid image of the institute). Most analysts are Ashkenazi (of Western origins) and secular, and they come from affluent families. Not surprisingly, most analysands of our candidates also come from middle- to upper-class families, and our contact with working-class individuals, with Arabs, with new immigrants, and with foreign laborers (the poorer groups in Israeli society) becomes quite limited.

The tendency to leave public facilities and focus on private practice and the views idealizing psychoanalysis proper in comparison to "inferior" psychotherapy (Kernberg, 1999) increase the danger that psychoanalysis will become elitist and reclusive — engaged in treating mental health professionals and some affluent individuals while turning its back on the majority of society, for whom emotional needs and emotional misery are, to say the least, no less pressing.

In recent years, I had the experience of supervising three analyses of individuals from a lower class background. I found it moving to follow these analysands' struggle to understand their emotional lives and to make use of the analytic relationship without having a foundation of psychological language and familiar psychological discourse — building their discourse from scratch, based on unformulated intuitions and innate capacities never cultivated in their families of origin. These analyses had a freshness, a sense of discovery, that is lacking at times in the analyses of mental health professionals and other analysands who have grown up in a sophisticated, psychoanalytically informed cultural milieu.

Here again we are reminded of Freud's inner contradictions. Although originating from a rather poor rural family and financing his medical studies with the aid of scholarships (Gay, 1988), Freud paved his way into a bourgeois existence and worked mostly with affluent patients.

At one point, in an elitist state of mind, Freud (1913) wrote, "One may . . . regret that analytic therapy is almost inaccessible to poor people, both for external and internal reasons. Little can be done to remedy this" (p. 132). But a few years later we hear a different tone, closer to Freud's (1910b) radical views:

> At some time or other the conscience of society will awake and remind it that the poor man should have just as much right to assistance for his mind as he now has to the life-saving help offered by surgery . . . When this happens, institutions or out-patient clinics will be started, to which analytically trained physicians will be appointed . . . [to help] men who would otherwise give way to drink, women who have nearly succumbed under their burden of privations, children for whom there is no choice but between running wild and neurosis . . . Such treatments will be free [Freud, 1919, p. 167].

The latter line of thought, influential in the early policlinics established by psychoanalysts in Vienna and in Berlin (Danto, 1999), was recently revived by Altman (1993, 1995) in his work.

But social understanding in psychoanalysis is not related solely to the populations we treat. We live in a world in which history and sociopolitical processes have visibly affected the life of so many individuals and in which analytic and therapeutic involvement often activates questions of national, ethnic, religious, and ideologic identity; issues involving gender and sexual orientation; and the subjective consequences of war, migration, and survival (Berman, 2002d). We cannot understand our patients, I suggest, if we are not attentive to the way history and politics shape their destiny in subtle and complex interaction with intrapsychic factors. We cannot understand ourselves without similar self-scrutiny, and this has implications for countertransference, for being clinically effective, and therefore for training.

Private patients, even if they are relatively affluent, are social creatures too, and they are not exempt from the influence of historical forces. Social reality forms an omnipresent layer in the mind of any analysand. Naturally, the particular form and intensity in which this "external" reality is represented differ enormously from individual to individual.[3]

Doing ahistorical analysis in our present reality may imply a degree of denial. Paraphrasing Ferenczi, I would suggest that keeping "political" issues out of the consulting room, in a society which experiences them with great intensity (especially at times of crisis, war, and massive controversy), may also be experienced by some patients as professional hypocrisy and become destructive for the analytic process. Exploring such aspects need not be seen as disruptive to analytic work. If transference is constantly influenced by countertransference, and self-disclosures and enactments naturally happen in most sessions, what is crucial is not the avoidance of contamination (the image of the sterile test tube, which Freud imported from the natural sciences) but free exploration on all levels (both individual and social) of this unavoidable reciprocal influence and use of this influence for the development of insight and of a deeper and richer analytic relationship.

Giving attention to historical, social, and political processes can help analysts and therapists better understand their own lives, the lives of their patients, and the juncture in which they and their patients meet — namely, the transferential relationship in its broadest sense. This too can become a focus of training.

I believe that fuller awareness of the social implications of our work, attention to the way history and culture shape the life of all our patients, interest in the impact of social processes on our own identity and therapeutic values, greater capacity to overcome

---

[3]I consider it a trademark of the psychoanalytic approach that it rejects generalizations and is attuned to the minute nuances of individual uniqueness. Overinclusive statements, be they about posttraumatic stress disorder or "second-generation" Holocaust influences, are out of place in psychoanalytic discourse.

elitism and reach wider populations, and better methods for working psychoanalytically with minorities, with poorer people, and with the victims of social violence—these are all neglected but crucial aspects of training psychoanalysts and psychotherapists for a future in which psychoanalysis could survive and continue to contribute to human well-being.

References

Abraham, K. (1922), The rescue and murder of the father in neurotic phantasy formations. In: *Clinical Papers and Essays in Psychoanalysis.* New York: Basic Books, 1955, pp. 68–75.

Aguayo, J. (2002), Reassessing the clinical affinity between Melanie Klein and D. W. Winnicott (1935–51). *Internat. J. Psycho-Anal.,* 83: 1133–1152.

Altman, N. (1993), Psychoanalysis and the urban poor. *Psychoanal. Dial.,* 3:29–49.

———— (1995), *The Analyst in the Inner City: Race, Class, and Culture Through a Psychoanalytic Lens.* Hillsdale, NJ: The Analytic Press.

———— (1997), Response to review [by Boticelli]. *Psychoanal. Dial.,* 7:547–551.

———— (2000), Black and white thinking: A psychoanalyst reconsiders race. *Psychoanal. Dial.,* 10:589–605.

Arlow, J. (1963), The supervisory situation. *J. Amer. Psychoanal. Assn.,* 11:576–594.

———— (1972), Some dilemmas in psychoanalytic education. *J. Amer. Psychoanal. Assn.,* 20:556–566.

Aron, L. (1992), From Ferenczi to Searles and contemporary relational approaches. *Psychoanal. Dial.,* 2:181–190.

———— (1996a), *A Meeting of Minds: Mutuality in Psychoanalysis.* Hillsdale, NJ: The Analytic Press.

———— (1996b), From hypnotic suggestion to free association: Freud as a psychotherapist, circa 1892–1893. *Contemp. Psychoanal.,* 32:99–114.

———— (1998), "Yours, thirsty for honesty, Ferenczi": Some background to Sándor Ferenczi's pursuit of mutuality. *Amer. J. Psychoanal.,* 58:5–20.

———— (1999), Clinical choices and the relational matrix. *Psychoanal. Dial.,* 9:1–29.

———— (2000), Ethical considerations in the writing of psychoanalytic case histories. *Psychoanal. Dial.,* 10:231–245.

———— & Harris, A., eds. (1993), *The Legacy of Sándor Ferenczi.* Hillsdale, NJ: The Analytic Press.

Bachrach, H. M. (1983), On the concept of analyzability. *Psychoanal. Quart.,* 52:180–204.

Balint, M. (1948), On the psychoanalytic training system. *Internat. J. Psycho-Anal.,* 29:163–173.

_____ (1954), Analytic training and training analysis. *Internat. J. Psycho-Anal.*, 35:157–162.

_____ (1958), Letter to the editor. *Internat. J. Psycho-Anal.*, 39:68.

_____ (1967), Sándor Ferenczi's technical experiments. In: *Psychoanalytic Techniques*, ed. B. Wolman. New York: Basic Books, pp. 147–167.

_____ (1969), *The Basic Fault: Therapeutic Aspects of Regression*. London: Tavistock.

Bar-Lev Elieli, R. (2001), Discussion of J. Schubert's paper on training models. *Psychoanal. Eur.*, 55:27–35.

Barron, G. C. (2003), Silent thoughts, spoken wishes: When candidate experience of the supervisor converges with patient fantasies. *J. Amer. Psychoanal. Assn.*, 51:155–175.

Basch-Kahre, E. (1984), On difficulties arising in transference and countertransference when analyst and analysand have different sociocultural backgrounds. *Internat. Rev. Psycho-Anal.*, 11:61–67.

Baudry, F. D. (1993), The personal dimension and management of the supervisory situation with a special note on the parallel process. *Psychoanal. Quart.*, 62:588–61.

_____ (1998), Kohut and Glover: The role of subjectivity in psychoanalytic theory and controversy. *The Psychoanalytic Study of the Child*, 53:3–24. New Haven, CT: Yale University Press.

Bauer, R. A. (1952), *The New Man in Soviet Psychology*. Cambridge, MA: Harvard University Press.

Benjamin, J. (1995), *Like Subjects, Love Objects*. New Haven, CT: Yale University Press.

_____ (1997), Psychoanalysis as a vocation. *Psychoanal. Dial.*, 6:781–802.

Bergmann, M. S. (1997), The historical roots of psychoanalytic orthodoxy. *Internat. J. Psycho-Anal.*, 78:69–86.

Berman, E. (1982), Authority and authoritarianism in group psychotherapy. *Internat. J. Group Psychother.*, 32:189–200.

_____ (1983), Orthodoxy and innovation in the history of psychoanalysis [in Hebrew]. *Yiunim Bahinuh*, 37:23–30.

_____ (1988a), Communal upbringing in the kibbutz: The allure and risks of psychoanalytic utopianism. *The Psychoanalytic Study of the Child*, 43:319–335. New Haven, CT: Yale University Press.

_____ (1988b), The joint exploration of the supervisory relationship as an aspect of psychoanalytic supervision. In: *New Concepts in Psychoanalytic Psychotherapy*, ed. J. Ross & W. Myers. Washington, DC: American Psychiatric Press, pp. 150–166.

_____ (1993), Psychoanalysis, rescue and utopia. *Utopian Stud.*, 4: 44–56.

_____ (1994a), Review of Etchegoyen's *The Fundamentals of Psycho-Analytic Technique*. *Psychoanal. Dial.*, 4:129–138.

_____ (1994b), Psychoanalytic training: Dynamics, social processes, pathology [in Hebrew]. *Sihot/Dial.: Isr. J. Psychother.*, 9:28–37.

_____ (1995a), On analyzing colleagues. *Contemp. Psychoanal.*, 31: 521–539.

_____ (1995b), Letter to the editor on "Confusion of tongues." *Internat. J. Psycho-Anal.*, 76:1045–1046.

_____ (1996), The Ferenczi renaissance. *Psychoanal. Dial.*, 6:391–411.

_____ (1997a), Hitchcock's *Vertigo:* The collapse of a rescue fantasy. *Internat. J. Psycho-Anal.*, 78:975–996.

_____ (1997b), Mutual analysis: Boundary violation or failed experiment? [Letter to the editor]. *J. Amer. Psychoanal. Assn.*, 45:569–571.

_____ (1997c), A basic lack of understanding? *Psychoanal. Eur.*, 49: 95–100.

_____ (1997d), Relational psychoanalysis: A historical perspective. *Amer. J. Psychother.*, 51:185–203.

_____ (1997e), Psychoanalytic supervision as the crossroads of a relational matrix. In: *Psychodynamic Supervision,* ed. M. Rock. Northvale, NJ: Aronson, pp. 160–186.

_____ (1998), Structure and individuality in psychoanalytic training: The Israeli Controversial Discussions. *Amer. J. Psychoanal.*, 58: 117–133.

_____ (1999), Sándor Ferenczi today: Reviving the broken dialectic. *Amer. J. Psychoanal.*, 59:303–313.

_____ (2000a), *The Scarlet Letter,* revised: Vicissitudes of the utopian fantasy of a New Sexual Person. *Psychoanal. Dial.*, 10:319–326.

_____ (2000b), Discussion of Warren Poland's "Witnessing and otherness." *J. Amer. Psychoanal. Assn.*, 48:41–48.

_____ (2000c), The utopian fantasy of a New Person and the danger of a false analytic self. *Psychoanal. Psychol.*, 17:38–60.

_____ (2000d), Psychoanalytic supervision: The intersubjective development. *Internat. J. Psycho-Anal.*, 81:273–290.

_____ (2001a), Psychoanalysis and life. *Psychoanal. Quart.*, 70:35–65.

_____ (2001b), Obituary: Stephen A. Mitchell. *Internat. J. Psycho-Anal.*, 82:1267–1272.

_____ (2002a), "Dora." In: *The Freud Encyclopedia,* ed. E. Erwin. London: Routledge.

_____ (2002b), The other's failures — And one's own. In: *Failures in Psychoanalytic Treatment,* ed. J. Reppen & M. Schulman. Madison, CT: International Universities Press, pp. 263–288.

_____ (2002c), The long journey: Introduction to S. Freud, *Psychoanalytic Treatment* [in Hebrew], ed. E. Berman. Tel Aviv, Israel: Am Oved.

_____ (2002d), Beyond analytic anonymity: On the political involvement of psychoanalysts and psychotherapists in Israel. In: *Psycho-*

analysis, Identity, and Ideology, ed. J. Bunzl & B. Beit-Hallahmi. Boston: Kluwer, pp. 177–200.

_____ (2003a), Ferenczi, rescue and utopia. *Amer. Imago,* 60: 429–444.

_____ (2003b), "Issues in Training" panel contribution. *Psychoanal. Dial.,* 13:419–427, 445–449.

_____ (2004), Sándor, Gizella, Elma: A biographical journey. *Internat. J. Psycho-Anal.,* 85:489–520.

_____ & Segel, R. (1982), The captive client: Dilemmas of psychotherapy in the psychiatric hospital. *Psychotherapy,* 19:259–265.

Bernfeld, S. (1962), On psychoanalytic training. *Psychoanal. Quart.,* 31: 457–482.

Bettelheim, B. (1969), *Children of the Dream.* New York: Avon.

Blass, R. & Simon, B. (1994), The value of the historical perspective to contemporary psychoanalysis: Freud's "seduction hypothesis." *Internat. J. Psycho-Anal.,* 75:677–694.

Bollas, C. (1987), *The Shadow of the Object.* New York: Columbia University Press.

_____ (1997), Supervision and intersubjectivity. Discussion at Tel Aviv University, Tel Aviv, Israel.

Bonomi, C. (1999), Flight into sanity: Jones's allegation of Ferenczi's mental deterioration reconsidered. *Internat. J. Psycho-Anal.,* 80:507–542.

Brabant, E., Falzeder, E. & Giampieri-Deutsch, P., eds. (2003), *The Freud–Ferenczi Correspondence, Vol. 1, 1908–1914,* trans. P. Hoffer. Cambridge, MA: Harvard University Press.

Brenman-Pick, I. (1997), Letter to Dan H. Buie. *Internat. J. Psycho-Anal.,* 6:32–33.

Brenneis, C. B. (2002). Apparitions in the fog? Commentary on paper by Harris and Gold. *Psychoanal. Dial.,* 12:987–999.

Breuer, J. & Freud, S. (1895), Studies on hysteria. *Standard Edition,* 2. London: Hogarth Press, 1955.

Bromberg, P. M. (1994), "Speak, that I may see you": Some reflections on dissociation, reality, and psychoanalytic listening. *Psychoanal. Dial.,* 4:517–547.

_____ Modell, A. H., Aron, L., Greenberg, J. R. & Hoffman, I. Z. (1991), Symposium: Reality and the analytic relationship. *Psychoanal. Dial.,* 1:8–105.

Brown, L. & Miller, M. (2002), The triadic intersubjective matrix in supervision. *Internat. J. Psycho-Anal.,* 83:811–823.

Bruzzone, M., Casuala, E., Jimenez, J. P. & Jordan, J. (1985), Regression and persecution in analytic training: Reflections on experience. *Internat. Rev. Psycho-Anal.,* 12:411–415.

Calef, V. (1982), An introspective on training and nontraining analysis. *The Annual of Psychoanalysis*, 10:93–114. New York: International Universities Press.

Caruth, E. (1990), Complexities and vulnerabilities in the supervisory process. In: *Psychoanalytic Approaches to Supervision*, ed. R. C. Lane. New York: Brunner/Mazel, pp. 181–193.

Casement, P. (1993), Review of Etchegoyen's *Fundamentals of Psychoanalytic Technique*. *Internat. J. Psycho-Anal.*, 74:393–396.

_____ (1997), Towards autonomy: Some thoughts on psychoanalytic supervision. In: *Psychodynamic Supervision*, ed. M. Rock. Northvale, NJ: Aronson, pp. 263–282.

Chasseguet-Smirgel, J. & Grunberger, B. (1986), *Freud or Reich?* New Haven, CT: Yale University Press.

Coburn, W. (1997), The vision in supervision: Transference-countertransference dynamics and disclosure in the supervision relationship. *Bull. Menn. Clin.*, 61:481–494.

Craige, H. (2002). Mourning analysis: The post-termination phase. *J. Amer. Psychoanal. Assn.*, 50:507–550.

Crastnopol, M. (1997), Incognito or not? The patient's subjective experience of the analyst's private life. *Psychoanal. Dial.*, 7:257–280.

_____ (2003), "Issues in Training" panel contribution. *Psychoanal. Dial.*, 13:379–389, 431–432.

Cresci, M. B. (2003), "Issues in Training" panel contribution. *Psychoanal. Dial.*, 13:391–402, 433–435.

Danto, E. A. (1999), The Berlin Poliklinik: Psychoanalytic innovation in Weimar Germany. *J. Amer. Psychoanal. Assn.*, 47:1269–1292.

Davies, J. & Frawley, M. (1992), Dissociative processes and transference–countertransference paradigms in the psychoanalytically oriented treatment of adult survivors of childhood sexual abuse. *Psychoanal. Dial.*, 2:5–36.

_____ & _____ (1994), *Treating the Adult Survivor of Childhood Sexual Abuse*. New York: Basic Books.

DeBell, D. E. (1963), A critical digest of the literature on psychoanalytic supervision. *J. Amer. Psychoanal. Assn.*, 11:546–575.

Decker, H. (1991), *Freud, Dora and Vienna 1900*. New York: Free Press.

Doehrman, M. J. G. (1976), Parallel processes in supervision and psychotherapy. *Bull. Menn. Clin.*, 40:3–104.

Drescher, J. (1994), Interview with Stephen A. Mitchell. *White Society Voice*, 6.

Druck, A. (2000), Organizational structure and the establishment of psychoanalytic identification: Commentary on paper by Sorenson. *Psychoanal. Dial.*, 10:889–907.

Dulchin, J. & Segal, A. J. (1982), The ambiguity of confidentiality in a psychoanalytic institute; Third-party confidences: The uses of information in a psychoanalytic institute. *Psychiatry*, 45:13–37.

Dupont, J., ed. (1988), Introduction. In: *The Clinical Diary of Sándor Ferenczi*. Cambridge, MA: Harvard University Press.

———— (1994), Freud's analysis of Ferenczi as revealed by their correspondence. *Internat. J. Psycho-Anal.*, 75:301–320.

Ehrlich, J. (2003), Being a candidate: Its impact on analytic process. *J. Amer. Psychoanal. Assn.*, 51:177–200.

Eisold, K. (1994), The intolerance of diversity in psychoanalytic institutes. *Internat. J. Psycho-Anal.*, 75:785–800.

Eissler, K. (1953), The effect of the structure of the ego on psychoanalytic technique. *J. Amer. Psychoanal. Assn.*, 1:104–143.

Ekstein, R. D., Wallerstein, J. & Mandelbaum, A. (1959), Countertransference in the residential treatment of children. *The Psychoanalytic Study of the Child*, 14:186–218. New York: International Universities Press.

———— & Wallerstein, R. S. (1972), *The Teaching and Learning of Psychotherapy*. New York: International Universities Press.

Ellman, S. (1991), *Freud's Technique Papers, A Contemporary Perspective*. Northvale, NJ: Aronson.

Epstein, L. (1986), Collusive selective inattention to the negative impact of the supervisory interaction. *Contemp. Psychoanal.*, 22:389–409.

Erlich, S. H. (1996), Discussion of P. Daniel's paper. *Psychoanal. Eur.*, 47:29–32.

Esman, A. H. (1987), Rescue fantasies. *Psychoanal. Quart.*, 56:263–270.

Etchegoyen, H. (1991), *The Fundamentals of Psychoanalytic Technique*. London: Karnac.

Fairbairn, W. R. D. (1954), *An Object Relations Theory of the Personality*. New York: Basic Books.

Falzeder, E. & Brabant, E., eds. (1996), *The Correspondence of Sigmund Freud and Sándor Ferenczi, Vol. 2, 1914–1919*, trans. P. Hoffer. Cambridge, MA: Harvard University Press.

———— & ———— (2000), *The Correspondence of Sigmund Freud and Sándor Ferenczi, Vol. 3, 1920–1938*, trans. P. Hoffer. Cambridge, MA: Harvard University Press.

Fanon, F. (1963), *The Wretched of the Earth*. New York: Grove, 1968.

Felman, S. (1991), Education and crisis, Or the vicissitudes of teaching. *Amer. Imago*, 48:13–74.

Fenichel, O. (1939), Trophy and triumph: A clinical study. In: *The Collected Papers of Otto Fenichel, Vol. 2*. New York: Norton, pp. 141–162.

Ferenczi, S. (1899), Spiritism. In: *Selected Writings*. London: Penguin, 1999, pp. 3–8.

_____ (1900), Two errors in diagnosis. In: *Selected Writings*. London: Penguin, 1999, pp. 9–12.

_____ (1901), Love within science. In: *Selected Writings*. London: Penguin, 1999, pp. 13–18.

_____ (1909), Introjection and transference. In: *First Contributions to Psycho-Analysis*. New York: Brunner/Mazel, 1980, pp. 30–79.

_____ (1919a), On the technique of psycho-analysis. In: *Further Contributions to the Theory and Technique of Psycho-Analysis*. New York: Brunner/Mazel, 1980, pp. 177–189.

_____ (1919b), Technical difficulties in the analysis of a case of hysteria. In: *Further Contributions to the Theory and Technique of Psycho-Analysis*. New York: Brunner/Mazel, 1980, pp. 189–197.

_____ (1921), The further development of an active therapy in psycho-analysis. In: *Further Contributions to the Theory and Technique of Psycho-Analysis*. New York: Brunner/Mazel, 1980, pp. 198–217.

_____ (1923), The dream of "the clever baby." In: *Further Contributions to the Theory and Technique of Psycho-Analysis*. New York: Brunner/Mazel, 1980, pp. 349–350.

_____ (1924a), On forced fantasies. In: *Further Contributions to the Theory and Technique of Psycho-Analysis*. New York: Brunner/Mazel, 1980, pp. 68–77.

_____ (1924b), *Thalassa: A Theory of Genitality*. New York: Psychoanalytic Quarterly, 1933.

_____ (1925), Contra-indications to the "active" psycho-analytical technique. In: *Further Contributions to the Theory and Technique of Psycho-Analysis*. New York: Brunner/Mazel, 1980, pp. 217–230.

_____ (1927), The problem of the termination of the analysis. In: *Final Contributions to the Problems and Methods of Psycho-Analysis*. New York: Brunner/Mazel, 1980, pp. 77–86.

_____ (1928), The elasticity of psycho-analytic technique. In: *Final Contributions to the Problems and Methods of Psycho-Analysis*. New York: Brunner/Mazel, 1980, pp. 87–101.

_____ (1929), The unwelcome child and his death instinct. In: *Final Contributions to the Problems and Methods of Psycho-Analysis*. New York: Brunner/Mazel, 1980, pp. 102–107.

_____ (1930), The principles of relaxation and neocatharsis. In: *Final Contributions to the Problems and Methods of Psycho-Analysis*. New York: Brunner/Mazel, 1980, pp. 108–125.

_____ (1931), Child analysis in the analysis of adults. In: *Final Contributions to the Problems and Methods of Psycho-Analysis*. New York: Brunner/Mazel, 1980, pp. 126–142.

_____ (1932), *The Clinical Diary of Sándor Ferenczi*, ed. J. Dupont (trans. M. Balint & N. Z Jackson). Cambridge, MA: Harvard University Press, 1988.

_____ (1933), Confusion of tongues between adults and the child. In: *Final Contributions to the Problems and Methods of Psycho-Analysis.* New York: Brunner/Mazel, 1980, pp. 156–167.

_____ (1955), *Final Contributions to the Problems and Methods of Psycho-Analysis.* New York: Brunner/Mazel, 1980.

_____ & Rank, O. (1924), *The Development of Psycho-Analysis.* New York: Dover.

Fleming, J. (1973), The training analyst as an educator. *The Annual of Psychoanalysis,* 1:280–295. New York: International Universities Press.

_____ & Benedek T. F. (1966), *Psychoanalytic Supervision.* New York: International Universities Press.

Fortune, C. (1993), The case of RN: Sándor Ferenczi's radical experiment in psychoanalysis. In: *The Legacy of Sándor Ferenczi,* ed. L. Aron & A. Harris. Hillsdale, NJ: The Analytic Press, pp. 101–120.

_____ ed. (2002), *The Ferenczi–Groddeck Correspondence, 1921–1933.* London: Open Gate.

Fowles, J. (1969), *The French Lieutenant's Woman.* London: Vintage.

Frankel, J. (2002), Exploring Ferenczi's concept of identification with the aggressor: Its role in trauma, everyday life, and the therapeutic relationship. *Psychoanal. Dial.,* 12:101–139.

Fraser, K. (1996). What goes on in supervision and isn't talked about: Beyond the didactic to the dyadic. Presented at annual meeting of the American Psychoanalytic Association, New York.

Frawley-O'Dea, M. G. (2003), Supervision is a relationship too. *Psychoanal. Dial.,* 13:355–366.

_____ & Sarnat, J. E. (2001), *The Supervisory Relationship: A Contemporary Psychodynamic Approach.* New York: Guilford.

Freeman Sharpe, E, (1937). *Dream Analysis.* New York: Brunner/Mazel, 1978.

Freud, A. (1954), The widening scope of indications for psychoanalysis: Discussion. In: *The Writings of Anna Freud, Vol. 4.* New York: International Universities Press.

_____ (1965), *Normality and Pathology in Childhood.* New York: International Universities Press.

_____ (1983), Some observations. In: *The Identity of the Analyst,* ed. E. D. Joseph & D. Widlocher. New York: International Universities Press.

Freud, S. (1905), Fragment of an analysis of a case of hysteria. *Standard Edition,* 7:7–122. London: Hogarth Press, 1953.

_____ (1908), "Civilized" sexual morality and modern nervous illness. *Standard Edition,* 9:181–204. London: Hogarth Press, 1959.

_____ (1909), Notes upon a case of obsessional neurosis. *Standard Edition,* 10:155–249. London: Hogarth Press, 1955.

_____ (1910a), A special type of choice of object made by men. *Standard Edition*,11:165–175. London: Hogarth Press, 1957.

_____ (1910b), The future prospects of psycho-analytic therapy. *Standard Edition*, 11:139–151. London: Hogarth Press, 1957.

_____ (1910c), "Wild" psychoanalysis. *Standard Edition*, 11:221–227. London: Hogarth Press, 1957.

_____ (1910d), Five lectures on psychoanalysis. *Standard Edition*, 11: 7–55. London: Hogarth Press, 1957.

_____ (1912a), The dynamics of the transference. *Standard Edition*, 12:99–108. London: Hogarth Press, 1958.

_____ (1912b), Recommendations to physicians practising psychoanalysis. *Standard Edition*, 12:109–120. London: Hogarth Press, 1958.

_____ (1913), On beginning the treatment. *Standard Edition*, 12: 123–144. London: Hogarth Press, 1958.

_____ (1914), Remembering, repeating and working-through. *Standard Edition*, 12:147–156. London: Hogarth Press, 1958.

_____ (1915), Observations on transference-love. *Standard Edition*, 12:157–171. London: Hogarth Press, 1958.

_____ (1919), Lines of advance in psycho-analytic therapy. *Standard Edition*, 17:159–168. London: Hogarth Press, 1955.

_____ (1926), The question of lay analysis. *Standard Edition*, 20: 183–258. London: Hogarth Press, 1959.

_____ (1933), Sándor Ferenczi. *Standard Edition*, 22:297–299. London: Hogarth Press, 1964.

_____ (1937), Analysis terminable and interminable. *Standard Edition*, 23:216–253. London: Hogarth Press, 1964.

_____ (1938), An outline of psycho-analysis. *Standard Edition*, 23: 144–207. London: Hogarth Press, 1964.

Fromm, E. (1970), *The Crisis of Psychoanalysis*. New York: Holt, Rinehart & Winston.

Gabbard, G. O. (1995), When the patient is a therapist: Special considerations in the psychoanalysis of mental health professionals. *Psychoanal. Rev.*, 82:709–725.

_____ & Lester, E. (1995), *Boundaries and Boundary Violations in Psychoanalysis*. New York: Basic Books.

Gaddini, E. (1984), Changes in psychoanalytic patients up to the present day. In: *Changes in Analysts and in Their Training*, Monogr. 4. London: International Psychoanalytic Association, pp. 6–19.

Gay, P. (1988), *Freud: A Life for Our Time*. New York: Norton.

Gediman, H. K. & Wolkenfeld, F. (1980), The parallelism phenomenon in psychoanalysis and supervision: Its reconsideration as a triadic system. *Psychoanal. Quart.*, 49:234–255.

262   References

Ghent, E. (1989), Credo: The dialectics of one-person and two-person
    psychologies. *Contemp. Psychoanal.*, 25:169–211.
_____ (1992), Paradox and process. *Psychoanal. Dial.*, 2:135–159.
Gill, M. M. (1982), *Analysis of Transference*. New York: International Uni-
    versities Press.
Gill, S. (2001), Narcissistic vulnerability in supervisees: Ego ideals,
    self-exposure, and narcissistic character defenses. In: *The Supervisory
    Alliance*, ed. S. Gill. Northvale, NJ: Aronson, pp. 19–34.
Gitelson, M. (1948), Problems of psychoanalytic training. *Psychoanal.
    Quart.*, 17:198–211.
_____ (1954), Therapeutic problems in the analysis of the "normal"
    candidate. *Internat. J. Psycho-Anal.*, 35:174–183.
Glenn, J. (1986), Freud, Dora and the maid: A study of countertrans-
    ference. *J. Amer. Psychoanal. Assn.*, 34:591–606.
Glover, E. (1924), "Active therapy" and psycho-analysis: A critical re-
    view. *Internat. J. Psycho-Anal.*, 5:269–311.
Godley, W. (2002), Saving Masud Khan. *London Rev. Books*, February 22,
    pp. 3–7.
Goldman, D. (1993), *In Search of the Real: The Origins and Originality of D.
    W. Winnicott*. Northvale, NJ: Aronson.
_____ (2003), The outrageous prince: Winnicott's "uncure" of Masud
    Khan. *Brit. J. Psychother.*, 19:486–501.
Greenacre, P. (1966), Problems of the training analysis. *Psychoanal.
    Quart.*, 35:540–567.
_____ (1971), *Emotional Growth*. New York: International Universities
    Press.
Greenberg, J. & Mitchell, S. (1983), *Object Relations in Psychoanalytic The-
    ory*. Cambridge, MA: Harvard University Press.
Greenson, R. R. (1960), Empathy and its vicissitudes. *Internat. J. Psy-
    cho-Anal.*, 41:418–424.
_____ (1967), *The Technique and Practice of Psychoanalysis*. New York:
    International Universities Press.
_____ (1971), The "real" relationship between the patient and the psy-
    choanalyst. In: *Classics in Psychoanalytic Technique*, ed. R. Langs. New
    York: Aronson, 1981, pp. 87–96.
Grinberg, L. (1979), Countertransference and projective counteridentifi-
    cation. *Contemp. Psychoanal.*, 15:226–247.
Grosskurth, P. (1986), *Melanie Klein: Her World and Her Work*. New York:
    Knopf.
Gumbel, E. (1965), Psychoanalysis in Israel. *Isr. Ann. Psychiat. Rel. Dis-
    cipl.*, 3:89–98.
Guntrip, H. (1973), *Psychoanalytic Theory, Therapy and the Self*. New York:
    Basic Books.

_____ (1975), My experience of analysis with Fairbairn and Winnicott. *Internat. Rev. Psycho-Anal.*, 2:145–156.

Hamilton, V. (1993), Truth and reality in psychoanalytic discourse. *Internat. J. Psycho-Anal.*, 74:63–79.

Harris, A. (2002), Minds and dialogues in analytic spaces — Negotiating certainty and uncertainty: Reply to commentary. *Psychoanal. Dial.*, 12:1001–1017.

_____ & Gold, B. H. (2001), The fog rolled in: Induced dissociated states in clinical process. *Psychoanal. Dial.*, 11:357–384.

_____ & Ragen, T. (1993), Mutual supervision, countertransference and self-analysis. In: *Self-Analysis: Critical Inquiries, Personal Visions,* ed. J. W. Barron. Hillsdale, NJ: The Analytic Press, pp. 196–216.

Haynal, A. (1988). *The Technique at Issue.* London: Karnac. Also published as *Controversies in Psychoanalytic Method.* New York: New York University Press.

_____ (1993), Ferenczi and the origins of psychoanalytic technique. In: *The Legacy of Sándor Ferenczi,* ed. L. Aron & A. Harris. Hillsdale, NJ: The Analytic Press, pp. 53–74.

_____ (1994), Review of *The Complete Correspondence of Sigmund Freud and Ernest Jones. Internat. J. Psycho-Anal.*, 75:1278–1283.

_____ (2002), *Disappearing and Reviving: Sándor Ferenczi in the History of Psychoanalysis.* London: Karnac.

Heimann, P. (1950), On countertransference. *Internat. J. Psycho-Anal.*, 31:81–84.

_____ (1954), Problems of the training analysis. *Internat. J. Psycho-Anal.*, 35:163–166.

Hertz, N. (1983), Dora's secrets, Freud's techniques. *Diacritics,* Spring, pp. 65–76.

Hirsch, I. (1998), Further thoughts about interpersonal and relational perspectives. *Contemp. Psychoanal.*, 34:501–538.

Hoffer, A. (1993), Ferenczi's relevance to contemporary psychoanalytic technique. In: *The Legacy of Sándor Ferenczi,* ed. L. Aron & A. Harris. Hillsdale, NJ: The Analytic Press, pp. 75–80.

_____ (1996), Asymmetry and mutuality. In: *Ferenczi's Turn in Psychoanalysis,* ed. P. L. Rudnytski, A. Bokay & P. Giampieri-Deutch. New York: New York University Press, pp. 107–119.

Holloway, E. & Wolleat, P. (1994), Supervision: The pragmatics of empowerment. *J. Educ. Psychol. Consult.*, 5:23–43.

Hopkins, L. B. (1998), D. W. Winnicott's analysis of Masud Khan: A preliminary study of failures of object usage. *Contemp. Psychoanal.*, 34:5–47.

Hornstein, G. A. (2000), *To Redeem One Person Is to Redeem the World: The Life of Frieda Fromm-Reichmann.* New York: Free Press.

Hughes, J. (1989), *Reshaping the Psychoanalytic Domain: The Work of Klein, Fairbairn and Winnicott*. Berkeley: University of California Press.

Hurwitz, M. R. (1986). The analyst, his theory, and the psychoanalytic process. *The Psychoanalytic Study of the Child*, 41:439–466. New Haven, CT: Yale University Press.

Isaacs-Elmhirst, S. (1982–1983), Thoughts on countertransference (with reference to some aspects of the therapy of colleagues). *Internat. J. Psychoanal. Psychother.*, 9:419–433.

Jacobs, T. J. (1983), The analyst and the patient's object world: Notes on an aspect of countertransference. *J. Amer. Psychoanal. Assn.*, 31: 619–642.

Jaffe, L., rep. (2000), Supervision as an intersubjective process: Hearing from candidates and supervisors. *J. Amer. Psychoanal. Assn.*, 48: 561–570.

Jones, E. (1957), *The Life and Work of Sigmund Freud, Vol. 3*. New York: Basic Books.

––––––– (1958), Response to Balint. *Internat. J. Psycho-Anal.*, 39:68.

Joseph, B. (1993), A factor militating against psychic change: Non-resonance. In: *Psychic Structure and Psychic Change*, ed. M. J. Horowitz, O. F. Kernberg & E. M. Weinschel. Madison, CT: International Universities Press, pp. 311–325.

Kahr, B. (1996), *D. W. Winnicott: A Biographical Portrait*. London: Karnac.

Kairys, D. (1964), The training analysis. *Psychoanal. Quart.*, 33:485–512.

Kantrowitz, J. L. (2002), The triadic match: The interactive effect of supervisor, candidate and patient. *J. Amer. Psychoanal. Assn.*, 50: 939–968.

––––––– Katz, A. L. & Paolitto, F. (1990). Follow-up of psychoanalysis five to ten years after termination: III. The relation between the resolution of the transference and the patient–analyst match. *J. Amer. Psychoanal. Assn.*, 38:655–678.

Kernberg, O. F. (1986), Institutional problems of psychoanalytic education. *J. Amer. Psychoanal. Assn.*, 34:799–834.

––––––– (1996), Thirty methods to destroy the creativity of psychoanalytic candidates. *Internat. J. Psycho-Anal.*, 77:1031–1040.

––––––– (1999), Psychoanalysis, psychoanalytic psychotherapy and supportive psychotherapy: Contemporary controversies. *Internat. J. Psycho-Anal.*, 80:1075–1091.

––––––– (2000), A concerned critique of psychoanalytic education. *Internat. J. Psycho-Anal.*, 81:97–120.

Kerr, J. (1993), *A Most Dangerous Method: The Story of Jung, Freud, and Sabina Spielrein*. New York: Knopf.

Khan, M. (1958), Introduction to Winnicott's *Through Paediatrics to Psychoanalysis*. New York: Basic Books, 1975.

King, P. & Steiner, R., eds. (1991). *The Freud–Klein Controversies, 1941–45.* London: Routledge.

Kirsner, D. (2000), *Unfree Associations: Inside Psychoanalytic Institutes.* London: Process Press.

Klauber, J. (1981), Elements of the psychoanalytic relationship and their therapeutic implications. In: *The British School of Psychoanalysis: The Independent Tradition,* ed. G. Kohon. London: Free Association Press, 1986.

_____ (1983), The identity of the psychoanalyst. In: *The Identity of the Psychoanalyst,* ed. E. D. Joseph & D. Widlocher. New York: International Universities Press, pp. 41–50.

Klein, M. (1921), The development of a child. In: *Love, Guilt and Reparation.* London: Delacorte Press, 1975, pp. 1–53.

_____ (1923), Early analysis. In: *Love, Guilt and Reparation.* London: Delacorte Press, 1975, pp. 77–105.

_____ (1925), A contribution to the psychogenesis of tics. In: *Love, Guilt and Reparation.* London: Delacorte Press, 1975, pp. 106–127.

Klumpner, G. H. & Frank, A. (1991), On methods of reporting clinical material. *J. Amer. Psychoanal. Assn.,* 39:537–551.

Kris, A. O. (1994), Freud's treatment of a narcissistic patient. *Internat. J. Psycho-Anal.,* 75:649–664.

Kvarnes, R. J. & Parloff G. H., eds. (1976). *A H. S. Sullivan Case Seminar.* New York: Norton.

Lacan, J. (1952), Intervention on transference. In: *Feminine Sexuality,* ed. J. Mitchell & J. Rose. New York: Norton, 1983.

_____ (1988), *The Seminar – Book 1.* New York: Norton.

Laing, R. D. (1961). *Self and Others.* New York: Pantheon.

Lampl-de Groot, J. (1954), Problems of psychoanalytic training. *Internat. J. Psycho-Anal.,* 35:184–187.

Langs, R. (1976), *The Therapeutic Interaction.* New York : Aronson.

_____ (1979). *The Supervisory Experience.* New York: Aronson.

Lazar, R. (2001), Subject in first person—Subject in third person: Subject, subjectivity and intersubjectivity. *Amer. J. Psychoanal.,* 61:271–291.

Lebovici, S. (1978), Presidential address in honour of the centenary of the birth of Karl Abraham. *Internat. J. Psycho-Anal.,* 59:133–144.

Lesser, R. (1984), Supervision: Illusions, anxieties and questions. In: *Clinical Perspectives on the Supervision of Psychoanalysis and Psychotherapy,* ed. L. Caligor, P. M. Bromberg & J. Meltzer. New York: Plenum, pp. 143–152.

Lester, E. & Robertson, B. (1995). Multiple interactive processes in psychoanalytic supervision. *Psychoanal. Inq.,* 15:211–225.

Lewin, B. D. & Ross, H. (1960), *Psychoanalytic Education in the United States.* New York: Norton.

Liberman, E. J. (1985), *Acts of Will: The Life and Work of Otto Rank*. New York: Free Press.

Lichtenberg, J. D. (1998), Experience as a guide to psychoanalytic theory and practice. *J. Amer. Psychoanal. Assn.*, 46:17–36.

Limentani, A. (1974), The training analyst and the difficulties in the training psychoanalytic situation. *Internat. J. Psycho-Anal.*, 55:71–77.

Lipton, S. D. (1977), The advantages of Freud's technique as shown in his analysis of the Rat Man. *Internat. J. Psycho-Anal.*, 58:255–273.

Litman, S. (1994), Memorandum to the International Psychoanalytical Association [circular]. Jerusalem: Israel Psychoanalytic Society.

Little, M. (1951), Countertransference and the patient's response to it. *Internat. J. Psycho-Anal.*, 32:32–40.

——— (1990), *Psychotic Anxieties and Containment*. Northvale, NJ: Aronson.

Lothane, Z. (1998), The feud between Freud and Ferenczi over love. *Amer. J. Psychoanal.*, 58:21–39.

Luber, M. P. (1991), A patient's transference to the analyst's supervisor. *J. Amer. Psychoanal. Assn.*, 39:705–725.

Lussier, A. (1991), Our training ideology. Presented at IPA Conference of Training Analysts, Buenos Aires.

Lynn, D. J. & Vaillant, G. E. (1998), Anonymity, neutrality and confidentiality in the actual methods of Sigmund Freud: A review of 43 cases, 1907–1939. *Amer. J. Psychiat.*, 155:163–171.

Mahony, P. J. (1986), *Freud and the Rat Man*. New Haven, CT: Yale University Press.

Marcus, S. (1975), Freud and Dora: Story, history, case history. In: *Representations*. New York: Random House.

Martinez, D. & Hoppe, S. K. (1991), The analyst's own analyst: Other aspects of internalization. Presented at meeting of the Society for Psychotherapy Research.

Mayer, D. (1972), Comments on a blind spot in clinical research. *Psychoanal. Quart.*, 41:384–401.

Mayer, E. L. (1996). Introductory remarks to panel "Supervision as an Intersubjective Process" at meeting of the American Psychoanalytic Association, New York.

McGuire, W., ed. (1974), *The Freud/Jung Letters*. Princeton, NJ: Princeton University Press.

McLaughlin, F. (1967), Addendum to a controversial proposal: Some observations on the training analysis. *Psychoanal. Quart.*, 36:230–247.

Meyer, L. (2003), Subservient analysis. *Internat. J. Psycho-Anal.*, 84:1241–1262.

Meyerson, A. & Epstein, G. (1976), The psychoanalytic treatment center as a transference object. *Psychoanal. Quart.*, 45:274–287.

Milner, M. (1950), A note on the ending of an analysis. *Internat. J. Psycho-Anal.*, 31:191–193.

Mitchell, S. (1988), *Relational Concepts in Psychoanalysis: An Integration.* Cambridge, MA: Harvard University Press.

———— (1993), *Hope and Dread in Psychoanalysis.* New York: Basic Books.

———— (1997), *Influence and Autonomy in Psychoanalysis.* Hillsdale, NJ: The Analytic Press.

———— (1998), The emergence of features of the analyst's life. *Psychoanal. Dial.*, 8:187–194.

Moi, T. (1981), Representation of patriarchy: Sexuality and epistemology in Freud's Dora. *Feminist Rev.*, 9:60–73.

Momigliano, L. N. (1987), A spell in Vienna — But was Freud a Freudian? *Internat. Rev. Psycho-Anal.*, 14:373–389.

Moses, R. (1992), A short history of psychoanalysis in Palestine and Israel. *Isr. J. Psychiat. Rel. Sci.*, 29:229–238.

Novick, J. (1997), Termination conceivable and inconceivable. *Psychoanal. Psychol.*, 14:145–162.

Ogden, T. (1983), The concept of internal object relations. *Internat. J. Psycho-Anal.*, 64:227–241.

———— (1995), Analysing forms of aliveness and deadness of the transference–countertransference. *Internat. J. Psycho-Anal.*, 76:695–709.

———— (1996), Reconsidering three aspects of psychoanalytic technique. *Internat. J. Psycho-Anal.*, 77:883–899.

Olinick, S. A. (1980), The gossiping psychoanalyst. *Internat. Rev. Psycho-Anal.*, 7:439–446.

Orgel, S. (1990), The future of psychoanalysis. *Psychoanal. Quart.*, 59:1–20.

———— (2002), Some hazards to neutrality in the psychoanalysis of candidates. *Psychoanal. Quart.*, 71:419–443.

Ornstein, P. (2002), Michael Balint then and now: A contemporary approach. *Amer. J. Psychoanal.*, 62:25–35.

O'Shaughnessy, E. (1987), Review of Grosskurth's *Melanie Klein. Internat. Rev. Psycho-Anal.*, 14:132–136.

Palgi-Hecker, A. (2003), Mother as subject: An absence in philosophical, psychoanalytic and feminist thought. Doctoral dissertation, University of Haifa, Haifa, Israel.

Paris Psychoanalytical Society (1994). *Institute of Psychoanalysis: Training Regulations* [circular]. Paris: Paris Psychoanalytical Society.

Peled, R. (2002), *"The New Man" of the Zionist Revolution* [in Hebrew]. Tel Aviv, Israel: Am Oved.

Pergeron, J. (1996), Supervision as an analytic experience. *Psychoanal. Quart.*, 65:693–710.

Phillips, A. (1988), *Winnicott*. Cambridge, MA: Harvard University Press.

Pigman, G. W. (1995), Freud and the history of empathy. *Internat. J. Psycho-Anal.*, 76:237–256.

Poland, W. S. (2000), Witnessing and otherness. *J. Amer. Psychoanal. Assn.*, 48:17–35.

Rachman, A. W. (1993), Ferenczi and sexuality. In: *The Legacy of Sándor Ferenczi*, ed. L. Aron & A. Harris. Hillsdale, NJ: The Analytic Press, pp. 81–100.

Racker, H. (1968), *Transference and Countertransference*. New York: International Universities Press.

Rangell, L. (1974), Presidential address. *Internat. J. Psycho-Anal.*, 55: 3–12.

Rank, O. (1924), *The Trauma of Birth*. London: Routledge, 1929.

Reider, N. (1953), A type of transference to institutions. *J. Hillside Hosp.*, 2:23–29.

Renik, O. (1999), Playing one's cards face up in psychoanalysis: An approach to the problem of self-disclosure. *Psychoanal. Quart.*, 68: 521–539.

Ricci, W. F. (1995), Self and intersubjectivity in the supervisory process. *Bull. Menn. Clin.*, 59:53–68.

Roazen, P. (1975), *Freud and His Followers*. New York: Knopf.

———— (1995), *How Freud Worked?* Northvale, NJ: Aronson.

———— (1998), Elma Laurvick: Ferenczi's stepdaughter. *Amer. J. Psychoanal.*, 58:271–286.

Rodman, F. R., ed. (1987), *The Spontaneous Gesture: Selected Letters of D. W. Winnicott*. Cambridge, MA: Harvard University Press.

Ross, J. M. (1999), Psychoanalysis, the anxiety of influence and the sadomasochism of everyday life. *J. Appl. Psychoanal. Stud.*, 1:57–78.

Rothstein, A. (1995), *Psychoanalytic Technique and the Creation of Analytic Patients*. Madison, CT: International Universities Press.

Roudinesco, E. (1990), *Jacques Lacan & Co.: A History of Psychoanalysis in France, 1925–1985*. Chicago: University of Chicago Press.

Rudnytsky, P. L. (1991), *The Psychoanalytic Vocation*. New Haven, CT: Yale University Press.

Rustin, M. (1985). The social organization of secrets: Towards a sociology of psychoanalysis. *Internat. Rev. Psycho-Anal.*, 12:143–159.

Sachs, H. (1947), Observations of a training analyst. *Psychoanal. Quart.*, 16:157–168.

Sandler, A. M. (1982), The selection and function of the training analyst in Europe. *Internat. Rev. Psycho-Anal.*, 9:386–398.

Sandler, J. (1976), Countertransference and role responsiveness. *Internat. Rev. Psycho-Anal.*, 3:43–48.

_____ Dare, C. & Holder, A. (1979), *The Patient and the Analyst*. London: Maresfield.

_____ & Sandler, A. M. (1983), The "second censorship," the "three box model," and some technical implications. *Internat. J. Psycho-Anal.*, 64:413–425.

Sarnat, J. (1992), Supervision in relationship. *Psychoanal. Psychol.*, 9:387–403.

Sayers, J. (2000), *Kleinians: Psychoanalysis Inside Out*. Cambridge, England: Polity Press.

Schachter, J. (1990), Post-termination patient–analyst contact. *Internat. J. Psycho-Anal.*, 71:475–485.

_____ (1996). Final overview panel: San Francisco Psychoanalytic Congress. *Internat. J. Psycho-Anal.*, 77:387–391.

Schafer, R. (1993), Five readings of Freud's "Observations on transference-love." In: *On Freud's "Observations on Transference Love,"* ed. E. Spector-Person, A. Hegelin & P. Fonagy. New Haven, CT: Yale University Press, pp. 75–95.

_____ (1997), ed., *The Contemporary Kleinians of London*. Madison, CT: International Universities Press.

Schröter, M. (2002), Max Eitingon and the struggle to establish an international standard for psychoanalytic training. *Internat. J. Psycho-Anal.*, 83:875–893.

Schwaber, E. A. (1998), "Traveling affectively alone": A personal derailment in analytic listening. *J. Amer. Psychoanal. Assn.*, 46:1045–1065.

Searles, H. (1955), The informational value of the supervisor's emotional experience. In: *Collected Papers on Schizophrenia*. New York: International Universities Press, 1965, pp. 151–176.

_____ (1962), Problems of psychoanalytic supervision. In: *Collected Papers on Schizophrenia*. New York: International Universities Press, 1965, pp. 584–604.

_____ (1979), The patient as a therapist to his analyst. In: *Countertransference and Related Subjects*. New York: International Universities Press, pp. 380–459.

Segal, H. (2001), Review of J. Kristeva's "La Genie Feminine" v. ii. *Internat. J. Psycho-Anal.*, 82:401–405.

Severn, E. (1933), *The Discovery of the Self*. London: Rider.

Shane, M. & Shane, E. (1995). Un-American activities and other dilemmas experienced in the supervision of candidates. *Psychoanal. Inq.*, 15:226–239.

Shapiro, D. (1976), The analyst's own analysis. *J. Amer. Psychoanal. Assn.*, 24:5–42.

Shapiro, S. A. (1993), Clara Thompson: Ferenczi's messenger with half a message. In: *The Legacy of Sándor Ferenczi*, ed. L. Aron & A. Harris. Hillsdale, NJ: The Analytic Press, pp. 159–173.

Simon, B. (1988), The imaginary twins: The case of Beckett and Bion. In: *Essential Papers in Literature and Psychoanalysis*, ed. E. Berman. New York: New York University Press, 1993, pp. 456–490.

_____ (1993), In search of psychoanalytic technique: Perspectives from the couch and from behind the couch. *J. Amer. Psychoanal. Assn.*, 41:1051–1082.

Skolnikoff, A. S. (1990), The emotional position of the analyst in the shift from psychotherapy to psychoanalysis. *Psychoanal. Inq.*, 10:107–118.

Slavin, J. (1992), Unintended consequences of psychoanalytic training. *Contemp. Psychoanal.*, 28:616–630.

_____ (1997), Models of learning and psychoanalytic traditions: Can reform be sustained in psychoanalytic training? *Psychoanal. Dial.*, 7:803–817.

_____ (1998), Influence and vulnerability in psychoanalytic supervision and treatment. *Psychoanal. Psychol.*, 15:230–244.

Sloane, J. (1986), The empathic vantage point in supervision. *Progress in Self Psychol.*, 2:188–211. Hillsdale, NJ: The Analytic Press.

Sorenson, R. L. (2000), Psychoanalytic institutes as religious denominations: Fundamentalism, progeny and ongoing reformation. *Psychoanal. Dial.*, 10:847–874.

Spence, D. (1998), Rain forest or mud field? *Internat. J. Psycho-Anal.*, 79:643–647.

Springmann, R. R. (1986), Countertransference clarification in supervision. *Contemp. Psychoanal.*, 22:252–277.

Stanton, M. (1991), *Sándor Ferenczi: Reconsidering Active Intervention*. Northvale, NJ: Aronson.

Stein, R. (1990), A new look at the theory of Melanie Klein. *Internat. J. Psycho-Anal.*, 71:499–511.

_____ (2000), Impressions from reading case presentations to the Israel Psychoanalytic Society in the past 20 years [in Hebrew]. *Psifas*, 2:1–20.

Stimmel, B. (1995), Resistance to the awareness of the supervisor's transference with special reference to parallel process. *Internat. J. Psycho-Anal.*, 76:609–618.

Stolorow, R. D. (1990), Converting psychotherapy to psychoanalysis: A critique of the underlying assumptions. *Psychoanal. Inq.*, 10:119–130.

_____ & Atwood, G. E. (1979), *Faces in a Cloud: Subjectivity in Personality Theory*. New York: Aronson.

_____ Atwood, G. E. & Brandchaft, B., eds. (1994), *The Intersubjective Perspective*. Northvale, NJ: Aronson.

_____ Atwood, G. E. & Ross, J. M. (1978), The representational world in psychoanalytic therapy. *Internat. Rev. Psycho-Anal.*, 5:247–258.

_____ Brandchaft, B. & Atwood, G. E. (1983), Intersubjectivity in psychoanalytic treatment. *Bull. Menn. Clin.*, 47:117–128.

Szasz, T. S. (1958), Psycho-analytic training: A socio-psychological analysis of its history and present status. *Internat. J. Psycho-Anal.*, 39: 598–613.

Szecsödy, I. (1999), Report on the follow-up responses received from the presenting supervisors/supervisees at the IPA Conference of Training Analysts. *Internat. J. Psycho-Anal.*, 8:20–23.

Talmon, J. L. (1952), *The Origins of Totalitarian Democracy*. London: Mercury, 1961.

Tansey, M. & Burke, W. (1989), *Understanding Countertransference*. Hillsdale, NJ: The Analytic Press.

Teitelbaum, S. H. (1990), Supertransference: The role of the supervisor's blind spots. *Psychoanal. Psychol.*, 7:243–258.

Temkin-Bermanowa, B. (2000), *An Underground Diary* [in Polish]. Warsaw, Poland: ZIH & Twoj Styl.

Thompson, C. (1950), *Psychoanalysis: Evolution and Development*. New York: Grove Press.

Turner, B. S. (1991), Introduction to K. Mannheim, *Ideology and Utopia*. London: Routledge.

Tyndale's New Testament (1989), New Haven, CT: Yale University Press. Originally published 1534.

Wallerstein, R. S., ed. (1981), *Becoming a Psychoanalyst*. New York: International Universities Press.

_____ (1986). *Forty-two Lives in Treatment*. New York: Guilford.

_____ (1989). Psychoanalysis and psychotherapy: An historical perspective. *Internat. J. Psycho-Anal.*, 70:563–591.

_____ (1993), Between chaos and petrification: A summary of the fifth IPA Conference of Training Analysts. *Internat. J. Psycho-Anal.*, 74:165–178.

_____ (1998), *Lay Analysis: Life Inside the Controversy*. Hillsdale, NJ: The Analytic Press.

Weisz, G. (1975). Scientists and sectarians: The case of psychoanalysis. *J. Hist. Behav. Sci.*, 11:350–364.

Werman, D. S. (1989). The idealization of structural change. *Psychoanal. Inq.*, 9:119–139.

Windholz, E. (1970), The theory of supervision in psychoanalytic education. *Internat. J. Psycho-Anal.*, 51:393–406.

Winnick, H. Z. (1977), Milestones in the development of psychoanalysis in Israel. *Isr. Ann. Psychiat. Rel. Discipl.*, 15:85–91.

Winnicott, D. W. (1935), The manic defense. In: *Through Paediatrics to Psychoanalysis*. New York: Basic Books, 1975, pp. 129–144.

_____ (1945), Primitive emotional development. In: *Through Paediatrics to Psychoanalysis*. New York: Basic Books, 1975, pp. 145–156.

_____ (1947), Hate in the countertransference. In: *Through Paediatrics to Psychoanalysis*. New York: Basic Books, 1975, pp. 194–203.

_____ (1951), Transitional objects and transitional phenomena. In: *Through Paediatrics to Psychoanalysis*. New York: Basic Books, 1975, pp. 229–242.

_____ (1958), *Through Paediatrics to Psychoanalysis*. New York: Basic Books, 1975.

_____ (1960). Ego distortion in terms of true and false self. In: *The Maturational Processes and the Facilitating Environment*. London: Hogarth Press, pp. 140–152.

_____ (1962a), A personal view of the Kleinian contribution. In: *The Maturational Processes and the Facilitating Environment*. London: Hogarth Press.

_____ (1962b), The aims of psycho-analytical treatment. In: *The Maturational Processes and the Facilitating Environment*. London: Hogarth Press.

_____ (1964), Review of Jung's *Memories, Dreams, Reflections. Internat. J. Psycho-Anal.*, 45:450–455.

_____ (1971). *Playing and Reality*. Harmondsworth, England: Penguin, 1974.

Winokur, M. (1982), A family systems model for supervision of psychotherapy. *Bull. Menn. Clin.*, 46:125–138.

Wolf, E. S. (1995), How to supervise without doing harm. *Psychoanal. Inq.*, 15:252–267.

Wolkenfeld, F. (1990), The parallel process phenomenon revisited: Some additional thoughts about the supervisory process. In: *Psychoanalytic Approaches to Supervision*, ed. R. C. Lane. New York: Brunner/Mazel, pp. 95–109.

Yerushalmi, H. (1992), On the concealment of the interpersonal therapeutic reality in the course of supervision. *Psychotherapy*, 29:438–446.

Zusman, W. (1988), Our science and our scientific lives. *Isr. Psychoanal. J.*, 1:351–377, 2003.

Index

Photo by Michal Heiman

Emanuel Berman, Ph.D. is a Professor of Psychology at the University of Haifa, a Training Analyst at the Israel Psychoanalytic Institute, and a Visiting Professor at the Postdoctoral Program in Psychotherapy and Psychoanalysis, New York University. He is editor of *Essential Papers in Literature and Psychoanalysis* (1993) and of Hebrew translations of Freud, Ferenczi, and Winnicott. Dr. Berman is the International Editor of *Psychoanalytic Dialogues: A Journal of Relational Perspectives* and a frequent contributor to the *International Journal of Psychoanalysis* and other journals.